MAX REINHARDT

[*Frontispiece*

THE THEATRE OF
MAX REINHARDT

BY

HUNTLY CARTER

BENJAMIN BLOM, INC.

NEW YORK

FIRST PUBLISHED IN 1914
REISSUED 1964 BY BENJAMIN BLOM, INC.,
L. C. CATALOG CARD NO.: 64-14700

Printed in U.S.A. by
NOBLE OFFSET PRINTERS, INC.
NEW YORK 3, N. Y.

PREFACE

WHATEVER we may think of the art value of the work of Max Reinhardt, one of the greatest masters of modern stagecraft, the comprehensiveness and optimistic tone of the whole are inspiriting. Its summary and revelation of the ideas which are now transforming the theatre in Europe, and its suggestion that the shoulders of the theatre will eventually be relieved of its present burden of ugliness, open up endless vistas on expansion which contrast curiously with the avenues of contraction now confronting the English theatre. Max Reinhardt has a genuine love for the theatre, and his attitude towards it is one of aspiration, whatever may be the peculiarity of his style. His optimism is not to be treated lightly, for, as it is the purpose of this book to show, it is not the optimism of inexperience, but of one who has travelled far in the theatre, has sounded its depths, has tried and tested its resources in all their width and variety, and who possesses a genuine passion for achievement and a belief in its artistic worth.

As to the precise value of his achievements in modern stagecraftsmanship there is, of course, a divided opinion. And this is largely due to the fact that very few persons outside Germany are fully acquainted with the wide results which he has attained.   How many dramatic critics are there in England who have surveyed the entire ground which Max Reinhardt has covered, have followed his daily experiments, have seen the definite plan at which he is quietly working in his own sphere of study ?   As far as I know, not more than two or three.   It is therefore not surprising that a misconception concerning the nature of his activities should have arisen.   Hence some English critics do not view his work with any great favour.   It has, they think, an effect in encouraging in this country a taste for mere spectacle, and discouraging a taste for the drama. Such critics emphasise, and very rightly, the importance of promoting the drama first, before all things, seemingly unaware that Reinhardt has been doing this from the very start, and that, strangely enough, a great deal of his popularity is owing to that circumstance.   They are not aware that he has been searching for first principles, and that in reintroducing impulse to the theatre, in reawakening the quest for intimacy, in striving to attain rhythmical unity, and in seeking to lift the many and varied activities of the theatre out of the local into the universal once more, he is inviting the theatre to become that which it is fitted to become, viz., a refined and highly efficient instrument for receiving and transmitting the spirit of the drama.   In short, he has served the drama not only by producing plays by all the most remarkable writers of the neo-Sturm und Drang period through which Europe has just passed, but by endeavouring to construct a theatre wherein he could recapture the first fine rapture of the eternal form of drama, and to restore that element which alone can seize the spectator, and bring him nearer to the profound secret of human existence. He has, in fact, sought to widen and deepen the power of the drama by preparing to give full play to its primitive, religious, and eternal elements, believing, no doubt, that the dramatic spirit resides in the subconscious element in mankind, and finds expression only through that element.

Probably students may derive the greatest advantage from the stagecraftsmanship of Max Reinhardt not by examining the strong evidences of German culture and scholasticism underlying it, but by the study of the personal element which it contains. Max Reinhardt himself has brought impression and impulse to our doors once more. His contribution to the current reform of the theatre and the drama in England cannot be overestimated when we remember that without impression to awaken impulse there can be no advance in the drama. Eliminate these two elements and the drama becomes as dull and wearisome as the literary and moral theatre has made it.

It should be mentioned that owing to the unavoidable postponement of the publication of this book certain facts call for revision, and they are accordingly dealt with in the " Supplementary Chapter."

HUNTLY CARTER.

CONTENTS

5

LIST OF ILLUSTRATIONS

INTRODUCTION

IN this book I propose to survey the process of
Max Reinhardt's development, beginning with the
forces which were waiting to receive him, and
which had been developing from the first STURM
und DRANG period onward. I reveal in these
forces the tendencies of a nation impelled towards
progress in the theatre rather by intellectuality, in
the form of a literary and moral ideal, than by
artistic intelligence. Thence I pass to the consideration of German and other influences on Max
Reinhardt's living individual development, passing
in turn from the naturalistic to the realistic movement, thence to the æsthetic and symbolic. In
doing so I seek to show that there is no real ground
for the charge of plagiarism which has been so
unjustly brought against the German producer in
this country. From the outset Reinhardt has
recognised the great potentialities of the theatre,
and for a number of years he has sought to realise
them. Many experiments have had to be tried,
many systems tested, some things accepted, others
rejected. His only crime has been that of working
with time and patience, armed with sensibility and
great concentration, towards one definite and practi-

cal end—his " Theatre of the Five Thousand " or
The Theatre of Actuality. In answer to the
charge of plagiarism, I produce evidence showing
that there is little or no relation between the
work of Gordon Craig and that of Max Reinhardt.
Each producer has his individual value, and that
is all that matters. Whatever value they may have
in common does not count.

I then proceed to survey the effect of Max
Reinhardt's development in :

1. His Aim.
2. His conception of Drama.
3. His conception of the Stage.
4. His conception of the Player.
5. His conception of Theatre Organisation.

His principal aim has been throughout to bring
the spectator into the action of the drama and to
make him live the actor's part in the tiny world
formed by the theatre, as he lives his own part in
the greater social world.

Reinhardt's conception of drama has been
founded upon this aim. With no new form of
drama to work upon he has been obliged to turn
to forms of great drama, having old and obsolete
structural purposes, and no relation or proportion
to each other, as the only material available for his
purpose—that of appealing through the primitive
human passions to vast heterogeneous masses of
human beings. In Max Reinhardt's view these
passions are the binding cords which the new form
of drama must contain. They have been eliminated
from the discussion drama. Some day he hopes to
create a dramatist in whose work will be found these

elements of kinship, the essentials of the Reinhardt theatre and drama. And when such a dramatist does arrive, he promises us to build a theatre for him.

This intimacy idea has also affected his conception of the stage, which it has altered in character in two ways :

(*a*) Formation.

(*b*) Working.

And thus we see Reinhardt's stage altering in form, and passing from one tradition to another. As the intimacy idea grows stronger, so the stage walks out of the enormous box with three sides in which the Italians placed it, and enters the arena which the Greeks bequeathed us. In this way it is seen encroaching upon the auditorium, first modestly, as the apron stage begins to project, and the earlier and simpler methods of Shakespearean staging becomes apparent, and then more boldly, as it plunges across and occupies the whole floor of the theatre.

The working of the stage is also affected by the same idea, and this in three ways :

(*a*) Scenery.

(*b*) Lighting.

(*c*) Changes of scenery.

As the scene steps out of the frame in response to the intimacy idea, so its character and materials change. It passes from the age of extravagant and complicated scenery to that of broad and simple effects. Painted canvas yields to solid doors, walls, and roofs. As the stage takes on spacious and ample proportions, so the " architecture " of the scene becomes more or less a substantial embodiment of these proportions, possessing architectonic elements in its structure that suggest a return to the pre-Italian period of stage scenery. These proportions are attained (1) by the use of the entire stage built out to the level of the first tier of boxes, and (2) by the use of the arena. In the latter case the main aim is to build in the audience, as at Olympia, so as to convey to each spectator the sensation of being a part of a great whole.

The new system of stage lighting is also bound up with intimacy. As the latter is largely based on emotional effects, so the main aim of stage lighting is to contribute as far as possible to the emotions of the drama. Lighting has, in fact, become an embodiment of emotion. It plays its emotional part in the drama, focussing and accentuating the emotions as they make their entrance, mostly by means of coloured rays. Colour is, in fact, fast deserting scenery and costumes for the limelights, owing no doubt to the discovery that the conventional system of stage lighting is obsolete and stupid. The impossibility of obtaining the right colour values by this system is now fully apparent to artists who find they can do nothing with batteries of lights placed at the most unsuitable angles, and producing dirty tones that ruin their finest effects. Decorators are in fact convinced that they can attain a far better result by the use of neutral surfaces and some coloured limes served by intelligent operators under their direction. To them it is more intelligent to prepare their palette with coloured limes and to paint each detail of scenery, costumes, and accessories with a single ray, or a mixture of rays of light and their reflections. Colours have not, however, entirely deserted the reform stage, and occasionally satisfactory results are obtained by mixing the coloured rays with the colours worn by the players and the scenery.

In short, the modern problem of costume, scenery, and light is being treated with special care by reformers like Max Reinhardt.

In order to preserve the mood of the drama in the spectator, it is highly desirable there should be as little friction in the representation of a play as possible. This principle has led to the modern problem of the reduction of the act-interval, which Max Reinhardt has attempted to solve in various ways, but mostly by the employment of ingenious mechanisms. The two principal devices employed by him are the revolving stage in use at the Deutsches Theater, Berlin, and the sinking stage used in *The Miracle*. Beyond these movable stages, a further solution has been sought in the Elizabethan alternate stages and in the Greek device of intervals filled in by the chorus. The said devices are also used in the attempt to solve the modern problem of unity in variety of stage-setting.

In turning to Reinhardt's conception of the player, I show that he had to do with a type that is intimately alive, a player in whom the intellectual rather than the artistic faculty has become sensitive and awake. This awakened faculty is, as I indicate, declaring itself in a psychological conception of acting and in a modernised idea connected with the drama, its significance and interpretation. The idea is that the actor should subordinate himself to the spirit or mood of the drama and aim before all things to convey that mood to the audience. That is, he should first assert the individuality of the play, and thereafter his own individuality. This ensemble idea also demands that all players concerned in a production shall submit to the direction of a producer.

Finally, with regard to Reinhardt's system of organisation, which falls broadly into two divisions—(a) the physique of the theatre, and (b) the mind of the theatre—I point out that it shows an intellectual ordering of the theatre and a comprehension of the component parts of the circle of intellect necessary to its working. The circle is, as will be seen, composed, comparatively speaking, of a new form, a body of co-directors animated by a full intellectual conception of the function of the theatre. We see them united for the purpose of exerting the Will of the Theatre, as an instrument for restoring a shapeless mass to something resembling uniformity and coherence.

THE NEW DIRECTOR

THERE is no doubt that the theatre has reached the culmination of culture ; the co-operation of activities springing up are clearly towards a freer expression. I remember reading somewhere that "there has appeared during the last half-century a voluntary organisation—co-operation. It has accomplished remarkable results in diminishing the misery of a great number of hand-workers, and in laying the foundation of a new system of production, distribution, and exchange, while giving new hope of social and economical amelioration, preparing the way for a larger organisation." This social organisation has, no doubt, its advantages. Autocracy is suppressed. The whole of civilised communities are brought into intimate connection. The group spirit is awakened, and individuals are encouraged to unite for the manifestation of group-sentiments, or the general will of the group. Such collective sentiments play many important parts. For one thing, intellectuals have banded together for the ordering of other people's lives, while the heterogeneous elements of the mob have united in groups for the ordering of the intellectuals' lives. Thus we find one class of reformer united and animated by a common purpose and desire, namely, the destruction of the obsolete machinery of government.

Alarmists tell us that the danger to be apprehended from this social exercise of ordering is the future ordering of the intellectuals by the mob : that is, the supremacy of the average commonplace person. There is a danger of Demos being enthroned as Almighty. If so, it is no wonder that the rise of a certain section of society has become a nightmare to the intellectual mind. But it is a false alarm. The greatest " danger " likely to arise from the present shuffling of social units is a governance by aristocracy—an aristocracy of intelligence. And this is as it should be. Intelligence belongs only to the highest order of mind. Intellect was a discovery of the Greeks. It has tyrannised the world ever since. Society should be ordered to suit the intelligent man. He is the exceptional man to whom scope should be given to experiment and create, so as to enable him to make the earth less of a rubbish heap than the intellectual and the average man would have it.

This movement towards an aristocracy of intelligence is invading all forms of social life. It is finding expression in the theatre. So far the theatre has been in the hands of the commercials and the intellectuals. The latter, following the general tendency, have made frantic efforts of a sort at organisation. They have formed groups representing the collective not the individual I, and brought bodies of workers together for the aggrandisement of the latter. These intellectual organisers are always divided among themselves. Each holds an exclusive point of view as to whether the function of the theatre is literary, moral, musical, picturesque, and so on. They never appear to agree that the theatre should be a house of vision only. Thus intellectual organisation of their sort is really slavery. It ignores the fact that beyond organisation there must be liberty. The great thing in organisation is, indeed, the preservation of individual liberty. What is needed are groups of workers expressing the individual yet the collective Will. We do not want bundles of human episodes.

There are signs that reformers are beginning to apply this conception of the collective volition to the theatre, which is equivalent to saying that we shall soon experience the unaccustomed sensation of the exercise of the Will of the Theatre. There will be a new rulership to exercise it, and the ruler who exercises it will be a collective body, composed of as many members as are required to produce the Will. Thus the theatre, like the Church, will promote association, and will draw together all classes of artists in one mutual endeavour, namely, that of making the theatre a house of vision, in which we may see the ideal Will in action unveiling Truth. But every reformer does not see the theatre in the light of social readjustments, arrangements, and combinations. Some who prefer the misinterpreted Nietzsche, demand the ruler-man, not ruler-men. Discussing the question of how to obtain unity in the theatre, Mr Craig explains how unity is lost. He says this:

" Let me make a list (an incomplete one, but it will serve) of the different workers in the theatre. When I have made this list I will tell you how many are head-cook, and how they assist in the spoiling of the broth.

" First and foremost, there is the proprietor of the theatre. Secondly, there is the business manager who rents the theatre. Thirdly, there is the stage-director—sometimes three or four of these ; there are also three or four business men. Then we come to the chief actor and actress. Then we have the actor and the actress who are next to the chief : that is to say, who are ready to step into their places if required. Then there are from twenty to sixty other actors and actresses. Besides this, there is the gentleman who designs scenes ; another who designs costumes ; a third who devotes his time to arranging lights ; a fourth who attends to the machinery (generally the hardest worker in the theatre) ; and then we have from twenty to a hundred under-workers—scene-painters, costume-makers, limelight manipulators, dressers, scene-shifters, under-machinists, extra ladies and gentlemen, cleaners, programme-sellers—and there we have the bunch." This precise cataloguing of theatrical odds and ends is interesting, and Mr Craig proceeds : " Now look carefully at this list. We see seven heads and two very influential members ; seven directors instead of one, and nine opinions instead of one.

" *Now, then, it is impossible for a work of art ever to be produced where more than one brain is permitted to direct, and if works of art are not seen in the theatre, this one reason is a sufficient one, though there are plenty more."*

This looks as though Mr Craig is rightly asking for the organising intelligence. But he explains still further the point, which he has selected from a former book, *The Art of the Theatre* : " Do you wish to know why there are seven masters instead of one ? It is because there is no one man in the theatre who is a master in himself : that is to say, there is *no one man capable of inventing and rehearsing a play ; capable of designing and superintending the construction of both scenery and costume ; of writing any necessary music ; of inventing such machinery as is needed, and the lighting that is to be used."*

Mr Craig is simply demanding whole theatres-full of da Vincis. Directors and producers must stop playing with decayed fallacies, especially those favoured by the intellectual mind. We must try to make an intelligent advance. We must leave thinking in pyramids to the misinterpreted Nietzsche, who, they say, was a philosopher, and as such was privileged to do much of his thinking in the Ark. Accordingly, he was entitled to get the world's wheels fairly stuck in the mud. He was privileged to talk about definitions and distinctions, and to reconstruct the modern world in the ancient form of a pyramidal tomb. It was his mission to see that the civilised world got this form upon the brain, with the poor, mad ruler-man as a type of remorseless Force for an apex, and myriads of slaves for a base. It was a part of his insanity to demonstrate that all artists are not artists, but some of them are ruler-artists.

All artists are equal in the sight of Heaven. Art is simply art, and an artist is an artist, and nothing short of the re-creation of the system of the universe will make him different. All the talk about ruler-art and ruler-artist is drivel. If producers really desire to make an advance, let them study Reinhardt, not Nietzsche, and learn how to think in terms of a circle, not of a pyramid. Reinhardt's contribution to the problem of the theatre is co-directorship. Except to the theatre, co-directorship is not a new thing to this mighty booby world, but outside the theatre dull persons are expounding it in the form of co-management and guild-socialism as *the* idea of the century. The new and significant thing in the theatre is the expression of the Will of the Theatre by co-ordinated minds, each artist taking the keenest interest in promoting the artistic work of the theatre, each artist desiring to attain the best effect, not only for his own sake, but also for that of his fellow-artists. This is what may be called the expression of the Will of the Theatre. It is individual and collective striving of the highest degree. Each artist wills to attain his best individual effect, yet wills to attain the same end as the other members of his group, an end which only collective volition can assure. Thus the Will of the Theatre springs from a common action and a common sentiment, the love of the artists for the theatre, and its function is to give the widest expression to the Will of the author. Thus Max Reinhardt interrogates the alternative which Mr Craig puts forward. Apparently he has no sympathy with the Napoleonic tyranny, and aims to replace Mr Craig's seven-headed director by a seven-headed group of sympathetic and efficient artists who will together produce something as great and individual as a Gothic Cathedral, with all its parts so powerfully and perfectly willed that its infinite worth is apparent to the least of men. I am not aware that Max Reinhardt consciously values Will so highly in the theatre, or is promoting co-directorship because he knows how stupid and purposeless is its counterfeit, Wilfulness, which long ago gave the theatre to chaos. But I am sure that Max Reinhardt is an experimentalist. I imagine the impatience of an imaginative temperament has led him to conceive a nobler state of things in the theatre, and to try processes by which he may occasionally call fire from heaven. It may be that he has found the co-directorship cure by accident, and by accident has exposed the one-man system of directorship as one that cannot possibly promote unity. In any case he has not eradicated the prevailing disease of inartistic will-lessness, the dominant spirit in the theatre which becomes every year more intolerant and obtrusive. Instead of applying Will as an aid to art, the one divinely appointed means to progress and illumination, he has applied it as an aid to culture, and thus made it the last resource for a very desperate case. In doing so he merely emphasises the fact that culture cannot give the theatre that unity which art inevitably produces. Turn in all directions and we shall find striking examples of it. Many of the European theatres are well equipped and well organised to give a complete expression to a fairly complete

outlook upon a literary and moral drama. But
nowhere is the theatre equipped or organised to
give the widest expression to the drama of the soul.
As it stands it is quite unable to serve as a house
of vision. All that it can do is to show artistic
intention, give hints, throw out suggestions, offer
scraps of vision and imaginative interpretation,
turn out pretty odds and ends of pictures, wonderfully pretty bits of imagination, wonderfully ugly
bits of so-called realism, wonderfully deft bits of
stagecraft. But nothing it has done or can do
in its present condition has brought it or brings
it within measurable distance of producing the
complete vision, the design of the poet filled in by
answering minds, unified and vital in all respects.
In fact, the theatre has never been constituted to
produce anything of the kind, and this because
dramatic authors have been accustomed fully to
cover the delicate skeleton which sustains every
precious work of art, instead of handing it over to
co-operators to have its parts articulated and related
and clothed in the flesh of the illusion of the
theatre. Thus the finest play ever written has
never escaped being butchered in some of its
essentials, or been prevented from sinking into a
shapeless heap. The demonstrable fact is that the
theatre always has been, and is still, a vastly inferior,
imperfect, and disjointed instrument of dramatic
expression. In England especially is this true.
There the surroundings of the theatre are grotesque
and degrading ; its construction is bad, its form
obsolete, its design and decoration serve neither to
preserve the gravity, dignity, nor simplicity of

beauty. Its auditorium is rudimentary ; its three-sided stage belongs properly to the Stone Age ; and its lighting, scenery, properties, and other mechanical aids, though effective on occasion, never escape the suspicion of being what they are —theatre stuff. And if the temple is imperfect, its priests, as Mr Craig rightly maintains, are imperfect also. If the construction and mechanical contrivances of the theatre are crude and bad, the human directing, controlling, and interpreting force is not much better. It lacks unity. In short, the great number of units engaged in the work of the production of a play are not properly organised as a body to give that play the widest and most complete expression. They have not a vision in common, but they interpret each in his own way. As a rule they are a spineless and disjointed crew, without the faintest conception of a possible unity.

The system of Max Reinhardt reminds us that what is needed is a new harmonious and intelligent body of interpreters in whose hands all the processes of interpretation are complementary and complete. Such interpreters may be briefly divided into seven classes—the artist-author, director-producer, stage-manager, musician, actor, decorator, and mechanician. As I am concerned here only with the director, it is not necessary to analyse the mental constitution of each member of the group. Broadly speaking, each should be constituted to form a related part of the complete interpretative mind. Perhaps the simplest definition of a director is a leader. When a number of persons come

together for an active purpose they usually select
a leader. In the theatre the term leader has various
offensive applications, such as shopkeeper. But in
the new sense it means organiser. In the theatre
the leader mostly chooses himself. Here, hitherto,
he has mostly been a tyrant imposing his personality
upon a number of persons gathered together for the
purpose. Of recent years the theatre - leader has
taken various forms—showman-impresario, author-
producer, director, actor - producer, producer, and
stage-manager. The impresario may be divided into
two classes, the class which has an appreciation for
the beautiful in the theatre (Astruc and Diaghilew),
and that which regards the theatre as a means of
satisfying an intense hunger after the commercial
nourishment. The latter, of whom Frohman and
Schubert are the extreme type, are distinguished
by a love of compromise with base things. They
are tradesmen dealing in contraband goods—contraband because they are opposed to the highest
spirit of the theatre. They import productions
wholesale, regardless of the fact that such productions very often have a pernicious influence
both in matter and manner ; and the great danger
in them lies in a crude and tasteless treatment of
vital subjects. The remainder of the theatre-leaders
may be lumped together. Briefly, these modern
types are the effect rather than the cause of the
intellectual or literary drama, just as the Frohman-
Schubert octopus type are the cause rather than the
effect of the commercial theatre. The leaders in
question are partly thinkers, partly men of action,
though more frequently they are men of action

first and thinkers afterwards.   They are the prototype of the interpreting conductor, just as the old
leader was the prototype of the time-beating conductor.   Thus, while the latter may be compared
with Berlioz's picture of an incompetent butcher of
masterpieces, either from a point of view of representation or interpretation, or both, the former
may be compared with those leaders of the modern
interpretative school of music, Richter, Wood,
Mottl, and Weingartner.   Their business is mainly
to interpret the " new " drama—a drama which
is often an individual, intellectual, highly com-
plex expression of human experience brought to
the level of consciousness.   They constitute the
first element of the organisation of their heterogeneous crowds of servile workers, and are expected
to see that their human " orchestras " give a faithful
reading—not of the author's intellectual, moral,
or imaginative ideas—but of their own personality
—their leadership, in fact.   Needless to say, such
leaders are more often led than leading.   They
are so obsessed by the idea of leadership that
everything is subjected to it, and they become
shackled to the false idea that they represent a
supreme conscience to which their slaves should
all do reverence.   Thus their function becomes a
superstition instead of a truth, and thus the four
characteristics which this function presupposes
continue to lie dormant.   As properly balanced
leaders they should exercise, first, an instinct for
Truth, the underlying truth of human nature in
thought and action as perceived by the poet.
Second, an accurate intimacy with the mode of

expression of each particular truth. Third, a union of reason with sensibility, and the power to transmit their own feelings to the actors, and to be a directing, not a tyrannical, influence in the essential mode of expression. Lastly and pre-eminently, the gift of imagination in the highest and strictest sense of the word (the fullest comprehension of the power, charm, and interest of the harmonies of line, colour, and composition, the perception of the finest melody of a work).

The English stage does not lack leaders who exert an influence on all concerned in a production. But the influence is always in the wrong direction. Take the author-producer, say Sir Arthur Pinero or Mr Granville Barker. Sir Arthur Pinero at work producing reminds one of a drill sergeant. Both he and Mr Barker leave no scope for creation. In their hands the actors are mummers. They dominate and tyrannise in all directions. They both desire real life on the stage, and in order to get it they kill off so much percentage of live actors. In plays produced by them, we can see the spirit of Pinero or Barker moving about directing the movements of the mummers, superintending the setting of the scenes, working the limes, doing everything, in fact, as though the theatre were a machine constructed to produce nothing—but themselves. To them human material is simply a piece of clay to be moulded as they direct. To them actors are automatons. It is no doubt for this reason that *The Mask* condemns the present type of English director-producer as a shopkeeper, a Whiteley or a Selfridge automatically directing vast bodies of workers. The use of Sir Herbert Tree is not of the true inspiriting kind. " For he is the worst enemy of the English Theatre to-day. Under the guise of friendship he undermines its very existence. When he should be feeling, thinking, and acting as an artist feels, thinks, and acts, he is instead performing like a shopkeeper." This is just of *The Mask*, though hardly generous, seeing that Sir Herbert carries on the tradition of Irving, the well-beloved of the forward journal from Florence. The position of the remaining classes of " leader " is similar ; and those who do not take it seriously enough are to be pitied. Seriously, these leaders are hypnotised by the power of a false tradition, according to which the methods of the Inquisition are employed to achieve certain ends. Both the actor-producer, the producer, and the stage-manager simply exist to assist the author with their stock-in-trade of stage technique. Their aim is to legalise a privileged position in the Inquisition. In short, this system of leader-producership consists of an individual placed at the head of a servile crowd that is unable to dispense with a master. It is individualism run to seed. One individual Will does not make a theatre.

Fortunately for the future of the theatre there are four new types of leader springing into existence—the poet-director, the director, the new actor - director, and the artist-director. A fifth type of leader should be mentioned for the reason that he has brought distinction and taste into the theatre, though he is no longer new. I refer to the

literary type, the progressive German Intendant (Dr
Loewenfeld, Leipzig), the critic-director (Brahm),
the literary-director (Dr Stahl, Professors Georg
Fuchs, William Poel, Hagemann, Gregor, Dr Kilian,
and Dr Alexander Hevesi.   These follow more
or less the example of Goethe, who gave his
company of titled aristocrats a free hand.   Three
at least of the new leaders do not attempt to wield
a despotic authority.   They do not treat their
fellow-workers as half-educated slaves, swayed this
way and that by authority or flattery.   They treat
them as persons who, on the whole, know their
own mind, and who are likely to do full justice to
the director's discernment.   Freedom rather than
tyranny is the keynote of their leadership, though
it is not quite clear in each case how this freedom
is transmitted to others.   In a conversation with
Mr Herbert Trench (the poet-director), Mr T.
Martin Wood slightly fogs this issue.   He is
considering the question of the staging of plays,
and says : " So well known a lover of pictures,
one so intimate with art as Mr Trench, participates
in a painter's advantages in this respect, and by
reason of his appreciation enters into the painter's
belief in unity of effect and design when it comes
to the task of realising in a plastic form the stage
directions of a play.   He is then fitted in almost
dual capacity for his task as stage-director, as
sympathetic interpreter of dramatic aspiration
through the stratagem of stage device."   This
sounds as though Mr Trench, being a lover of
pictures, understands the painter's business, and,
having a sympathetic appreciation of drama, under-

stands the author's business.   Then comes a comparison with Goethe.   " It is not improbable that
he is the nearest approach to an ideal director there
has been since Goethe's time."   But Goethe was
not a dual-headed director.   He was more like
what follows.   " His extreme practicableness comes
as a surprise in a great poet, the combination of
the rarest nature, and everything is to be hoped for
from it—from the submission of every detail to
illuminative mind.   Every step taken in the production of *The Blue Bird* was personally attended
to by Mr Trench.   It is easy to understand how
little of all the florid convention that overwhelms
the stage was permitted to filter through. . . .
Mr Trench was very anxious to put from himself
on to Mr Lyal Sweete as much as possible of the
credit of the success of staging *The Blue Bird*. . . .
Napoleon's generals often won his battles for him,
and his genius was in his preference for these
generals, the *noble 'pieces' in the place of pawns.*
And the great man would use Murat and Ney
together to produce an effect upon the field, as
Mr Trench would use the art of Mr Cayley
Robinson and Mr Sime to produce an effect upon
the stage.   He told me that he would go to one
man for his statuesque and architectural qualities
and another for his fantasy, and so on, seeking
sometimes a possible combination."   What are
we to make of all this ?   Simply that Mr Trench
is not the supreme dominating head, as Mr Wood
would have us believe.   He is the architect of the
production, who draws up the plan and selects the
" noble pieces," not the pawns—the Neys and

Murats whose wills are equal to Napoleon's, but whose organising capacity is not so great—to fill it in to the best of their capacity. Mr Wood proves this in the next passage, where he says: "If I understand Mr Trench aright, instead of the painter-producer staging a play as if the stage was his huge canvas and the materials the recalcitrant ones we know, a director should stand again behind that painter, himself a super-painter, as it were, choosing specialists as he might choose his brushes, using one man's qualifications against another's to achieve a larger end. Such a programme obviates the likelihood of the presentment being one-sided and failing in the universality of appeal which the stage must make. In spite of this admission, however, all my own beliefs are with the advantages of making use of a painter-producer whose scheme the play shall be from beginning to end, as once set forth, I think, by Mr Gordon Craig." Obviously Mr Wood prefers the autocrat in the theatre. But his conversation was recorded in 1910, and the world has moved since then and tied another knot in grandma Past's apron-strings. The artist-director will also obey the dictates of freedom. If he has a true knowledge of art he will know that whenever art has been a ruling power in the world it has been the expression of freemen, not slaves.

Art shackled is a contradiction in terms, and artist-directors and producers must understand that if their fellow-artists are denied full liberty of action they can no more produce works of art than they themselves can. Art will only be possible in the theatre when art is free. I believe Wyspianski demonstrated that. He was the Admirable Crichton of Mr Craig's dreams. It comes to this, then, that the new director is an individual multiplied by many individuals all working in harmony. This is the type of director that Max Reinhardt represents. He is a leader only in name. I imagine he asks for a balance of temperament, but no discipline, recognising, no doubt, that when one temperament attempts to discipline another temperament friction is the result. He bears no resemblance to the leader-tyrant, he who believes in the divine rulership of directors. He suggests rather the director of the future, who will be the master-builder of the theatre, recognising that fine drama represents the lyrical impulse of the soul, and that its fullest expression should be the work of finely co-ordinated creative minds making their protest in spontaneity against everything disciplinary and formal. When creation becomes the whole object of the theatre, discipline will cease to exist. Such a director will know that the theatre and drama have to make their fight hardest against the men who have their hands at the throat of art, the culturists. I cannot conceive of such a director surpassing his co-directors in Will and Spirit. Both Will and High Spirit will indeed be the hall-mark of the director, as well as of those that co-operate with him. This is precisely where he will differ from and be an advance upon the director, workers and slaves of the materialistic and realistic theatre. For materialism and realism are always linked with low-spirited endeavour. Thus the new spell which he will weave will be stronger than the old spirit, because it will call forth the joy of life in us. Max Reinhardt has both Will and Spirit, but he has borrowed the mechanical chant of culture, and that chant hangs like a dense creeper about the theatre, and, creeper-like, keeps creation out. The greatest thing a director can do is to create a creative poet. His line of advance is, however, strongly marked. As I have indicated, Max Reinhardt stands for the assertion of the Will of the theatre. He has also made an advance on the ancients, inasmuch as he is adding artistic impulse to the intellectual spell which the Greeks have cast over us moderns. It remains to be seen whether the theatre and drama will cease to try to advance through the cultural past and will be delivered by the pure intelligence of the present. The advance that Max Reinhardt is making in the true direction may be seen in a survey of his progression, as well as in an examination of the influences which have produced him.

HIS ORIGIN

Most remarkable men live in their work. It is because Max Reinhardt gives us so much of himself in his work that it is not necessary to investigate either his spiritualism or his biology or his sociology. Even if there were a need, there is not much to help us. The plain matter-of-fact statements contained in various English and foreign *Who's Who's* and Green Room books are like geographically distributed peoples. They do not match. Even if one employs the police-court method of extracting the truth by comparing the statements of a number of witnesses, the result is meagre. This method reveals that Max Reinhardt was born at Baden near Vienna, on the 9th of September 1873. So that to-day he is forty years of age. He was educated at the Untergymnasium, and was in a banking business till seventeen. He studied for the stage under Emil Burde. In 1893 he made his first appearance at the Stadt Theatre, Salzburg. In 1894 he made his first appearance at the Deutsches Theater, Berlin. He founded a Cabaret (Schall und Rauch), and afterwards the Little Theatre, the Kammer-spielhaus, then went to the Deutsches Theatre.

Has played Mephisto, Philip II., Oberseer Strömer. Married Elsa Heins, etc. etc. This is a sample of the human budgets published for the guidance of the unsuspecting.

Let me pump some blood into these anæmic and slovenly details. Turning to German sources of information, I find that Max Reinhardt came from Austria, the birthplace of so many prominent artists of the theatre. As for his temperament, training, and physique, there is very little record. I may banish these subjects with a few words. All men have some genius ; and some men are gifted enough to appear all genius. One is never quite certain how much of this precious quality Max Reinhardt possesses. It is clear he has the ability to plan on the largest scale and in accordance with the most advanced ideas. He knows how to bring up-to-date grist to his mill. He has vitalising force, and everything he touches he vitalises so far as his peculiar methods will permit. To an extraordinary capacity for organisation he unites tremendous energy. Physically he is of the vital type. Somewhat below the average height, he is of conspicuous sturdiness and possessed of unusual power of endurance. His well-known portrait reveals certain notable characteristics, such as emotional intellectuality, strength of character, modesty, and restless ambition. There is an expression of sensuality to which no doubt could be traced his tendency towards art, and especially his love of rich sensational colour. The dominant note of the man is power.

It does not matter greatly whether he set out

consciously to pass through all the necessary stages to complete self-realisation, or whether he progressed unconsciously stage by stage, seizing instinctively each point of advantage as it appeared, and assimilating the significant things of the moment as he went. All intelligent men assimilate. We can hear them saying, "There is something for me in the very latest achievement of that man. He is great enough for me to steal from. I see how right he is in what he is doing. I see something that is a step beyond my own work. Others will see it, but will only seek to imitate it. I am intelligent and will try to build on it." Loftiness of aim justifies plagiarism. Coming to the true story of Reinhardt's career, we find that throughout and above all he is an actor. From first to last he has stimulated the acting potentialities of the drama and theatre. It was as an actor that Otto Brahm discovered him when, in 1890, that famous critic-director was hunting for talent in Austria. At the time, the latter was visiting the School of Acting of the Vienna Conservatorium, and his object was, no doubt, to watch a performance given by the students. During the course of the performance his attention was drawn to a student who was giving a remarkable interpretation of an old man. Brahm, with that profound perception of talent which has marked his directorship, noted that this short, somewhat stodgy actor had in him the material for a character-actor of the first order for his own school of realism. There was in the young man an unusual mingling of originality and force which promised interesting results. He did not, however, engage Reinhardt at once, but waited till he had gained professional experience by a year's playing at Salzburg. In 1892 Brahm visited Salzburg and found Reinhardt interpreting old men with the technical skill of an old, experienced actor—being dramatically effective yet naturalistically correct in every detail. As a result Brahm offered him an engagement at the Deutsches Theater, then, as now, the foremost German theatre, whose prestige among German actors is as great as that of the Comédie Française among French actors. The selection was fully justified. At the Deutsches Theater, Reinhardt soon made his strong personality felt, and in a theatre where all the actors were equal in the sight of the director, he was not long in satisfying his ambition. Reinhardt, it seems, is composed of that ambitious material which makes for success. Unlike so many professionals who sit down and wait for likely things to turn up, he knew how to prepare for opportunities, and to make the most of them when they came. On the stage it is the unexpected that always happens. In English theatres a great deal is left to chance. There is no organised system of promotion. It is to this element of chance that many of our foremost actors and actresses owe their position. They have patiently waited and watched for the right part, and persevered in choosing and mastering each suitable part that offered in readiness for the opportunity to play it. Possibly one of the wise habits of Max Reinhardt was that of closely watching parts which he felt he was suited to play. To practise this habit in a theatre presided over by a director who had an intelligent system of promoting the members of his company was to encourage happy results. So it was with Reinhardt. His chance came and he seized it. The story goes that among the actors cast for the production of Gerhard Hauptmann's *The Beaver Fur* was one named Müller. Müller, who was cast to play the old skipper, committed suicide on the eve of the production. Brahm was in a fix. The part was an important one, and no understudy had been rehearsed for it. An indefinite postponement entailing loss of time and money seemed inevitable. At this moment Reinhardt came forward word perfect and fully prepared to go on. Brahm permitted him to do so, and Max Reinhardt gave Berlin a new sensation in acting. In one scene of Hauptmann's merciless satire on Prussian bureaucracy, the old skipper has only a thinking part. Reinhardt endowed the interpretation with such remarkable silent by-play that it afterwards became the gem of the representation. From this moment his progress was assured. He pursued his acting career with ardour and enthusiasm, broadening those characteristics which Brahm had noticed when, as a twenty-year-old amateur, he had appeared at the Vienna School of Acting, and afterwards as a professional at Salzburg. A sure instinct for character and philosophical types led him to develop along these lines, and to interpret successfully many well-known parts. Ibsen's old man Foldal, Hauptmann's Baumert in *The Weavers*, Tolstoy's Akim in *The Power of Darkness*, the depraved cabinetmaker Engstrand in Ibsen's *Ghosts*, the philosophic Mortensgard in Ibsen's *Rosmersholm*, the old skipper in Hauptmann's *The Beaver Fur*, the moody headmaster Störmer in Dreyer's *Probationers*—these were some of the rôles that Reinhardt created.

Naturalism was the keynote of his interpretation. It was just about the time of his joining the Deutsches Theater company that naturalism was making itself strongly felt in German acting. Brahm had promoted it in the Deutsches Theater, and the distinguished work of some of its exponents, Josef Kainz (the first to introduce psychological acting at the Deutsches Theater), Rudolf Rittner, and Agnes Sorma, served to fire Reinhardt's talent in this direction, and to give him rich impressions which he has never forgotten. Thus at the Deutsches Theater he fully assured his future as an actor. But his thirst for progress impelled him to seek a wider sphere of action.

Accordingly we find him joining the " Freie Bühne," a dramatic institution answering in some respects to the London Stage Society. Here he remained, giving his naturalistic and psychological renderings of parts, and acquiring craftsmanship that was destined to carry him to heights. So he continued to interpret the naturalistic methods of this particular stage society, till, finding that its naturalism had drifted into a rut and was fast becoming mere photography, he broke away. We next find him infected by the " Ueberbrettl " (or, so-called, " Cabaret ") movement which had suddenly sprung up, and was attracting the attention of live exponents of the new spirit in drama, art, and literature throughout Germany. An example of this " artistic cabaret " movement has just made its appearance in England. In " The Cave of the Golden Calf," London's first Cabaret Theatre Club, or midnight restaurant-theatre, are found many of the features in a revised form contained in the earlier German theatrical clubs or combined music-hall and Montmartre Cabaret. It is decorated by advanced artists, including Eric Gill, Spencer F. Gore, and Wyndham Lewis. Its object is " to provide throughout the night a refuge place, an atmosphere of vivid colours, music, and motion." Moreover, it provides representations and interpretations of high merit, and it is designed to promote a desirable intimacy between all artistic classes. As Mr Austin Harrison, editor of the *English Review*, explains somewhere : " Our stage is small enough to bring the artists into close and intimate touch with the audience, making it more of a social affair of the drawing-room than of the theatre." This is just the sort of intimacy between artists and the public that is needed to stimulate a much desired spirit of intimacy in the theatre, similar to that which is springing up in the German theatres. An increase of drama cabarets such as " The Cave of the Golden Calf " in England might help the dramatic movement in the theatre. But of course the Intimate Theatre will be quite a different affair from the Intimate Cabaret. In the former there will be no feeding while the performance is on.

Being badly bitten by this theatrical club movement, Reinhardt, and a number of sympathisers, among them Christian Morgenstern, Friedrich Kayssler, Richard Vallentin, and Martin Zickel, met together in a restaurant in the Lessingstrasse, where they founded the " Brille," much as Whistler and his *confrères* used to meet in the Six Bells at Chelsea, where the Chelsea Arts Club was founded. The " Brille " was conducted privately, only members, mostly comedians, and their friends being privileged to participate in the sing-songs and the Bohemian entertainments directed by Reinhardt. It was here that Reinhardt first became possessed of the idea of intimacy. The " Brille " flourished. It gave Reinhardt full scope for his original ideas, and its members grew in number and quality. Soon this tavern-born example of originality, sense, and imagination outgrew its design, and a larger and more ambitious one, equally instinct with life and motion, was outlined. It emerged under the title of " Schall und Rauch " (Sound and Smoke), and proved to be based on more solid qualities than its title implies. This choice of a larger design did not at first interfere with the private character of the entertainment. It removed to the Künstlerhaus in the Bellevuestrasse, continued to maintain its Bohemian aspect, and to keep the moods going from midnight to dawn. But fame will out, even Künstlerhaus fame, and if a company of amiable entertainers have anything good to give away they cannot expect the world to remain long in ignorance of the fact. Accordingly the Berlin world was soon knocking at the Künstlerhaus door, and as it refused to be argued into going away, Reinhardt and his *confrères* consented to come out and have popularity thrust upon them. So they departed for Unter den Linden, where they built one of those little intimate theatres which are destined to be a form of the theatre of the future. The ambition of the " Schall und Rauch " grew. But its fresh outburst had a commendable practical basis. Beyond its expression of vaudeville vigour of body and mind, in parodies of well-known authors—Maeterlinck, Stefan George, and Hofmannsthal—in one-act social satires, in grotesque song and dance—beyond these it had a discerning, understanding, and sympathetic eye for unknown players to whom the Berlin Theatre was a closed door. Among these was Gertrud Eysoldt, who made her entrance upon the " Schall und Rauch " stage one December evening in 1901, and swam into instant favour on some Danish gutter-songs. Her " star " has never set. A second appeared, also without engagement. This was Emanuel Reicher. A third was " discovered," the immensely clever Rosa Bertens. In this way Reinhardt gave to the German stage talent which otherwise might have been lost to it, as so much is lost in England.

Throughout the " Freie Bühne," " Ueberbrettl," and " Schall und Rauch " period, Reinhardt had remained under the formative influence of Brahm, without which it is conceivable his activities would have suffered a certain lack. What had chiefly characterised him so far had been his steady pursuit of naturalism and culture. His naturalism and culture were, in their own way, offshoots of Goethe's, who long ago had set the tone of the German theatre. Thus, as Reinhardt's person-

ality unfolded, it was bound to take deep root in
the literary movement to which Brahm had added
a decided impulse. Vaudeville had played its
essential part in the long course of preparation
Reinhardt was undergoing. It was necessary that
the comedic no less than the dramatic instinct should
be fully developed in him. If he was destined to
be a director-producer, one, moreover, aiming to
revolutionise the culture theatre, it was necessary
he should be an all-round man, able to touch the
highest and lowest note of dramatic life ; able to
navigate the variegated stream of drama from its
source in time, through the past, present, and
possible. So, having established a useful record
of work in vaudeville, he began to turn to serious
things, and exhibited an eager taste for literary
drama. As his literary ambition grew, so the
character of his entertainments changed, and we
find him in 1901 deserting the variety stage for
the literary theatre. With characteristic boldness
he marked his new departure by producing Strindberg — whose greatness both as a revolutionary
dramatist, as a power of the new movement in
Swedish literature, and as a many-sided profound
thinker, is only just becoming known in England,
now that he is dead. Two one-act pieces by
Strindberg were given, to be followed four weeks
later by a longer piece. With the beginning of
the new season the name "Schall und Rauch"
was inurned, and the Kleines Theater sprang from
the ashes. One of Reinhardt's first successes at
this theatre was Strindberg's *Rausch*. This was
followed by the *Salome* sensation. It seems it

had been arranged to give a public performance of Oscar Wilde's *Salome*, but the censor banned it, thus proving that censorship is sometimes a sanctuary from badly behaved women. Thereupon Reinhardt, seizing his chance, resolved to produce the piece privately, as it is now the custom to produce censored pieces in England. He did so, and with a remarkable cast, including Eysoldt as Salome, Kayssler, Louise Dumont (now intimately connected with the Düsseldorf Theater), and Reinhardt himself, who impressed everyone with the episode of the praying Jew. The first performance staggered even Berlin. It is curious to note that the production inspired Richard Strauss to write his *Salome* opera. From this we gather that, audacious as the production was, it contained the precious life-blood of artistic inspiration. The highest function of drama is to inspire art ; otherwise it is sapless and voiceless. Apparently Reinhardt had conceived the notion that it was time the Berlin Theatre left the hospital for the sanatorium. Having given Strindberg, Wilde, and Wedekind immediate Berlin popularity and lasting fame, so to speak, and hung their culture with the votive offering of art, he began to search in wider fields for any author who gave evidence of intellectual force, in whatever kind, above the average literary and theatre quality. He did not seek names in the literary domain that were only names. He sought authors whose work would keep one in the stalls or by the fire by their strength of originality and fullness of content, if not altogether by the magnetism of the creative imagination. That he succeeded is fully shown by the list of authors and plays published at the end of this volume.

He was now beginning to focus his energies. On the 1st of January 1903 he left the Brahm *ensemble* for good, in order to concentrate upon directorship and to continue his acting for a time. Beyond this he was beginning to work under a different sky. The spirit of style had taken possession of him, and, as some persons contend, had carried him beyond Brahm to the point where he turned from the latter's form of naturalism (which, however, was not Brahm's distinguishing feature) to artistic realism or " style," as it is termed. According to the publication *Das Deutsche Theater*, the naturalism which preceded this was no style (" stillos "). It may be mentioned here that for the last ten years, at least, a number of European reformers have been actively engaged in the attempt to bring style into the theatre. Among these are Reinhardt, Georg Fuchs, Professor Littmann, Craig, Adolph Appia, Bakst, and Stanislawsky. These enthusiasts agreed that the note of style was to be sought and found in coherence and uniformity, in simplification and synthesisation. Accordingly each play was to be given its own character ; its peculiar mood was to be developed and preserved throughout. Of course the methods employed to attain style were different, varying from the relievo-stereoscopic ideas of the Künstler Theater to the deepening suggestiveness of Mr Gordon Craig.

Max Reinhardt's conception of " style " is said

to have appeared in his production of Gorky's
Lower Depths. But it is extremely doubtful
whether Reinhardt produced this formless, incoherent piece of realism. Indeed, the wonderful points
which characterised the production revealed the
hand of the very highly gifted Richard Vallentin,
who unfortunately died too young to realise fully
the splendid promise he gave as a producer. It
may be that Reinhardt learnt a great deal from
Vallentin, who was the most original producer
of his time, and is not known to have had a
predecessor in his own line of realism. In any
case, I believe I may safely say that Reinhardt
had but an acting acquaintance with the *Lower
Depths*, playing the part of the old pilgrim
" Luka." This synthesis of Brahm and Vallentin,
of naturalism and realism, ran for five hundred
performances, excluding imagination, and attracting
the Berliners by the sheer force of unthinkable
brutality.

Owing to the long run of the *Lower Depths*,
and in order to fulfil other contracts, Reinhardt
was compelled to seek a larger theatre. In 1903
he took over the " Neues Theater," still, however,
retaining the Kleines Theater. Here he began to
give full expression to his talent for play-production.
He maintained and widened his Kleines Theater
aim by abandoning his earlier naturalistic methods,
taking part in the realistic revival in Berlin, and
devoting himself to the application of Vallentin's
realistic principles, while at the same time widen-
ing their artistic bases. He now began fully to
realise the importance of appealing to the eye of

the spectator by unity of form, colour, and movement. He also felt the return to mysticism and symbolism inaugurated by Hofmannsthal and Stefan George, and sought to give the spoken word its largest significance—that of illuminating the soul of the drama. In this way he was led to add Maeterlinck's *Pelleas and Melisande*, which four years previously had been a failure at the Theatre Royal, to his repertory of successes, thus claiming four victories in less than a year—*Rausch, Salome, Nachtasyl*, and *Pelleas and Melisande*. That Reinhardt was successful in following the author's intentions was admitted by Maeterlinck, when in 1909 he wrote to Reinhardt congratulating him on his fine efforts on behalf of the art of the theatre—efforts which appeared to him to be the most remarkable in the world. He confessed that he owed Reinhardt a great debt of gratitude, because the latter alone had dared to produce two or three of his plays which were thought to be unplayable.

It seems as though Reinhardt has never considered a piece unplayable. The more difficult the play to be produced, the more boldly he has emerged. He embodies, in fact, the modern militant spirit—a spirit marked by audacity and fighting force. No one in this century has expressed this spirit in the theatre more persistently and thoroughly, exhibiting a certain kind of unchained energy that made progress meteoric but certain. As a dynamic figure, as a revolutionary who has fired all cultural points in a vigorous endeavour to exalt the Will of the Theatre, where of recent years emotionless intellect has alone been enshrined, in his effort to bring himself face to face with a new theatrical world, the elements of which he has eagerly absorbed so far as it is possible, and to justify the demands of his emotional nature, as well as to render himself master of a chaotic domain, by reducing its chaos to order, he probably has no equal in the contemporary theatre.   In purely artistic endeavour alone, he has been surpassed.

At the " Neues Theater " we find him actively engaged weaving the new spell out of the hints and suggestions of the old one.   Realistic romance had touched him, and we find him adapting the methods of realism to romantic subjects.   Thus he transforms Shakespeare into a blend of realist and Parnassian, and, strangely enough, the Bard stood the experiment very well.   Shakespeare has the business merit of standing anything well.   I believe if someone came along and bade him put on evening dress, Shakespeare would do it and walk down Piccadilly or Unter den Linden without being mistaken for a waiter.   Mr Gordon Craig recently put him in dark grey trousers with side pockets, and still Shakespeare did not look like a shop-walker.   Shakespeare has been treated so often as a man who does not know his own mind that he can now adapt himself to any emergency.   However, he had not much to complain of in his appearance in *A Midsummer Night's Dream*.   If there is one thing that Reinhardt understands, it is the child-like spirit of fantasy which is contained in Shakespeare's comedies.   So strong is the spirit in these comedies that I believe

they were meant for children to interpret. I am not
alone in this belief ; Mr William Poel profoundly
shares it.   He once produced one of Shakespeare's
plays in which only East-End school children took
part.   Two things struck me about the representation, the joy of life spirit with which the children
invested their parts, and the wonderful preservation
of the mood of the play throughout.   The child-
actors simply enjoyed the thing, played with perfect
ease, and left one with the impression that the dull,
gloomy old world was not so dull and gloomy after
all.   I have ever since been drawn by a mighty
affection towards that representation of Shakespeare
by children.   The secret of Reinhardt's success in
producing Shakespearean comedy lies in the fact
that he enjoys himself.   He certainly did so when
staging *A Midsummer Night's Dream.*   And he
called in the aid of others who were also under the
spell of its child-like charm.   And so by means of
appropriate music, acting, and decoration, this delightful fantasy took Berlin by storm, as we are
usually bidden to say in trade terms.

In this way Reinhardt continued his perfectly
logical development, giving expression to the force
that was working from underground into the light.
He had passed in turn from the unnatural discipline of the school of acting into the beginnings
of a professional career where he began to gaze
more clearly on natural methods of acting ; thence
to a new form of naturalism under Brahm and
the Freie Bühne ; thence we turn from this, as
it lost its freshness for him, to the artistic realism
of Vallentin, the symbolism of Maeterlinck, the

romance of Shakespeare, to an artistic naturalism, and thence to the new æsthetic synthesis of movement, colour, and sound, upon which he got soundly drunk without developing the usual theatre symptoms of unlovely liverishness. Throughout this period he encountered and gradually overcame the opposition of the Berlin press. By this time he was seeking even a wider field of expression, and his good fortune did not fail him. In 1905 we find Adolph l'Arronge seeking a new man for the Deutsches Theater. His choice fell on Reinhardt, who was no stranger to the house, having commenced his Berlin experience there but a few years previously. But it was not the actor Reinhardt, but the producer Reinhardt, that l'Arronge chose for the Deutsches Theater. In the autumn of 1905 Reinhardt transferred his activities to the famous Schumannstrasse playhouse. In doing so he relinquished the Kleines Theater and retained the Neues Theater for a season longer. At the Deutsches Theater he continued to widen his policy, and gradually began to touch his highest development as a producer. He focussed on organisation, made the theatre a cosmopolitan centre for English, Belgian, Austrian, German, Russian, Scandinavian players, and a centre for the plays of the younger Sturmer und Dranger of his time, including French authors, and thus established a Continental reputation for it. He widened the scope of symbolical representation and interpretation, and provided a framework for plays which was intended to invest realistic forms with a symbolic meaning, such as, for instance, two empty thrones occupying an empty stage, and placed face to face, so as to suggest a universe divided against itself. And he stimulated the invention of mechanical devices, which have added materially to the resources of one of the best equipped theatres in Europe. Besides this, he laid a surer foundation for the intimate theatre. Finding the Deutsches Theater too large, and the distance between the audience and the actors too great to produce and preserve the essential mood of plays which by their nature can only appeal to a limited and highly cultured audience, Reinhardt determined to build a small theatre suited to the purpose of producing such plays. Adjoining the Deutsches Theater was a dance-hall which he converted into a small theatre, to which he gave the name of Kammerspielhaus. The physical features of the theatre are notable. The auditorium is constructed to hold only three hundred spectators, and but three feet separate it from the stage. Its warm rose-colour walls and ample red upholstered seats, its thickly carpeted floor, and its rich decorations tend to give it the air of a precious theatre. Here are produced literary plays, including a peculiar order of conversational pieces that do not lend themselves to decoration, but merely require a round table and some chairs so that (figuratively speaking) the audience may sit among the actors and take part in the dissections or discussions. It is a modern advance on the old condition, when the audience used to sit on the stage grouped round the actors. The Kammerspielhaus was opened in 1906. *Das Deutsche Theater* wrongly gives the date as 1896.

Thus favourably equipped, Reinhardt found no difficulty in pursuing the various problems of representation and interpretation. His experiments in perspective, colour, and lighting, in the proper relation between the actor and spectator, the actor and scenery, do not exhaust the work of the Deutsches Theater. Throughout and above all his chief work here has been the splendid chances of development he has designed his system to afford to some of the most gifted authors, actors, and actresses who in the atmosphere of the Deutsches Theater have risen to unexpected heights. Reinhardt will always be remembered for his un-exampled loyalty to the unknown actor. From first to last he has helped those who stand looking in at the window of the theatre for chances which no one will offer them. To-day his strenuousness is unabated. But it is in the direction of early and colossal Greek expression rather than in that of wideness and intensity of vision. He has taken to thinking in the arena. His first utterance was naturalistic ; his last should be mystic. I say last advisedly, because we can only survey his beginning as yet.

INFLUENCES ON HIS DEVELOPMENT

DISPARAGEMENT is the soul of levity. It is a common complaint of Max Reinhardt's detractors that he stands for many things of which he is not the originator. It is the common fault of remarkable men that owing to the peculiarity of their temperament and the uncontrollableness of the circumstances in which they are placed, they help themselves freely to whatever ideas happen to be lying about. In fact, they assimilate, in many instances, unconsciously, and thus set the long arm of coincidence waving in the face of their jealous opponents, who are not slow to set up a charge of plagiarism. There is nothing that is so often mistaken for plagiarism as coincidence. Perhaps it is because every individual is a potential plagiarist. Thus De Quincey's charge of plagiarism against Coleridge is as much a revelation of De Quincey as Gordon Craig's charge against Reinhardt and the whole of Europe and the United States of America is of Gordon Craig. Great and important men cannot help being responsive to the influences which surround them. And some have been guilty of conscious plagiarism. It breaks one's heart to think of it, but it's true. Some of Max Reinhardt's

critics go so far as to suggest that he is as " an un-
conscionable plagiary as Byron." It is not my
purpose here to answer criticisms, but one comment
deserves notice. Herein disparagement reaches the
point of levity.

A signed article in the *Sketch* of June 1912
maintains that Max Reinhardt really stands for
nothing. The sources from which he has helped
himself are endless, and apparently he has no more
claim to any of his materials than Shakespeare to any
of his plots. He has associated himself with the
Saxe-Meiningen Court Company's crude ideas, with
" the uplifted hands and crinkling fingers used in
Ben-Hur," with lighting effects that were ancient
before Gordon Craig heard of them, with the
novelties of the Greek, Morality, and Shakespearean
stages, and with the Craig notion of an autocratic
producer. The writer concludes that Max Reinhardt may have ideas of his own, but "after seeing
several gushing articles about him, and seeing all
the specimens of his art *in London*," he believes that
Reinhardt may be dismissed with a kick. The
reply to this sort of wind-bagging is that the writer
has been reading " gushing articles " whose writers
are as imperfectly acquainted with Max Reinhardt's
development as he evidently is, and that he has had
the misfortune to witness samples of the German
producer's work in London—that is, in theatres
imperfectly equipped for their production. He
has, in fact, proved himself to be " an uncon-
scionable plagiary " in borrowing the opinions of
others, and misrepresenting both Reinhardt and the
aforesaid imperfectly housed productions.

The truth about Reinhardt is that he is a sensitive. At every turn of his career he has encountered a flow of influences striking against him and producing various responses. Some of the influences he has rejected, some he has accepted, culled their essential features, broke from them or gone beyond them. If we examine the ladder up which he has passed to his present position, we shall find that it is composed of an infinite number of stimuli and responses; of attractions, acceptances, and repulses, of experiments and results.

Let us begin with the lowest rung of the ladder and pass along with Reinhardt to the position he has attained, noting as we go the influences and what he has extracted from them.

NATURALISM

It will be remembered that Reinhardt was first discovered walking on at a school of acting, and that he afterwards played professionally at Salzburg for a year. He then passed under the direction of Otto Brahm. At this point he may be said definitely to have assumed the robe of naturalism which Goethe bequeathed to the German theatre some generations before. The influences that produced Reinhardt then seemingly began with Goethe, as well as with Schiller. Strictly speaking, they originated with Shakespeare, if we consider the English and French influences which influenced the work of Goethe and Schiller and resulted in the transference of supremacy in drama during the following generations to Germany. This hardly agrees with Mr H. B. Irving's distinction, when he speaks of

Stage Setting for Brutus Garden (Julius Caesar)

Julius V. Klein

the seventeenth century being noteworthy for great drama, the eighteenth for great acting, and the nineteenth for great stage-mounting. Though the nineteenth century had some noteworthy stage-mounting, the great stage-mounting has yet to come. Goethe reflected the naturalism of the Sturm und Drang period, he was also influenced by the nature-philosophy of Spinoza, Schelling, and Rousseau ; but he did not go to Rousseau's length of breaking with culture. Indeed, both culture and nature were equally important to him. His naturalism took the form of turning his face to the purely human aspect of mankind, and demanding a naturalistic expression from the theatre. Schiller laid emphasis on the cultural or educational aspect of the theatre. He saw the theatre as a medium of mental and moral development, as a means of focussing the reading and thinking mind of the nation and disseminating the academical wisdom of this said mind throughout the land.

Both Goethe and Schiller were present at a transitional period in the literary and dramatic history of Germany, when men had found a new touch with nature and life and were setting forth in quest of new adventures, with vital theories of poetry, drama, and art, to urge them on. Some were accompanied by the ideas of J. L. Tieck, the two Schlegels and Novalis, the leaders of the new Romantic School ; while others were caught up later by the more positive and naturalistic aspect of the " Young German movement." If we consider that Heinrich von Kleist, a dramatist of the romantic movement, and the German Shakespeare, as he has been called, left no successor, that his principles lay dormant till rediscovered by the Austrians and French some years later, we may conclude that the naturalistic movement soon took the lead.

This naturalistic tendency found expression in the Freie Bühne movement at Berlin. The Freie Bühne was established to give effect to the movement towards a closer union of the theatre and literature which has marked the close of the nineteenth and the beginning of the twentieth century in Germany, and which has found expression elsewhere in, for instance, Antoine's Free Theatre and the Incorporated Stage Society. It was one of the earliest steps towards the formation of that arena in which literary battles were to be fought out. Accordingly it became actively engaged in the propaganda of the work of what may be termed the Freie Bühne group, Ibsen, Hauptmann, Max Halbe, and O. E. Hartleben. Its first production was Ibsen's *Ghosts*, and this was followed a month later by Hauptmann's *Das Friedensfest*. In short, it stood for the production of unconventional plays acted in a naturalistic fashion which gradually became ultra-naturalistic. Thus it constituted a strong and beneficent break from stilted artificiality and cloying conventions. It drew its actors from the best sources and gave its performances on Sunday afternoons, that being the only time when the said actors were at liberty. The performances were given at different theatres, as is the case with the Incorporated Stage Society of London. The latter is, in fact, an imitation of the vigorous Freie Bühne, but it has not led to

similar developments by initiating a Freie Volks-
bühne movement answering to that which was
undoubtedly stimulated by the Freie Bühne.

To-day the People's Stage Societies are flourishing
in Germany, exerting an influence for good and
stimulating progress, whereas in England they are
still lacking. In London the Stage Society is still
our sole example of a Freie Bühne. It resembles a
respectable, highly educated parrot running round
begging for a perch in unsuitable theatres, and
interpreting " masterpieces " in an inglorious
fashion by means of a Home and Colonial assort-
ment of actors. Generally speaking, it does not
exert the influence of a parrot. It has been urged
by way of excuse that the Stage Society has
been killed by the Press ; that Germany possesses
intelligent critics who work enthusiastically for
the welfare of the theatre, while England has
not yet given birth to a dramatic critic. The
unfortunate person who is asked by his editor
to attend a Stage Society festival invariably
misrepresents the character of the entertainment. If he witnesses a thoughtful play he
goes home and spills columns of ink in describing
it " gloomy," " depressing," and so forth. And
because he tells the truth, forthwith he is labelled
fat-head. If it is uncertain whether we do possess
dramatic critics, or only literary critics called forth
by the literary " drama," there is no doubt that
Germany not only does possess them, but helps
some of them to a directing and improving position
in the theatre. Thus it was that Otto Brahm was
promoted from critic to critic-director.

ENSEMBLEISM AND PSYCHOLOGY

Otto Brahm came into active co-operation with the work of the theatre at a moment when Germany was beginning to manifest a remarkable literary activity, and when the drama was once more beginning to command chief interest in Germany. The permanent repertory of the theatre was being enriched by writers of brilliant and suggestive ideas, and new forms of drama were springing up out of the experiments made by the older writers who were not content to rest on their successes. It was a moment made memorable by the names of Ibsen, Hauptmann, and Sudermann. Both Brahm and Schlenther started as critics and from critics became successful managers. Brahm was moreover fitted to take part in the literary movement in the theatre by his wide knowledge of German literature and foreign movements and literatures. He recognised that the future belonged to the new-comers, and as a critic he fought for their interests, while as a director he practically promoted them. There is no finer proof of this than his amazing loyalty to Ibsen and Gerhart Hauptmann. Perhaps his loyalty was partly due to his whole-hearted love of the psychological drama. His contribution to the modern theatre was indeed ensemble acting derived from the Meiningers, and modern psychological acting derived from Josef Kainz, one of his predecessors at the Deutsches Theater. Soon after becoming one of the leaders of the Freie Bühne, he was appointed director of the Deutsches Theater, where he remained ten years, till 1904, when he became director of the Lessing Theater. At the Deutsches Theater he obtained full scope for applying his reforms. It was here that Reinhardt came under Brahm's influence, and through Brahm, under that of the Freie Bühne, thus developing in this naturalistic school till he found it necessary to break fresh ground. From Brahm he also derived ideas of ensemble and psychology. Brahm succeeded Adolf l'Arronge at the Deutsches Theater. The latter was a playwright and critic and exponent of the classical school of drama of the 'seventies. Brahm did not continue l'Arronge's tradition, but occupied himself with the production of modern plays, in the interpretation of which none but the most cultivated players were permitted to take part. He persistently sought psychological uniformity, and had even the smallest parts played by thoroughly efficient players. Under his direction every player was deprived of his mere stage personality and subjected to the will of the author; all the subordinate instruments were tuned to accord with that of the master-musician. Thus he promoted the Will of the drama, while regarding his theatre as the highest culture-centre.

Thus in time he surrounded himself with a group of modern and cultured men and women, who not only could play the parts allotted to them, but knew how to subordinate themselves to the main interest of the piece, and thoroughly understood the intellectual character of that which they were interpreting. As a contrast to this I may point to the London stage, where half the modern plays—especially

those by Mr Bernard Shaw—are interpreted by
actors who do not understand what they are doing
and saying. The result is that, as many of these
plays are on the level of consciousness and quite
devoid of emotion, and the players are mostly in
the subconscious region, we are offered amazing
examples of cine-gramophonitis. This distressing
state of affairs seems to have impressed itself
upon the brain of more than one person connected with the English stage. Though not
possessed of vast erudition, and entirely lacking
the artist-vision, Mr Charles Frohman has discovered that " if you can find an actor that looks
a part, be thankful ; if you can find an actor that
acts a part, be thankful ; but if you can find an
actor that looks and acts a part, get down on
your knees and thank God." Some day, when
Mr Frohman has ceased from scraping in the
shekels, he may pause to think. Then, may be,
he will add the essential tailpiece to his dictum.
If you find an actor who illuminates a part, get
down on your knees and worship his genius. But
this will not happen till we have abolished a
pernicious system whereby authors in this country
select players with but one view, namely, to match
parts, as women match pieces of dress material, and
to speak and move automatically at the direction of
the author. " All the activities of the theatre are
group activities, and the Art of the Stage is the
Art of Ensemble," says Carl Hagemann in his
comprehensive *Regie*. It was on the application of
these two principles, then, that Brahm rose to fame.
Brahm has, in fact, reached a perfection of ensemble

never before attained. He has gathered together a body of players who act harmoniously together, and act into each other's hands. They consider the play as a whole, and allow no part of it to protrude. In fact, they give it a collective individuality and quicken it with the collective Will of the Theatre, so far as this Will can be expressed under the Brahm system. There is no over-emphasis. Indeed, some critics say that Brahm has so abolished over-emphasis that the interpretation is too subdued. Be this as it may, the ensemble system is an immense advance on the one-man system in England—a system under which stars bulge over the footlights, players are taught to fight for the centre of the stage, and the limelight man beams incandescently on the leading actor or actress. Examine the centre of the stage of any of our London theatres and it will be found to be worn into a slippery hollow. The hollow worn in the centre of the English stage is the symbol of the Limited Individuality Company. It may be possible that Brahm was influenced in some directions by the Comédie Française. To a great extent he answers the description which Georg Brandes has given of Edmond Thierry, the director of the Théâtre Français : " A conversation with him was a regular course in Dramaturgy." And he succeeded in making first the Deutsches Theater, and afterwards the Lessing Theater, centres to which actors went for their diplomas. He, of course, has given distinction to the German Repertory system, and has always been highly accessible to the demands of new talent. He never hesitated to advance very small part people in important parts, and in so doing discovered many players of talent.

But I think Brahm will live chiefly through the loyalty he has shown to Ibsen, and the great praise he has bestowed upon the Norwegian. Just as Turner praised nature as painter had never done before, and Ruskin praised Turner as critic had never praised artist before, so Brahm has praised Ibsen in a manner far above that of contemporary producers. It is not too much to say that the representation and interpretation of Ibsen in England has been and still is a disgrace to the civilised world. According to the English method, Ibsen is interpreted backwards, following a singular defect in Sir J. M. Barrie's method of working, according to which, as Mr Frohman is kind enough to inform us, Sir James begins to write his plays by entering at the back door, thus starting with the climax first. Leaving for a moment the consideration of this miserably enervated and disjointed system of interpretation and the tendency of English players to treat Ibsen as a joke, let me return to Brahm. The latter's aim was to reach his audience through the psychology of Ibsen. Whether he did so in a manner to reach the collective intelligence of the audience so that it responded simultaneously is not a question to enter into here. It may be that psychological interpretations are not the most generally effective ones, seeing that what is one man's psychology is another man's poison. And though in a psychological world the science of mind makes its appeal, in a sensible world sense

alone counts.   All that Brahm strove for was to
bring out the full psychological significance of the
part and the whole of each of Ibsen's plays.   He
made everything direct and simple in its appeal.
But the appeal was through the brain.   All his
players were chosen for this purpose, to make their
appeal not through the senses but through the
intellect.   All the subconscious element of which
Ibsen's plays are so full was left out.   Perhaps
Brahm made a mistake in interpreting Ibsen solely
as a psychologist.   We shall see.   Perhaps Ibsen
himself contributed to the mistake.   We shall see.
In any case, Brahm regarded Ibsen as worthy of
his highest efforts.   If he did not look upon
him altogether as a musician, he got more music,
more rhythm out of him than any other producer
has done.   But he did not go far enough.   He
was the first to give a complete and faithful
rendering of Ibsen—according to modern psychological conception and method.   Such a conception
and method did not enable him to bring out the
finest shades of the dramatist's meaning.   It is
only possible to obtain this meaning by re-interpreting Ibsen as a symbolist.   When we come
to understand Ibsen thoroughly we shall find
that we should not concern ourselves about his
meaning so much as about the manner of obtaining
the meaning.   On the stage the rule should be, take
care of the manner and the meaning will take care
of itself.   It is a commonplace that wise men sometimes do stupid things.   All things considered, this
is unwise of them, since stupidity is the thing that
other men are apt to imitate in them.   Ibsen was

no exception to the rule. He did stupid things, and fools rushed in and imitated them. One piece of stupidity was that, in breaking with a form of drama that had been degraded to talking waxworks and building a new one out of symbolic materials, and with enormous capacity casting his plays so that everything assumes its due place and proportion, and the whole mood of each play is expressed in perfect equilibrium, he smeared this form over with real realism. In other words, he buried his symbolism under a form of realism and became "purveyor of drama of the middlings." This stupidity not only robbed him of prestige, but it took the middlings of Europe by storm, and, as we are painfully aware, it sent the English middlings crazy. One of the middlings was Mr Bernard Shaw who, together with Oscar Wilde, has given birth to a deadly illegitimate drama of modern times that it will take centuries to stamp out. Mr Shaw saw his way to a cheap triumph by retailing Ibsen's misrepresentation of himself to an incompetent public. Accordingly, he proclaimed Ibsen as realist, social reformer, the master of miscarriages in drama, of a crude and superficial form of work that anyone can produce with a limited five-shilling camera and unlimited cheek. Mr Shaw's crowning effort in this direction is to be found in the obituary notice of Ibsen with which he draped the memoriam number of the *Clarion*. In this mass of stupidity we get a fresh evidence of the extent to which the critical opinions of the so-called advanced critics conform to the public opinions which uphold the narrow prejudices of sects, societies, and nations. The article is a foolish attempt to throw a false light upon the origin of Ibsen's ideas and the nature of his technique. Speaking of Ibsen and death, he says : "What was worse, Ibsen seems to have succumbed without a struggle to the old notion that a play is not really a play unless it contains a murder, a suicide, or something else out of the *Police Gazette*." The italics are mine. He continues : "The great men born early in the nineteenth century were all like that ; they visited the Morgue whenever they went to Paris ; and they clung to Ruskin's receipt for a popular novel—Kill a baby." If this proves anything, it is that Mr George Bernard Shaw is one of the middlings. He views Ibsenism as a bit of real realism. It is not the reality of the visionary—that is, a reality which lies beneath the excrescences of life—but it is the unreal thing which lies on the surface all the time. It also proves that Mr Shaw is anxious to cloak his own incompetency. "Only professional playwrights," he tells us, "can realise how old-fashioned it (Ibsen's technique) was in its imitable and traditional qualities." Those who are acquainted with Mr Shaw's early writings will know that in the above respect Ibsen is only surpassed by Mr Shaw. Further, it was a confession that Mr Shaw did not understand the tragic significance of death. Being challenged by Mr William Archer in the *Tribune* to exhibit his knowledge of this profound subject, he forthwith set to work and produced a work called *The Doctor's Dilemma*, which not only showed that he was lacking the power to

confute Mr Archer's argument, but was lacking
the dramatic sense on which to found a confuta-
tion.   In short, his attempt to express death on
the stage was too silly for words, and all he
succeeded in doing was that of pricking the bubble
of his pretence to superiority.   The stupidity of
Ibsen, then, consisted in laying himself open to
misrepresentation by dramatists with the Shaw
mind.   He had a vision, and saw more in the
thing than the thing itself.   Thus the thing
became a symbol of what Ibsen really saw.   But
the symbolic side was never emphasised by him.
For instance, he neglected the background and left
it to be interpreted as a part of the physical man
or woman.   Thus the background became, in the
hands of certain producers—the literary and moral
ones, for example—simply an excrescence.   By
them it was composed not of those essentials springing out of the inner necessity of the action and
standing as a part of the spiritual man or woman,
but filled with excrescences with which the physical
man and woman love to surround themselves—
that is, the odds and ends of an auctioneer's catalogue
that look like wreckage littering a shore after
the tide has ebbed.   Thus it was the fault of
Brahm to give Ibsen a local rather than a
universal character.   He emphasised the three
things in Ibsen which have determined the trend
of the modern drama—Ibsen's habit of treating
apparently small everyday types as such and not
as cosmic realities, his photographic realism, and
his neglect to use the background as a means of
giving the widest expression to the fundamental

idea.   But throughout, Brahm has upheld faith in Ibsen's greatness.   He has contributed to that greatness in bringing out the important fact that Ibsen was, before all, a patriot.   Underlying Ibsen's plays there is a fierce burning love of his own country, of his own people, that will force him to reveal their fundamental defects even at the risk of banishment two or three times over.   This was where Ibsen's political greatness lay.   He loved his country so much that he would have sacrificed his soul for its liberty.   It is because he was a visionary-patriot that, like Wyspianski, he towers above contemporary dramatists.   Unfortunately, we have not this spirit of patriotism in England.   And it is because we lack it that   our drama is crude and nasty, trivial and irrelevant.   It is because Mr Bernard Shaw is not a patriot that he misses Ibsen's patriotism and exhibits Ibsen's apparent inferiority in the curious tone of complaisancy which is prevalent in suburban society.   It is noteworthy that explorers are at work rediscovering Ibsen in other directions.   Thus the Municipal Theatre at Düsseldorf, under the intelligent directorship of Louise Dumont and Lindemann, is actively engaged with the symbolic staging of Ibsen. Soon there will be a general re-interpretation of Ibsen's ideas.   For one thing, Ibsen will be taken out of the Morgue where Mr Shaw placed him, and his notion of death spiritualised.   I think the deaths of Hedda and Lövborg will be represented as being the result of a spiritual compact between Hedda and Lövborg which can only be realised through physical death.   Lövborg has

degraded his work by collaborating with a commonplace woman, Mrs Elvstedt.   Some persons may
call this new interpretation, spiritual eugenics—
that is, individuals doing on the spiritual plane
what scientists are endeavouring to do on the
physical one—acting on the conclusion that you
cannot have a perfect idea without a perfect union.
If we examine Ibsen's plays closely, it appears as
though he believed that the spiritually minded
person is he who ought not to be born, but, being
born, there is no need for him to make the best
or worst of a material world.   There is always an
avenue for escape.   Ibsenism maintains that self-
effacement is self-realisation.   Brahm never rose
to this conception of Ibsen's ideas.   Still, his failure
to recognise the symbolist in Ibsen is atoned for
by his recognition of the patriotic spirit which
pervades Ibsen's plays and by the inauguration of
Ibsen cycles.   There was once a talk of Brahm
conducting such a cycle at His Majesty's Theatre,
London.   But it was only a talk.   There is no
hurry in England ; England was made for the
obsolete.

To sum up.   Reinhardt has learnt from Brahm
the principle of the ensemble—no stars, no tricks,
no incompetence, all the players guided by a central
figure, the director, all the acting subordinated to
a central idea, the author's.   To study the poet's
work, and give the poet his due, so far as experience
allows ; " not to misunderstand the poet, or to falsify
him for the sake of the vulgar mob," as the *Blätter
des Deutschen Theaters* says ; to understand delicacy,
refinement, judgment ; to abolish all useless tradi-

tions ; to promote talent and not eliminate it,
as in England ; to promote acting, and to kill
off ranting and melodramatic speech and action :
all this he learnt from Brahm.   There is, however,
this difference noticeable in the work of the two
men.   Brahm's productions were distinguished by
a most delicate intellectual refinement.   Everybody
was in tune.   Reinhardt is not so delicate.   He
also seeks to orchestrate his instruments.   But
the instruments are sometimes of unequal value.
Brahm sought to kill off the one-part actor.   Reinhardt goes further.   He has produced the actor
of forty or fifty different parts.   It may be mentioned that the ensemble is now growing hoary-
headed in Germany.   It came there to roost when
the star-system of England was in its swaddling
clothes.   We know that only in recent years it has
made its appearance in England, where it is beginning to exhibit the extravagances of a dying system.
For one thing, it is seen that the intellectual ensemble does not allow players to project their
imagination into the characters, but compels them
to work to a rigid pattern set by the producer.
For another, it is opening the door on abuse by
encouraging authors to sketch out their plays in
soulless talk, leaving them to be filled in by acting.
Efficient acting is in fact giving rise to a glut of
bloodless dialogue.

INTIMACY

Reinhardt was no doubt influenced in his idea
of intimacy by Goethe, who, with other critics,
sought to attain a naturalistic *rapprochement* between

actor and audience. He began to develop it at the " Brille " and the " Schall und Rauch." The Ueberbrettl cult (and " Brille ") was initiated by the German troubadour, Baron Ernst von Wolzogen. The movement was associated with the well-known lyricist O. J. Bierbaum. For a few years it enjoyed extraordinary popularity ; it spread rapidly throughout Europe, and variety halls or combined music halls and Montmartre cabarets sprang up everywhere. In serving the purpose of bringing poets, actors, painters, and all sorts and conditions of men together, they were studio intimate theatres in the true sense. These places provided an entertainment which caught everybody simultaneously, and everybody responded simultaneously. There was no exalting of psychology. The floodgates of feeling were opened, and everybody was engulfed. The following description of the inauguration of the " Schall und Rauch " illustrates how intimacy was quickened by the kind of entertainment provided. Under the name of " Schall und Rauch " the members of the Café-theatre Society removed their nightly meetings to the Künstlerhaus in the Bellevuestrasse. Here they invited guests, to whom they offered, between midnight and dawn, their triple bill: music, colour, and motion. In the year 1901 they were led to give up the intimate evenings at the Künstlerhaus, and to transfer them elsewhere. They rebuilt for their purpose a hall in a hotel in Unter den Linden. This hall they hung with drapery and decorated with grinning Böcklin masks. Having commissioned Orlik to design a poster, they began their " Schall und Rauch " performances in public, in spite of being warned "not to waste an abundance of good ideas having harmony and style upon an audience of snobs."

On the first night (9th October 1901) the audience was received by attendants dressed in white pierrot costumes with black pom-poms. After a prologue written by Kayssler there came cabaret songs, caricatures of the products of culture and civilisation, and grotesque dances, followed by a satirical dream-poem by Max Reinhardt, in which the horrors of the *Brettleiter's Hollenfahrt* (the cabaret manager's descent to hell) were described. Thus the entertainment rushed forward at high speed and in high spirits. Here the somewhat crudely applied principle revealed is, that intimacy resides in high-spirited, not in low-spirited drama.

REALISM

When I visited Moscow in the autumn of 1911, I had an opportunity of learning a great deal about the aims, methods, and influence of the Moscow Art Theatre. I was received by M. Stanislawsky, the distinguished director, and by him handed over to the secretary, M. Michael Lykiardopoulas, who, in turn, introduced me to the working members of the theatre organisation, and also gave me some essential facts and figures. From him I gathered that there had been a logical development of the theatre, from its smallest beginnings as an amateur society to its present dimensions as a financial undertaking clearing over £10,000 profit yearly. One of the

facts that he sought to impress upon me was that
for some years the Moscow Art Theatre has been,
and now is, exercising a strong influence on the
European theatre and drama. I received this piece
of information with a smile, knowing that he had
been understudying Mr Gordon Craig. Statements
of this kind are certainly as numerous in Europe
as the oft-mentioned flies round the sugar bowl.
From Paris, Berlin, Munich, Buda-Pesth, Cracow,
and elsewhere the claims to discoveries, initia-
tions, and innovations in the theatre are unend-
ing. But in most cases such discoveries prove to
be nothing more than remarkable coincidences
and correspondences. Ideas are let loose ; we
are unable to say whence they come, and they are
received in various quarters by individuals specially
equipped for the purpose. It would be interesting to know how much the Moscow Theatre
owes to the Theatre of Wyspianski, and to hear
what is the forcible influence which Mr John
Balance, writing in the *Mask*, suggests that Mr
Gordon Craig has exerted over the Moscovian
management. In going through my notes on
the stages of the development of the Moscow
Theatre, I find these stages correspond to some
of those of Max Reinhardt's career. There is
the initial stage of the founding of a society by
art and literary enthusiasts, answering to the Freie
Bühne. There is the " Ueberbrettl " and literary
movement, which spread to Russia, disseminating
the idea of intimacy. There is the founding
of a small theatre, the Moscow Kleines Theater.
There are public and press prejudices to overcome.

There is a passing from naturalism to artistic naturalism, to realism and ultra-realism, thence to artistic synthesis, symbolism, and now to ultra-symbolism. From this it looks indeed as though Max Reinhardt, and the various movements in which he has been caught up, have been in Moscow the whole time.

But, as I pointed out to Mr M. Lykiardopoulas, I had found there are more original art theatres in Europe than are dreamt of at the Moscow Art Theatre, and it is quite possible that these have evolved their own system of literary and artistic organisation without a great deal of outside aid. At the same time, it may be admitted that some outside influence has affected their originality. It may be possible that Max Reinhardt is indebted to the Moscow Art Theatre in small ways. When that theatre toured through Europe in 1896, it appears to have created a sensation by its realistic methods of representing and interpreting certain Russian plays. In particular, the extreme emphasis placed upon the minutely worked out details of characterisation in everyday plays of the Gorky class was followed with close attention, while the absolute realism of the scene must have produced delirium in those who admire house-to-house duplication. In fact, the absolute realism of the Moscow Art Theatre, which culminated in the £15,000 production of *Julius Cæsar*—a production that sent the theatre staff to Rome for local colour, and brought down real rain, called forth real wind, especially from the local press, and gave employment to a host of persons who are accustomed to

copy stage costumes with R.A.-like fidelity—this
sort of realism, no doubt, greatly impressed the
open-mouthed public. It may have impressed
Max Reinhardt. But, in point of fact, it was
not till some time afterwards that he broke with
naturalism, and gave a realistic representation of
The Lower Depths, wherein Vallentin's principles
established themselves. It is possible, too, that
some of the details of the organisation of the
Moscow Theatre reached Berlin. But there is no
evidence to prove this. Again, it may be thought
that the idea of the revolving stage came from
Moscow. But Lautenschläger of Munich was the
first to construct such a stage in Europe, and we
know there were revolving stages in Japan long
before Lautenschläger's time. All things considered, it is doubtful how much realism Max
Reinhardt derived from Moscow ; it is clear, however, that he derived a great deal from Wagner
and the Saxe-Meiningen company. Indeed, as we
shall see, Reinhardt was largely concerned in
carrying on the improvement in the artistic
technical and economic condition of the German
stage—an improvement due, on the one hand, to
the reforms introduced by the Duke of Meiningen
in the Court Theatre at Meiningen, and, on the
other hand, to the ideals realised at Bayreuth by
Richard Wagner.

ARTISTIC INFLUENCES

The artistic influence exerted upon the German
stage by the company of actors in the service and
under the direction of Duke George of Saxe-

Meiningen, at the Meiningen Theatre, was at its height between 1874 and 1890. The company created a great effect by its performances throughout Europe, contributing to the German stage improvements in crowd effects, speech, scenery and decoration, and above all attaining an extraordinary perfection of ensemble. The Meiningen Theatre was, and still is, a Court Theatre, and belongs to the reigning Grand Duke of Saxe-Meiningen, now in his eighty-fifth year. It stands in a town of 10,000 inhabitants. Franz von Dingelstedt, the director at Weimar, and contemporary of Duke George, also promoted the scenic reform. It was Dingelstedt who first produced Shakespeare's historical plays upon the German stage. He startled the Weimarians by producing these plays in an unbroken cycle on seven consecutive nights. At the time of the said scenic reform the German " scene " was in a very primitive condition. Representation was, in fact, at such a low pitch, and speech so bad, that an audience with the best imagination in the world could make nothing of the caricatures that haunted them like nightmares. Under the intelligent direction of the Grand Duke of Saxe-Meiningen this wretched state of affairs was altered. The Meiningen company began to reform the scene and the culture stage. Influenced by Charles Kean, it introduced to Germany the ideas of his revivals. Carefully organised by the Grand Duke, it sought to obtain effects by minute realism, and aimed to make the " scene " and everything in it a reproduction of historical correctness. The scenic artist,

the costumier, and the actor were faithful repro-
ducers of detail.   In the opinion of some authorities
the Meiningen company derived many principles
from Charles Kean, who was occupied with the
archæology of play-producing.   "The Shakespearean productions at the Princess's under Charles
Kean's management were," as Miss Ellen Terry tells
us, "the real beginning of a serious attempt to clear
the air of anachronisms.   Charles Kean had had a
classical education, and he could not share the
complacency of most actors at the sight of antique
Romans in knee-breeches, and other inaccuracies
in dress and architecture.   Planche, to this day
considered the best general authority on historical
dress, was his right-hand man.   I made my first
appearance as Mamillius in the middle of an outburst of care and erudition, of which it would be
absurd to deny the importance, because the actresses
of the time still loved their crinolines so much that
they would not discard them when they put on
their Greek dresses."   The view that Kean preceded
the Meiningen company in archæological reform
is held by Dr Ernst L. Stahl, and is developed
by him in a book *Das englische Theater im neun-
zehnten Jahrhundert*, published by R. Oldenburg
of Munich.   We must not forget that Kean had
reason for his reform.   In his day there was a
decline in passion and eloquence.   He himself had
no voice to speak of, and has been marked off accordingly.   His example has been followed by managers
who have substituted scenery to conceal defects of
speech and action.   Whether Kean did or did not
greatly influence George II. of Meiningen, the re-

forms undertaken by the latter were conscientiously carried out. He thoroughly organised and managed his own famous theatre ; he gathered together a really first-class troupe of players ; he directed the productions and he designed the costumes and scenery ; he brought the acting more into harmony with the scenery ; in fact, he had a true apprehension of scenic and acting ensemble, as well as the ability to do everything himself. In addition to the reform of the scene, the Meiningers gained a great reputation for their reform of speech and the stage-crowd. In these two particulars at least they exerted a great influence over the European Theatre. Grand Duke George was one of the modern Old Masters who, like the famous actors Iffland and Schröder, introduced a more natural method of speaking, just as Macklin, Talma, and Phelps did in their turn. The Meiningers really formed a company of speakers. Every member was an artist in this respect. The dialogue of the drama was spoken by each so that it could be heard and understood. How different it is in England to-day ! Here the theatres represent so many voice tombs where the players come to bury the noises which they make in their throats, within the unholy precincts of the stage itself, what time the spectator sits watching with an indescribable air of foolish melancholy. Irving set the fashion of barking at the spectator, and we find this raw material of the Hyde Park school of elocution recast and subtilised in the speech of our distinguished players. There are but one or two leading players who do not belong to the voiceless band, among

whom may be mentioned Arthur Bourchier, Forbes
Robertson, D. Lyn Harding, and Lewis Waller.
But it was in the handling of stage-crowds that
Duke George was pre-eminent.   He appears to
have understood the composition of the crowd and
to have solved one at least of the problems arising
therefrom.   The two main problems of the stage-
crowd lie in the manner of bringing the crowd on
the stage and taking it off again, and the management of it while it is on.   Again, there are two
forms of stage-crowd—the crowd in the mass, or
classical crowd, and the crowd composed of individuals or individualistic crowd.   Like Wyspianski,
Duke George was occupied with the classic crowd.
His crowd indeed formed a Greek chorus.   It had
a mental unity and spoke and acted as one person.
Such a crowd answers to the psychological crowd,
whose striking peculiarity is described by Le Bon.
Whoever be the individuals that compose it, however
like or unlike be their mode of life, their occupa-
tions, their character, or their intelligence, the fact
that they have been transformed into a crowd puts
them in possession of a sort of collective mind
which makes them feel, think, and act in a manner
quite different from that in which each individual
of them would feel, think, and act were he in a
state of isolation.   There are certain ideas and
feelings which do not come into being, or do not
transform themselves into acts except in the case
of individuals forming a crowd.   The psychological
crowd is a provincial being formed of heterogeneous
elements, which for a moment are combined,
exactly as the cells which constitute a living body

form by their reunion a new being which displays characteristics very different from those possessed by each of the cells singly. It was this organised or collective crowd representing " a creature acting by instinct " that Shakespeare had in mind when he wrote the Forum Scene of *Julius Cæsar*, and the attempt to compose the Forum Scene crowd in detail instead of in mass is utterly wrong. Duke George must have been of this opinion, for he rendered unto Shakespeare that which is Shakespeare's. For the Forum Scene he formed a classical chorus, composed of intelligent supers, and thus obtained the best general effects. In so doing he went far beyond the London manager, who composes his crowd of half-baked walkers-on, who slouch on and off the stage and throw everything out of gear.

The Meiningen company travelled about Germany and England, creating a tradition. In due course it came to London, and gave that city a taste of the finest example of a stage-crowd. *Julius Cæsar*, its greatest success, was staged at Drury Lane, transforming this theatre for the time being into a source of inspiration. But it is curious to note that though, as Miss Ellen Terry tells us, " from that moment there was reform amounting to revolution," it was the Meiningen company that exerted the influence and not Kean. Apparently Kean, " who had admirable stage-crowds," did not go beyond or as far as the German company. He merely gave a new life to classical and historical correctness and a fresh impulse to the modern " immoral " pruning of Shakespeare. Miss

Terry is of the opinion that "the standard imposed upon us by the Meiningen company has not been maintained of late years." The classical standard has not been maintained at all. Though Max Reinhardt learnt a great deal from the Meiningers' methods of handling a crowd, he also followed its fresh courage in breaking away from tradition. Finding that of the Meiningers growing out of date, he broke away from it. Reinhardt then turned his attention to the so-called naturalistic and realistic methods of modern crowd management, the aim of which is to get "voices." Thus a voice starts at one point, is followed by another in an opposite direction, and this in turn is followed by others, and so the cackle spreads like an infection. The individualisation of crowds is no doubt legitimate and logical up to a certain point. Though there are psychological, organised crowds, possessed by one dominating idea, there are also crowds which are divided on the main issue. Such are, for instance, electoral crowds. The members of these do not act collectively, but indulge in individual cries, to say nothing of the face-scratching of rivals. The distinction among crowds is either not understood or not sufficiently applied, with the result that there is a tendency to travesty the individualisation of the super. Mr Louis Calvert is very successful with his individualised crowds, his best result being that attained in the *Julius Cæsar* crowd scene which he produced a few years ago for Sir Herbert Tree. Mr Granville Barker's crowds are effective but blurred by exaggeration. His crowd in *Votes for*

Women had an essential political atmosphere ; but both the crowd in *Strife* and that of the Forum Scene, one of the items given at the coronation performance at His Majesty's Theatre, were dismal failures. The first was lacking in a proper conception of the behaviour of a working-class crowd moved by an issue in the hands of different "leaders." The second was a ludicrous attempt to edit Shakespeare. Mr Barker practically rewrote the Forum Scene. The parts were handed to the individuals of a crowd composed of all the leading lights of the London Stage. The learning and rehearsing of these parts put such a limit to the good nature of the individualised "supers," that towards the conclusion of the rehearsals they forgot to love and respect Mr Barker. Chaos flew down from the prehistoric flies, and Sir Herbert Tree took the conductor's chair.

STYLISATION AND SYNTHESIS OR UNITY

As I have pointed out, Max Reinhardt was born in Austria, where a powerful artistic development has been going on for some years. Government art schools for the enlightenment of the classes, and the art movement in the theatre have done much to produce in individuals a great accessibility to artistic ideas. It is possible that Max Reinhardt owes much to this renaissance both in and out of the theatre, and in subsequent years it largely helped him to feel the full force of the various currents of the artistic pressure and to appreciate their value. It is not surprising, therefore,

that style, or stylisation, as it is called, should make a
successful appeal to him.   It first manifested itself
in his attempt to obtain coherence and uniformity,
and it had characteristics similar to those which
M. Meierholdt gave to it.   M. Meierholdt, who
was manager of Madame Kommisarzhevsky's artistic
St Petersburg theatre, interpreted the meaning of
the term as follows : " I consider it is impossible
to separate the ideas of ' stylisation ' from the ideas
of generalisation, convention, and symbolism.   By
the ' stylisation ' of a period or a phenomenon,
I mean the use of all means that bring out the
inner synthesis of the period or phenomenon, and
that enable the latent characteristics of artistic
works to be clearly presented."   Simply stated,
this is a demand for the representation of the soul
of the drama by every means available.   The
secretary of the Moscow Art Theatre told me that
this theatre was the first to realise the element of
stylisation.   The Moscow Theatre discovered it in
Tchekoff's *Seagull*.   It consists, he said, in a subtle
mood which cannot be transmitted by any medium,
say acting, alone, but requires a unity of every
means employed on the stage—and everybody,
from leading man to " limes."   Apparently, however, Meierholdt was first with the idea that the
drama is to be represented and interpreted in a
" spiritual theatre " by means of an outer synthesis
expressing an inner synthesis.   Such an end
Wagner had in view when he sought to transport
himself and the spectator into the enraptured
world of imagination of the *Nibelungen*, and the religious world of *Parsifal*.   To Wagner the operas

of his time were unreal, presented in detached pieces, instead of in big, simple masses. There was no attempt made to preserve the spirit or mood which the poet-musician had created. So he set to work to change all this, and establish a new tradition. According to this tradition, music-drama was to be produced in a new style having unity and coherence. We know what that style was, and many of us know how antiquated it is to-day. But when Wagner first made known the theory of his synthesis of music, chant, and colour, it came as a revelation to most men. Here was a means indeed of realising the secrets of the spiritual world. Here was a way to express the subtlest nuances of the poetry of life. When chant failed there was music ; when music failed there was decoration to carry on the action. Or so it seemed. Gradually, however, reformers began to detect a serious flaw in the " Master's " scheme. It was found he had invented not a unified design, but a threefold one, composed of music, chant, and decoration running simultaneously. Then the complaint arose : " This is wrong ; you cannot hear the chant for the music, and you cannot enjoy academic scenery while the music and chant are going on. None the less, the Wagner synthesis has invaded and held the stage till to-day. The sins of the poet of the *Nibelungen* are still re-peated, and even Max Reinhardt repeats the fallacy of the Wagnerian threefold motive. He gives us music, song, speech, acting, dance, and decoration, repeating instead of expanding and supplementing each other. All that Reinhardt received from

Wagner he has retained, except one particular. He has quietly buried Wagner's ultra-realism derived from the Meiningers—his scenic aids and atrocious circus effects—in the dustheap. He prefers Böcklin to Brückner. Now the Festspielhaus orchestral flashes of lightning wedded to the magnesium flashes are to be found at His Majesty's Theatre, London.

THE IMPRESSIONISTIC SCENE

Max Reinhardt's period of seeking and earnest effort led him in time to the reform of the scene. The Meiningen company called upon the scenic artist for interesting colour photography. Wagner's scene-painter belonged to the German Royal Academy, while his animated properties came out of the Ark. Reinhardt has gone beyond this in his search for a simplified scene. He was the first to call to the service of the scene the aid of distinguished plastic artists and painters, selecting with judgment those who are specially gifted for the work : such as Arnold Böcklin, with his wonderful sense of atmospheric form ; Emil Orlick, with his love of Japanese form and colour ; Edward Munch, the Ibsen of Norwegian painters ; Ernst Stern, with his mastery of bold colour. That painting could legitimately be called in to serve the scene is clear when we remember that the modern movement in painting is largely decorative. I use the word decorative in its old sense : that is, of decoration being an accretion. In the new sense it is not decoration, seeing that what we call decoration is something which is an essential part of character and

which is added merely to give the widest expression
to that character. Reformers of the scene have
recognised the value of the decorative movement
in painting and have encouraged painters to serve
the theatre. Thus the application of the principles
of Neo-Expressionism was made both at the
Théâtre des Arts under the direction of M. Jacques
Rouché and by the decorators of the Russian Ballets
during their seasons in Paris and London, 1910–
12. By the intelligent use of line and colour,
the scene designed by the latter attained two
qualities : unity and continuity. Costumes and
scenery were designed to harmonise, and costumes
were designed to harmonise with each other. The
scene thus treated had a basis of fantasy, and all the
hues and colours helped to build up and maintain
the sensation of the fantasy. But the great aim
of these decorators was to create the dynamic scene,
in which everything is presented to the spectator
as a moving whole and having one big effect. So,
the scene became an outward synthesis of the
inner synthesis of the soul of the dancers. These
principles are not yet understood in England. Till
they are we shall not rise above the scenic conceptions of the studio artist. Mr Charles Ricketts
has treated Wilde's *Salome*, *Don Juan*, and *King
Lear*, in the latter calling forth Mr Craig's wrath.
Mr Cayley Robinson and Mr Sime have made
designs for *The Blue Bird*, and Mr Norman Wilkinson, armed with designs, has followed Mr Granville
Barker from theatre to theatre. But these painters
have asked us to accept pictorial work which,
though admirable in some respects, is incomplete

as stage decoration.   With regard to Reinhardt, I believe that he has helped himself to the new traditions of mass-impressionism which the Berlin and Munich Secessionists have been creating.   By this means he has given the scene a "feeling" part instead of a "thinking" part in the play, and enabled it to contribute to the general effect or sensation, in mass and not in wearisome detail. Thus he has come nearest to the newer unity in variety of stage-setting.

Symbolic Staging

Stylisation is a keynote of symbolic staging. The credit of initiating this form of staging in German progressive theatres has been given wrongly, I think, to Jocza Savits, who several years ago invented and used a new Shakespearean stage at the Court Theatre, Munich.   Herr Savits' book, *On the Aim of the Drama*, reveals indeed that he was not so much occupied (if at all) with symbolic staging as with simplified staging.   He would do away with scenery altogether.   As Mr Archer says in his contribution to the symposium on the Deutsches Theater : " Herr Savits has written a very solid and very thoughtful treatise, which is nothing but a systematic attack upon the whole principle and practice of calling in painting to the illustration or decoration of drama.   Herr Savits writes with a special view to Shakespeare, and to performances on the so-called Shakespeare-stage in Munich ; but if I understand him aright, he considers scenery the bane of all drama what-ever, and would not have the ear and mind distracted by any sort of appeal to the eye." Mr Archer then proceeds to examine Herr Savits' theory of non-stop Shakespeare, and puts in a plea for the act-interval. Having condemned the English practice of using this interval " to cumber the stage with ostentatious scenery," he comments on Max Reinhardt's employment of symbolic staging. Let me quote his words : " I have seen only one of Herr Max Reinhardt's Shakespearean revivals at the Deutsches Theater, Berlin ; but that struck me as a model of good taste in mounting. The play was *The Winter's Tale*. Almost all the scenes in Sicily were played in a perfectly simple yet impressive decoration—a mere suggestion, without any disturbing detail, of a lofty hall in the palace of Leontes. For the pastoral act in Bohemia, on the other hand, a delightful scene was designed, for all the world like a page from a child's picture book. The grass was bright green velvet, spangled with conventional flowers. A blossoming fruit-tree shadowed a toy-cottage ; and in the background some quaint masts and pennons showed the proximity of the sea. The whole effect was charmingly fantastic and admirably in keeping with the action of the scene." Following Mr William Poel's example, Herr Savits did Shakespeare in curtains only. Reinhardt, besides doing Shakespeare in curtains, added symbolic " decoration," while maintaining the simplicity of the " curtain " method. His vision of *The Winter's Tale* was that of a child, and he used such natural symbols to express natural objects, the masts and pennons suggesting ships and the sea, as a child would

choose. I do not say this to depreciate Max
Reinhardt's ability as a producer. On the contrary, I think that it testifies to his insight into the
first demand of the spectator, namely, that there
shall be a simple and intimate approach to the soul
of the play.

It is more correct, then, to credit Reinhardt with
being a pioneer of the modern form of symbolic
staging, the old form of which really dates back for
many centuries. This staging movement has spread
in Germany, and to-day there are many theatres aiming to abolish the realistic representation of drama,
consisting of a hair-to-hair fidelity to materialistic
details. Thus the very progressive theatre at
Düsseldorf, under the management of Louise
Dumont and G. Lindemann, have replaced the
realistic frame by the symbolic setting or frame
designed to emphasise the rhythmic mood of the
piece by broad outlines and symbolically applied
line, colour, light, and shade. During my visit
to Düsseldorf, I visited the Dumont-Lindemann
Schauspielhaus and found it had several interesting innovations designed to preserve the artistic
impression throughout. One is the disappearance
of the back cloth and the substitution for this
artificial and stupid background of a more obvious
and more useful decoration, namely, the whitewashed wall. I failed to notice whether this
wall corresponds to the round horizon in use
at the Deutsches Theater, Berlin. By the use
of this wall the silhouettes of the people are
shown more clearly than is the case before the
everlasting panorama of lawn and country scenes

to which we are accustomed.   In fact, it adds
to the importance of the characters.   Again, it is
claimed that many effects can be got from behind
this wall that are not possible behind the ordinary
painted cloth.   Another innovation is the attempt
to focus attention on the centre of the stage, not,
of course, after the manner of the English actor-
manager, who takes the centre of the stage and
never leaves it, but in a much more artistic
way.   The management believes that the supreme
point of the stage is the centre.   This is the point
from which movement should radiate, and also the
point of visual attraction, and all decorations are
made accordingly to lead to this point.   In consequence, everything is given a direction of line leading
to this one point of view.   All lines, in fact, converge
on the centre.   By this means a feeling of immensity
is created which is entirely lacking in the common
or garden scene.   But what struck me most about
the Düsseldorf Schauspielhaus was the attitude of
the audience.   One of the pieces I saw was Ibsen's
Hedda Gabler, the artistic interpretation and the
ensemble acting of which was only equalled by that
of the Lessing Theater Company under Brahm.
Throughout the performance the audience sat silent
and still.   There was no applause, no demand for
curtains, no rush for refreshments.   Though there
was no music between the acts, there was no idiot
gabble of the Stage Society sort which recently called
forth a strong protest from a suffering member.
Beyond this, there were no attendants buzzing
about the auditorium with doubtful liquid refreshments and sealed sixpenny programmes.   The pro-

gramme made its appearance not in the unlovely guise of an advertising tout, but in an artistic get-up, and accompanied by a readable literary sheet, *Masken*. It should be mentioned that the silent audience, the no-music entr'acte, and the no-call system, are not confined to Düsseldorf. They are to be found at Moscow also. I believe the object of the Düsseldorf Theatre management in introducing these three reforms was in pursuit of its idea that the theatre should be a place of meditation, where that portion of the theatre-going public who have the time and inclination for meditation might go instead of going to church. This is one of the many attempts towards making the theatre serve the purpose of the church in the matter of mental rest and enlightenment.

Gordon Craig's Symbolism

Of recent months we have heard a great deal about Mr Gordon Craig's influence on the artistic development of the German Theatre, and more especially on the work of Max Reinhardt. Mr Craig and his enthusiastic band of followers who contribute their opinions to that live journal, *The Mask*, contend that the influence exerted by Mr Craig has been considerable and not always acknowledged. In fact, they support the usual charge of plagiarism. To deny a charge of plagiarism would require a philosopher with a mind of an antique cast, and I am not going to attempt it. I can only repeat that "divinely" appointed minds have the bad habit of "lifting" each other's goods, and, as we shall see, Mr Craig himself, being " divinely " endowed, has fallen into the same class with Coleridge, whom De Quincey accused of stealing Pythagoras' wretched dogma about beans. Perhaps the charge against Reinhardt is not altogether just ; for, as facts can show, there is very little resemblance between his work and Mr Craig's, and there have been acknowledgments. In Germany it is generally admitted that Mr Craig's influence in the theatre has been felt. There are persons in Germany who would, no doubt, seriously consider the implication contained in the following note to a design for *Hamlet* published in his *On the Art of the Theatre*. Says Mr Craig : " It was this design which I carried over to Germany in 1904, when I first went to Weimar at the invitation of Count Kessler, one of the men who have done most for the German Theatre. If we had even one such enthusiast of like culture and practical energy in England, the theatre would be in a more living condition than it is to-day. This design seems to have given pleasure to my few German friends— and I remember that their pleasure gave me more. I am not particularly fond of German art, except for its early music, but I am never forgetful of German enthusiasm and of the titanic energy displayed from one end of the land to the other. And nowhere was there more promise in all Germany than in Weimar in 1904, when Count Kessler lent himself to the task of guiding the taste of the people who were eager to follow him. In fact, the success of Professor Reinhardt in Berlin is in a large measure due to the influence and enthusiasm of Count Kessler." The implication underlying this note is that Count Kessler did much to promote ideas, one at least of which Craig now admits to be out of date. For has not Craig told us that he has discarded the setting (with which he set Count Kessler in action), consisting of a set of curtains suspended from a great height with a narrow opening between, through which the moon peered, at a vast interior, in favour of a great grey screen for receiving light, against which the coloured limelights may move beautifully. A further implication is that Count Kessler pushed Max Reinhardt on. But this is extremely doubtful. I am more inclined to think that Reinhardt is made of the stuff that does its own pushing.

There was a great deal of artistic work going on in the German Theatre before Mr Craig arrived. As early as 1830 Goethe had conversations with Eckermann about the art of the theatre. Though Germans are ready to admit that there are some traces of Mr Craig in Reinhardt's production of *The Winter's Tale*, there can scarcely be any in *Pelleas and Melisande*, seeing that this piece was produced long before Mr Craig's aforementioned visit. As far as I remember, Brahm was the first German manager who tried to apply Mr Craig's ideas, but without success. The only two sets of scenery designed by Mr Craig himself for the German Theatre were done for Brahm, one of them being for *Venice Preserved*, by Otway, a piece adapted for the German stage under the title of *Das Gerettete Venedig*, by Hofmannsthal ; the other being the scenery for *Le Mirage*, by Georges Rodenbach.   Both plays were failures, and therefore but few details of Craig's artistic methods and still fewer of his designs are likely to have influenced the German style.   Indeed, his influence does not appear to have gone beyond the use of curtains, experiments in lighting, and inviting the artist to aid the producer.   Of course this is a great deal, and may be the root of a very widespread reform.

It is also true that his *Hamlet* has been produced at Moscow and the production has set new ideas running round the universe.   But Mr Craig had something to be thankful for.   Had M. Stanislawsky and his co-operators been in a hurry and not able to devote three years to the work of the production, had he been an Irishman or a Turk, or someone with less patience, Mr Craig and his ideas might have still been waiting to be brought to earth.

Having indicated to what extent Mr Gordon Craig has influenced Reinhardt and the German Theatre, it may be of interest to note the character of Mr Craig's ideas, together with the sources of their inspiration.   Mr Craig is a decorator of genius in search of light.   The light is, of course, limelight disguised as daylight.   For years he has concentrated on the problem of stage-lighting, and the nearer he gets to a working solution apparently, the farther away he gets.   It is for the light of the infinite he hungers, and he searches eagerly for the incandescent lamp that shall bear him towards it.   Let there be daylight !

cries Mr Craig.　And the pitying angels hear and
weep ; for they know that the light which Mr
Craig demands for the theatre will never be forthcoming, — unless indeed the theatre be born
again as Mr Craig insists it shall be.　Then Mr
Craig asks for suggestion, not representation.　To
him suggestion is the only open door to the
soul's liberation on the stage.　Representation is
more of a photographer's and less of an artist's
ideal.　He wants simplicity, but it is doubtful
whether he has not confused simplicity with elimination.　Elimination is the taking out of details or
unessentials ; simplicity is seeing and putting down
only the essentials.　In the composition of his
big, lonely, and sombre settings he eliminates the
human interest.　Man is made to appear impotent,
feeble, a microbe.　His mentality and vitality
are eliminated.　In fact, Mr Gordon Craig's stage
is so much space for a design, whereas it should be
so much space for the expansion of the mentality
of man.　It would be unfair to deny that there is
something tremendously big in Mr Craig's settings.
They are very arresting in their way, usually big
in conception, though monotonous in treatment.
He has an idea of getting a light here and
there against masses of black or shadow.　He
searches for movement and gets it so far as
stage mechanics will allow.　He tries for mystery
and gets mistiness.　His " scene " is in consequence all mist and vague atmosphere.　He is
searching for a scene " with as many moods as the
sea."　It sounds, coming from Mr Craig, indefinite.
Reinhardt is far more tangible.　He believes in

Original Sketch by KARL WALSER for a Scene in Shakespeare's "A Midsummer-Night's Dream," produced at The Deutsches Theater.

massiveness, scenes carved out of solid blocks, as by sculptors. If he uses symbols, they are at least serviceable ones. Mr Craig makes for atmospheric unity and gets style by the methods already described. Among Mr Craig's many ideas must be mentioned the famous Reckitt's blue background, which used to follow him about like Mary's lamb in the fable, and which he believed he had invented. Nature could, however, supply him with an improved copy. Perhaps it was Nature who obliged Max Reinhardt with a copy, and, if so, there is no need to deny it. We have all heard of Mr Craig's ideal stage-director, whose function is apparently that of a pattern-designer.

" He does not merely sit down and draw a pretty or historically accurate design with enough doors and windows in picturesque places, but he first of all chooses certain colours which seem to him to be in harmony with the spirit of the play, rejecting other colours as out of tune. He then weaves into a pattern certain objects—an arch, a foundation, a balcony, a bed—using the chosen object as the centre of his design. Then he adds to this all the objects which are mentioned in the play, and which are necessary to be seen. To those he adds, one by one, each character which appears in the play, and gradually each movement of each character, and each costume." After pointing out that the director-designer is liable to mistakes and must not mind going back several times, the passage continues : " Slowly, harmoniously must the whole design develop, so that the eye of the beholder shall be satisfied. While this pattern for the eye is being devised, the designer is being guided as much by the sound of the verse or prose as by the sense or spirit."

In this passage lies the keynote to Mr Craig's old conception and method of production. Instead of the scene growing out of the fundamental rhythm or note of the character or play, which slowly expands till it fills the frame and carries us beyond the theatre, the spirit of the play is to be matched with certain harmonious colours and a design outlined, into which every conceivable object is to be poured. Coming to the theatre, we found Mr Craig at one time busy with an entirely new form of playhouse, of which we were offered a glimpse in words which said : " I see a great building to seat many thousands of people. At one end rises a platform of heroic size, on which figures of a heroic mould shall move. Scenes shall be such as the world shows us, not as our own particular little street shows us. The movements on these scenes shall be noble and great: all shall be illuminated by a light such as the spheres give us, not such as the footlights give us, but such as we dream of." The new theatre is indeed Mr Craig's great dream.

He appears to think that we have already had a theatre, for he is repeatedly saying, " The theatre must be destroyed." The truth is, however, that we have never had a theatre and there is nothing to destroy. The institution I refer to elsewhere as the existing theatre is practically a stage, which I hope will develop into a theatre where the Will of the Theatre may be fully exercised. We have had stages, and we are still aspiring to a theatre by stages. This is Mr Craig's position. He will go a stage further. But this will be determined by his conception of a drama. At present Mr Craig and his followers are not clear concerning the materials for their new theatre. Ask Mr Craig what he is after and he will tell you, a new theatre, a new scene, a new kind of seven-headed director, a new electrician. Ask him what he is going to do with these materials, and he will reply perversely, "Wait and see." His words mean, "I have invented a theatre, but have nothing to put in it, that I can talk about." He believes that in time something will come. But as his editor, Mr John Semar, says, "You who are sympathetic towards us must not assist this (aim) forward by hastily rushing at our pupils and ourselves and demanding what this new drama is going to be. Nobody on earth can know till it is here."

From this it will be gathered that till this un-known and unheard-of drama arrives, Mr Craig must go on performing something, that something being Shakespeare. "*Hamlet*," Mr Craig tells us, "will go on being performed for some time yet, and the duty of the interpreters is to put their best work at its service. . . . But the theatre must not for ever rely upon having a play to perform, but must in time perform pieces of its own art." I wonder how Shakespeare likes being pasted in Mr Craig's scrap-book. Evidently Mr Craig is convinced that the drama must be born of the theatre. Some day he will say that the only drama is the Cosmic drama, and this is born outside the theatre, passes through the theatre, and carries the spectator out of the theatre with it, reappearing in time in the form of an enlarged Cosmic consciousness. Then he will be nearer the truth of his words, " Why, there are tremendous things to be done. We haven't yet got near the thing. Über-marionettes and wordless plays and actorless dramas are the obvious steps to a far deeper mystery." In thus banishing plays and actors and scenery from the theatre, in specialising in masks and marionettes and imaginative space, and asking for nothing more than symbolic gesture, Mr Craig aims to reintroduce art to the theatre. He is the one man in the world who is making art as accessible to the theatre as possible, and who recognises that drama is all a matter of impulse and movement.

The origins of Mr Craig's ideas are many and varied. Mr Craig, like Reinhardt, is a sensitive. He receives every moment artistic stimuli to which he yields a certain number of responses. He assimilates as he goes. He is a blend of art and theatre. He was, in a sense, born in the theatre, and he lived at Chelsea for several years. For a time he shared rooms with Mr Martin Shaw, the musician, and it would be interesting to know to what extent Mr Shaw brought him into touch with the melody and rhythm of the beautiful music of the old English masters, Purcell, Byrd, and the rest, " rhythm which is the very essence of dance." Mr Martin Shaw, I remember, conducted the music at the performance of Mr Laurence Housman's nativity play, *Bethlehem*, at South Kensington, and was very successful in bringing out the religious rhythms. Mr Craig's early impressions of theatre

reform were gained through his mother, Miss Ellen
Terry.   Her engagements with Kean, who started
the archæological reform of the " scene," doubtless
helped Mr Craig to a feeling for archæology,
which, as time proceeded, changed its name to
Craigology.   Miss Terry also had a great admiration for E. W. Godwin the architect, who, like Kean,
was deeply interested in matters that are included in
the general term " archæology."   Godwin designed
the scenery and dresses for plays in which Miss
Terry appeared.   "The production of *The Merchant
of Venice*," she tells us, " at the old Prince of Wales',
under the Bancroft management, in which I made
my first appearance as Portia, was in the hands
of Mr Godwin, and was, from many points of
view, the most beautiful production with which I
have ever been connected.   It was all very stiff
and stately, very Italian, and it necessitated what I
may call a Renaissance interpretation of the play."
This was in 1875.   Holding this high opinion of
Godwin's work (inspired by Greece and Flaxman),
Miss Terry would not fail to impress its importance
on Mr Craig.   Godwin's scrupulous exactness, with
which Irving and Sir Herbert Tree became bitten,
may help to explain for us Craig's sense of thoroughness, certain architectonic qualities of his settings,
and the great part which Godwin has been playing
in *The Mask*.   According to Miss Terry, Godwin
laid down the principle " that if you don't have
everything right, it is better to have nothing right
—to have either realism in every detail or pure
fancy applies to the garden, the heath, and the wood,
as well as the room."   Mr Craig took the thorough-

ness into the region of pure fancy. In a highly eulogistic " Note on the Work of E. W. Godwin," Mr John Semar places Godwin among the most remarkable of the " great men " of the modern theatre. He contends that Godwin " fathered the new movement in the European Theatre, and founded that race of theatrical artists of whom the theatre of the future shall be born. The services which he rendered by his earnestness, his thoroughness, by the talents which he brought to the assistance of the theatre, and the learning which he devoted to its cause, were incalculable." In pursuit of thoroughness " he searched in museums and libraries." Godwin then was of the learned type of mind. I was under the impression that the theatrical artists of the future were to be creators. I hope I am not mistaken. Probably Mr Semar means to imply that what is considered theatrically artistic to-day will not be considered so to-morrow. Like Ibsen, he may have discovered that everything is liable to change, and youthful truths to-day are hoary-headed lies to-morrow. Nor is it different with naturalism. Once upon a time Kean's acting was regarded as fairly natural, then came Macready and gave the lie to Kean's naturalism, then Irving appeared, and his artificial stage-stalking took away the breath of the naturalistic student, and then followed Mrs Patrick Campbell, Eleonora Duse, Antoine, and others, to put Irving's " naturalism " out of court. Ellen Terry's long and close connection with Irving opened up another source of inspiration to Mr Craig. Irving's leadership and characteristics must have exerted a tremendous formative influence upon Mr Craig's ideas of the theatre. It accounts for the exercise of big imagination in his work, for his ideas of directorship, for his conception of a synthesis of music, words, and colour, and for a certain pictorial sense. Mr Craig was further assisted in his conception of the new æsthetic synthesis by Wagner, and it is conceivable that he derived something from Adolphe Appia's suggestions for reforming the Wagnerian background by means of carefully detailed and differentiated lighting effects. The designs for these backgrounds were published in 1899. Böcklin too, who could make nothing of Wagner, may have led him into the region of pure fancy. Whether Irving afforded Mr Craig an insight into the problem of stage-lighting is not clear. It is possible that Mr Craig accepted the problem in his own way. Or he may have consulted da Vinci, who emphasised the value of lighting figures from above, but overlooked the fact that light is reflected from the ground as well as from a thousand natural objects. Mr Craig overlooked this question of reflection when trying to do away with the footlights. From da Vinci also came the idea of the all-round man of Mr Craig's dreams. Then the lighting system of Fortuny has been largely advertised and offers suggestions to the modern alchemists of stage-light. Then there are everyday sources of inspiration. Mr George Calderon suggests somewhere that Mr Craig has cribbed his notion of overhead lighting from the barn-theatre, where they hang stable-lanterns on hooks.

A rather tantalising charge. Other circumstances which count for much in Mr Craig's development are these. He lived at Chelsea, where he would have every opportunity of coming into contact with the artistic ideas which he has applied to the theatre. Godwin the architect was a friend of Whistler—Whistler married Godwin's wife after Godwin's death,—also of Burgess, who did the wonderful restoration work for the Marquis of Bute, and he was intimately acquainted with Burne-Jones and William Morris. It is not difficult to understand that Mr Craig became at an early period of his life fully acquainted with the work and principles of these and other artists and architects. It is certain that he was largely influenced by Whistler's Eastern æstheticism, and derived from that painter's Nocturnes, Moonlights, and Japanese subjects some useful qualities, such as a conception of atmospheric treatment, a feeling for the silver greys that Whistler discovered haunting the Thames by Chelsea Bridge, a certain quality of monumental design, and a unity of purpose. From the chapter on " Scene and Movement " in *On the Art of the Theatre*, where Mr Craig discusses at some length a two-colour scheme, and a rock and a cloud of mist, it may be gathered what Whistler taught his unseen pupil, and how near Mr Craig has got to the Whistlerian manner and technique. Blake was another source of inspiration. It would be interesting to know the names of all the artists who have been influenced by Blake. Look through his illustrations and there spring forth memories of Watts, Burne-Jones,

Puvis de Chavannes, Cayley Robinson, the Pre-raphaelites, Augustus John, the Post-expressionists —every artist of note, in fact, who has had anything to do with the imaginative, symbolic, and heroic. Blake saw more in a thing than the thing itself, and everything expanded under his hand. Thus an ordinary scene touched by him would become at once tremendously big in design. I have some-times thought that if Blake lived to-day what fine work he might do for the theatre. I do not think he would do good interior work. But I should like to see him do some simple, big exteriors. He might even treat *The Blue Bird*, poor material though it be, and if he did he would make it far more impressive than it has been made as yet. Then Blake and *Hamlet*——? I do not think *Hamlet* has ever been treated as it will be one day, when we get the Blake-like decorator with his vast yet simple, child-like vision. Again, if he were alive to-day, I am sure he would be the first to congratu-late Mr Craig on having seen so much that is of value in his (Blake's) own work. And he would doubtless blame Mr Craig for having overlooked the greatest thing—his big-minded space. Possibly, too, Blake might appreciate the plain curtained stages of Herr Savits and William Poel and find a correspondence in the curtain scenery of Mr Craig. And if we were to point to Mr Craig's handling of light and shade, and his use of black, Blake would whisper, " That's Rembrandt for certain." Then Mr Craig's vast doorways and arches and use of low tones contain a strong reference to James Pryde, in whose studio Mr Craig has worked.

Then there is the screen idea, which to me has a resemblance to the folding screens used by the Tuscan players. Perhaps it has an ancestor in that old dramatic screen, the " Sacre Rappresentazioni " of Florence. Or it may have had an ancestor in the Japanese screens and turn-tables which once were so much in the air at Munich. Or it may be the outcome of Mr Craig's imagination. We do not know. In any case, screens have been on the carpet, as in *The Mask*, for many moons, and maybe it is to *The Mask* we must turn for certain facts on Mr Craig's more recent development. Looking abroad, as far as Moscow, one perceives another source of influence. The Russian decorators, busy with the renaissance of the line, have crossed Mr Craig's path and left their mark. I happened one day to be in Bond Street, and, having some time to spare, I went, in my capacity of art and drama critic, to Messrs Colnaghi's gallery to sample some studies by Gordon Craig. Among these were two studies for Hamlet, noticeable for their extraordinary resemblance to the Egyptian figures designed by Bakst for his masterpiece, *Cléopâtre*. Hamlet himself was conceived as an Egyptian. The action of the limbs, the position of the parts and the whole body, and the lines of the drapery were distinctly Egyptian. But the most remarkable coincidence was the strong development of the line. It was the sharp, bold, moving line of the Russian decorators. Clearly, Mr Craig was re-interpreting Shakespeare as an Egyptian. I thought, " if this is to be the fundamental note of the production, then the whole production will be Egyptian." Previous to this I had seen the Russian Ballets both in Paris and London. In one of the productions, *Pétrouchka*, I came across Mr Craig's über-marionette idea applied with a great deal of intelligence by Nijinski. The latter played the part of a puppet, and certainly succeeded in expressing a wide range of emotions. M. Georges Banks, a penetrating artist and a great believer in the future of Mr Craig's marionette idea, wrote in *Rhythm* (now defunct) of Nijinski's performance as follows : " I have never seen anything which suggested sentiment, passion, and the inevitable sequence of things, produced by movement and sound alone, without consciousness of the elimination of dialogue, as this production does. Conveyed by puppets and visualised by the forms of the finest human material in the theatre to-day, it suggests to one that the idea of Mr Gordon Craig's übermarionette is not a dream but a possibility of great meaning." But, then, Mr Craig says it is a dream, and I am not going to contradict him on this occasion. Moreover, puppets are as old as China and Punch and Judy, and *Pétrouchka* is based on Russian folklore. So here is further evidence that Mr Craig moves in a well-inhabited universe.

Mr Craig has been seriously experimenting for years. But his achievement in comparison with that of Max Reinhardt is, to say the least of it, small. Miss Terry first helped Mr Craig into the light of exclusive recognition, then the seventeenth-century Purcell followed with his first opera, *Dido and Æneas*, and, I believe, *The Masque of Love*. Then came Handel with his pastoral, *Ace Galatea e*

Poliferno, or *Acis and Galatea*, as it is called. After this followed Mr Housman with *Bethlehem*, a company of authors with *Sword and Song*, Ibsen with the *Vikings*, and Shakespeare with *Much Ado about Nothing*, a production remarkable for its church scene. Duse accepted his decorative ideas for *Rosmersholm* and *Electra*. The latest to give Mr Craig an artistic lift is M. Stanislawsky, whose three years' struggle with *Hamlet* has now passed into history. But it has not been " roses, roses all the way." There were obstacles. In all probability Mr Craig would not have had so much achievement as the above to his account but for the loyalty of his mother. She backed him freely with her money and gave him the fullest opportunity to do his best. In *The Story of My Life* she refers to the fiasco at the Imperial Theatre, where she had her " financially unfortunate season in 1903."

By the foregoing examination of sources of ideas, I do not seek to obscure Mr Craig's individual value, which is, as already stated, an æsthetic one. Nor do I seek to diminish Mr Craig in order to expand Max Reinhardt. There is no need to do so. Though there are resemblances and differences, the work of each man is distinct. Both are aids to progress in the theatre. Both draw their inspiration from personal sources. Gordon Craig is perhaps a creative artist in a truer sense than is Max Reinhardt. Yet of four classes into which leaders may be divided, precursors, initiators, continuators, and re-initiators, I would unhesitatingly say that Mr Craig belongs to the third. He is a continuator of fine traditions, which he treats with marked originality. Culture, with which he is occupied, is an entirely artificial product. The word culture is derived from cultus, signifying the state of being cultivated. Thus the seeds of culture may be in a person, but the seeds by themselves are valueless. They need cultivating by cultural aids. Look at the effect the awaking of intellect had upon the seeds of Greek culture. Fascinated by the new occupation of thinking, the Greeks gave themselves up to nothing else. Thus the Greek type of mind was essentially an intellectual one, and never rose above intellect ; it never attained intelligence. It has been the tyranny of ages. To-day men are beginning to throw off this tyranny and to attain intellect plus emotion. That is, they demand an intuitive rather than an intellectual perception of things. The cultured person is occupied with existing things ; and it is from such things that he draws his inspiration. The purely creative mind works in an x world. It is impelled to create by sheer inward necessity. One day the rhythmic stream of life, passing unhindered through such a mind, touches a note of music. Gradually this tiny seed-note expands, attains form, and is thus born to provide a key to one of the great mysteries of life and death.

Since this chapter was written Mr Craig has moved—and I think moved rightly—in the direction of the realisation of his aims. By the financial support of Lord Howard de Walden, he has been enabled to realise his long cherished scheme of founding a School of the Art of the Theatre. He has also published his big and immensely important book of designs, *Towards a New Theatre.* There is much in this book which goes to bear out my statements regarding the origins of his ideas. Mr Craig, for instance, acknowledges his debts to Rembrandt, Ruskin, Blake, Fra Angelico, to Irving, Yeats, Whistler, Pryde, Max Beerbohm, Nicholson, Beardsley, to Tiepolo, Guardi, Crawhall, Hugo, Piranesi, Vitruvius, Whitman, Andreini, Ganassa, Martinelli, Gherardi, Delsarte, Otway, Vecellio, to Raphael, Nietzsche, Pater, E. K. Chambers, and to his father and mother. It will be seen that he is spiritual heir to a goodly company. The book represents the period of Mr Craig's development, between 1900–1913. It reveals that he does not stand still, but has passed many of his old ideas. His progress has been mainly in the direction of scenography, and we find him happiest in the creation of purely suggestive surroundings for players. This pursuit brought him into contact with Max Reinhardt in 1905, the latter having repeatedly asked him to co-operate in the production of a play. In 1905 he had some conversation with Reinhardt over the production of *Cæsar and Cleopatra.* It seems that it was Mr Craig's production of *Dido and Æneas* which gives birth to the celebrated plain blue background and the grey proscenium, which have become so popular with reformers. Another fact of some interest is this, that Mr Poel and others made the attempt some years ago to employ curtains in place of scenery ; and Mr Craig improved on their efforts by coming forward and showing how the curtains were to be hung.

The Endowed Theatre—Organisation and Repertory

As though anticipating the coming of Max Reinhardt, certain factors have long been at work in Germany preparing the ground for him. The principal of these is the multiformed Endowed Theatre, to which he owes a vast and cultured theatre-going public. In Taine's view, " In Germany the public which judges intellectual products is the entire nation ; it is the society of the large towns, the youth of the schools, the artisan, the peasant, everybody. In Germany the theatre, generally speaking, is organised to be one of the most powerful agencies for educating the people, and Germans have long endeavoured to establish theatres that shall not be entirely dependent on the box-office returns, nor on public taste, but shall be in a position to supplement the one and to guide the other, as well as to be free to come within the reach of all purses." Though the modern German stage is said to have begun with Goethe and Schiller, the movement towards an Endowed Theatre was of much earlier date. It came from England, and was initiated by or through the English comedians (Englische Komödianten) at the close of the sixteenth and at the commencement of the seventeenth century, at a time when wealthy and cultured German princes kept companies of English actors at court to amuse themselves and their subjects. These players, who were among the foreign actors of various nations who filtered through the innumerable courts of the empire, and appeared at Cassel, Wolfenbüttel, Berlin, Dresden, Cologne, and elsewhere, influenced the German Theatre in two or three ways. They were the means of initiating the Repertory Theatre. They brought English plays which gave form to the drama, and they introduced a style of acting which gradually became stereotyped by the use of masks. To-day the German Emperor, as King of Prussia, has five private theatres in his main provinces : two at Berlin, one at Wiesbaden, one at Cassel, one at Hanover, and these theatres are not in every case the most artistic in the towns to which they belong. Thus the idea of " Fürsten," kings or dukes endowing the theatre, is fairly old in Germany. Later came the movement towards a National Theatre. The German National Theatre sprang out of the literary movement known as the Sturm und Drang, the actual founder of which is said to be J. G. Herder (1744–1803). Theatres were established in several centres, and from this it may be gathered that the idea of one National Theatre was never seriously considered in Germany. At the outset it was held to be impossible owing to the division of the country into states. Thus Berlin, Hamburg, Mannheim, and other cities each clamoured for its own State Theatre, such theatre to serve the purpose hitherto fulfilled by the Court Theatre, that of being in the best sense a centre of dramatic progress. Besides these Court and National Theatres, there have sprung up of more recent years numerous Municipal Theatres in the cities and towns aiming to follow the lead of the Court and State Theatres. Besides these there are other Repertory Theatres and People's Stage Societies, dimly recalling those initiated in a rudimentary way by Morris, Crane, Ruskin, Watts, and other art and social reformers, which have become so indispensable that no city or town is considered complete without them. In this connection Düsseldorf may be mentioned. Though only a town of 300,000 inhabitants, it possesses, besides a large variety theatre, the Apollo Theater, and a sort of Vaudeville (Lustspielhaus) ; two theatres doing serious work ; the usual Municipal Theatre, one of the best financially supported of its kind in Germany ; the State Theatre, with its two stock companies, one for drama and one for opera ; and a Reformbühne —that is, a provincial parallel to Reinhardt's reform theatre. This Reformbühne is called the Schauspielhaus, and it has one stock company for drama and comedy.

The endowed theatre system has offered many advantages. It has been a distinct cultural influence ; it has established a national gallery of drama, wherein the history and development of the drama is fully illustrated ; it has afforded new-comers a hearing ; it has established a desirable system of theatre organisation ; it has given birth to the Repertory movement, and it has lent itself to the artistic movement It is not necessary here to go into the working details of the system. The subsidising is done in various ways, by the reigning duke, by the State, by the corporation, who appoint a director, or leases its theatre to a manager, who receives certain concessions for the purpose of enabling him to keep his eye on art and off the box-office, and

by private individuals who band together as share-
holders to provide a suitable theatre for good
plays in their centre. The latter method has
been adopted in England in the admirably conceived Liverpool Repertory Theatre and at the
Glasgow Repertory Theatre. The German Court
Theatre has also produced the German Intendant,
in whom its loftiness of purpose may be said to be
in some instances reflected. We have nothing in
this country answering to this type of "leader." The
Intendant of the Court Theatre is rather a person
of quality than of actual theatrical experience. His
chief qualification is that he stands well with the
Court. This is generally speaking. Occasionally a
Court Intendant emerges who is the directing force
in the Theatre—such was the case with Goethe at
Weimar. But mostly he is an ornamental director
with a staff of efficient co-operators who produce
the plays for him. The King of Prussia (the
Emperor), the King of Saxony, and the Duke of
Saxe-Weimar nominate their own Intendants. The
Intendants of the Municipal Theatre are usually
men qualified for directorship by a knowledge
of the practical work of the theatre. They are
sometimes critics, but more frequently actors and
producers. Thus Max Behrend, who was leader
of the German Theatre in London a few years
ago, was chosen from among many applicants
Intendant of the Municipal Theatre of Mainz. In
France, M. Jules Claretie at the Théâtre Français,
and M. Antoine at the Odéon, occupy the position
of a German Intendant, though M. Antoine has a
free hand in the administration of his theatre.

Max Reinhardt is, on the contrary, an independent manager, being only responsible to himself, and probably to his financial supporters. He is not hampered by any of the impositions of the subsidised theatre, like those of Royal Opera House, Paris, where the Press and Parliament claim seats on gala nights. The present financial position of the endowed theatre deserves to be noticed, especially as the example of Germany has drawn wide-spread attention towards the supposed necessity of establishing a National Theatre and other forms of subsidised theatres in this country. Until within thirty years ago, the State and Municipal Theatres paid fairly well, some of them exceptionally well. To-day, however, practically none of them pay. At first the sum given to the director of the State Theatre was small, but it increased as time went on. Now there are cities and towns in Germany losing from 150,000 to 200,000 marks a year owing to the high standard which they try to uphold in their own theatres. Among these cities and towns may be mentioned Mannheim, Düsseldorf, Freiburg-im-Breisgau, the latter being a town of but 85,000 inhabitants.

The Court Theatres are no exception to the rule. Every reigning Duke in Germany possesses at least one Court Theatre. For instance, the Grand Dukes of Baden, Hessen, Saxe-Weimar, the Dukes of Altenburg, Saxe-Coburg-Gotha, have one each, the Kings of Bavaria, Würtemberg, Saxony, two each. The deficit yearly on the two Munich Court Theatres is 420,000 marks, on the Darmstadt Theatre, 210,000 marks, on the Berlin Opera

House, 1,000,000 marks, and the Dresden Opera House, 500,000 marks. The privately subsidised theatres are no better off. The Düsseldorf Schauspielhaus, a private enterprise endowed by wealthy tradesmen of the Lower Rhine, has (roughly speaking) a yearly deficit of about £6000. Towards the upkeep of this theatre the Düsseldorf Corporation also contributes £2500. It should be mentioned that this sort of private theatre, with its private and official endowment, is rare in Germany. The financial decline of the endowed theatre can, perhaps, only be understood and justified from the German point of view. The German will tell you that he loves the theatre ; that if the theatre is necessary as a medium of mental and moral education, it is quite as valuable as the University, the Museum, or the Church, and should be placed on the same economic bases as these. If it is to be a centre of art illumination, then the difficulties of its financial organisation are of no importance. He is thoroughly convinced that the theatre endowed and to a certain point controlled by the Court, State, or Corporation has made the German public what it is—far more cultured than other peoples.

That the endowed theatre system has cultivated a taste for the intellectual theatre in the German public is perfectly true. And it may be urged by the opponents of the National Theatre scheme that the absence of this system argues for the indifferent attitude of the English public towards the intellectual theatre in England. It is not that the English public would not go to an established intellectual theatre. It would not go because it has not been given the same opportunity as the Germans of cultivating the necessary taste. If the classic and literary theatre had been accessible to the English public for generations, as it has been to the German public, the taste for it would have been awakened and an increasing demand by large audiences would have been met by a corresponding supply. The difficulty now is that it is too late to apply the German methods of cultivation of taste. For one thing, there is springing up everywhere a revolt against mere intellectualism ; the attempt to convert the theatre into an arena for literary battles has broken down, and on all sides there is an increasing demand for lyrical forms of expression in which emotion and imagination shall play predominant parts. And the revolt affords another interpretation of the increased financial difficulties of the endowed theatre : it is that the German public are getting sick of mere culture. History and archæology are all very well in their place, in a museum, but transferred to the theatre for a long number of years, they begin to act as a soporific. Culture has created a gulf between the theatre and creative forms of art which it will take centuries to bridge. It is the outcome of our peculiar civilisation and of our prehistoric mode of thinking. Maybe the Germans have noticed this and are now demanding art as an antidote. They do not ask that the endowed theatre shall be abolished, only that it shall be served by an intelligence which is beyond the intellectual individuals and groups now occupying the theatre. That the prevailing taste of the

German public is for a new form of representation is proved by the immense success, financially and other, of Max Reinhardt. Though Reinhardt is, I believe, the culmination of the culture movement in the theatre, he is also an initiator of the artistic movement. That he is largely indebted for ideas to the subsidised theatre system he himself would not deny. It has given him a public, has inspired the spirit of organisation, and has handed him the secrets of the Repertory Theatre. Perhaps it may lead him to put an end to the educative theatre and to lay the foundations of the Theatre of Illumination.

HIS AIMS AND PRINCIPLES

"THE Theatre is neither a moral nor a literary institution."

"The Theatre and literature are separate from one another."

"Two directors whose rank and importance could hardly be questioned have seen the theatre at its finest epoch : one was the greatest German writer, the other the greatest German stage-manager—Goethe and Schröder."

The reference to Goethe is doubtless intended to call attention to his association with the turbulent phase of the Sturm und Drang which Goethe stamped with his individuality at the moment when the theatre was fostering a drama which was throwing off the shackles of literary artificiality and becoming free, spontaneous, and creative.

The Schröder here meant is Friedrich Ludwig Schröder, tragedian and author, born 3rd November 1744 at Schwerin, and died 3rd September at Hamburg, where, in 1771, he became director of the theatre. His great achievement was that of making Shakespeare familiar to the German public, and it is principally to his efforts that Shakespeare has since become a German classic. In Germany, "at the side of Shakespeare," as Sir Sidney Lee reminds us,

" stand Schiller and Goethe and Lessing, the classical dramatists of Germany ; Molière, the classical dramatist of France ; and Calderon, the classical dramatist of Spain." It may have been due to Schröder's efforts that Germans have come to regard Shakespeare as born at Stratford-on-Avon, Germany. Schröder, it may be noted, was largely influenced by the epoch-making criticisms of Lessing, and learnt much from his *Hamburgische Dramaturgie*, for instance. To continue the extracts : " Our Lanterna magica will exhibit a mass of illuminating forces. Rich as that of the world should be the life shown on our stage, and as such life is contained in art and poetry, we aim to offer these inexhaustible riches without stint for the delectation of actor and public alike : the appalling power of the Greek tragic poets, the unlimited fancy of Shakespeare, the rebellious yet highly refined beauty of our classic poets, the mad caperings of Aristophanian mirth, the piquant mockery of Nestroy—in one word, the whole scale of Tragedy and Comedy, from the profound seriousness of the German soul-painters, to the spooks of Wedekind, Eulenberg, and Bernard Shaw. The stage should hold the mirror up to nature, and its repertoire should be as rich and kaleidoscopic as life itself. Here it is where the whole scale of Fate, from the depths of its horrors to the dizziest heights of its joys, should be played upon ; where men and women should sob and laugh ; where colour, now dull and dismal, now bright and joyous, should scintillate ; where orchestra and chorus should sometimes revel, sometimes mourn, where actors should play the tragedian

to-day, to-morrow the clown.   In such ways we
seek to widen the scope of the theatre of to-day,
to elevate its work and to tighten its hold upon the
public.   It was not by chance that we passed from
the Little Theatre to the Greek Arena.   We
encourage the belief, not without ground, that
those who follow us will enjoy a new vision."

I cull these extracts from the *Blätter des
Deutschen Theaters.*   This little sheet was issued
by the Deutsches Theater about two years ago,
and has been published fortnightly since.   Like
the official organ of the Düsseldorf Theatre,
it is a literary venture aiming to propagate
the ideas of the Deutsches Theater, and to give
the public an all-round view of certain authors
and plays.   It is edited by Arthur Kahane, the
literary director of the Deutsches Theater, and
Felix Hollaender, the manager of the Kammerspielhaus.   But though it aims to expound the
ideas of Max Reinhardt and his theatre, oddly
enough it has a tendency to leave the reader
puzzled as to the meanings of certain of Reinhardt's
aims.   For instance, I have looked in vain for
the meaning attached by Reinhardt to rhythm
and to distillation, two elements for which he has
sought throughout.   Still this little sheet is of value
to those who desire to come into communication
directly with the theatre, instead of through an
outside medium.   To the foregoing extracts I am
led to add the following literal translation of Herr
Arthur Kahane's " Glossen zum Theater der Fünf-
tausend " as being notes on Reinhardt's great dream
—the Theatre of the Five Thousand—which reveal

some of the ideas that are actuating the collective mind of the theatre as represented by Reinhardt himself.

" One of the marked characteristics of that strangely beautiful goddess, the theatre, is that she only yields herself freely to those who entirely serve and worship her.   Love is ever monomania ; all else is prostitution and business.   He to whom the theatre is not the whole world, its mirror and its centre, has nothing to seek or gain therein. The theatre is a jealous goddess ; she tolerates no other goddess.   But she richly recompenses him who devotes himself entirely to her, offers him a world, presents him with a vision of the cosmos, and creates in him a world-idea—in fact, forges for him a connecting link with his time, closer, finer, more intimate, more mysterious than can be obtained by other means.   From such a love of the theatre and such a union with the time has the idea of the Theatre of the Five Thousand arisen.

" On every side there are signs that the theatre is in a transition state.   It is seen in the creative activities of dramatists as well as in the taste of the public.

" Old traditions pale and petrify, and interest in them is lost.   Old ' genres ' (forms) die.   New ones arise, bad ones as yet.   But the worker must be optimistic and remember that the bad only influences the crowd because the good that is in the crowd has not yet become fertilised.   And this potential good is the living contact with the time. Only in its worst periods does the theatre lose its connection with the time.   If the senile art of

court theatres fades, dramas of the epigones fail,
and social comedies divorced from social life die
in the background, it is because they have missed
the open road to the soul of the time.   Revues,
operettas, pantomimes only draw the public in
crowds because there is to be found in them,
though not always in the best taste, a striving
after actuality, an attempt to set up a contact
with the modern spirit that is stirring our hearts
and minds.

"Should not the tremendous changes which
our entire mode of life is undergoing find an
echo on the stage ?   The technical revolution,
the expansion of all dimensions, our electric
existence, the discovery of society as a living
organism, the re-awakened joy in the struggle to
conquer the elements, the heightened consciousness of physical power, the love of nature and
the cosmos, the growth of a new mythology—all
these found singers and rhapsodists in Walt Whitman, Verhaeren, Johannes V. Jensen, Hamsun,
Stefan George ; and should nothing of this be
expressed on the stage ?

"Here, in the Theatre of the Five Thousand,
we have, I believe, the first attempt at such an
expression.   It arises, to my mind, from a similar
feeling for our time, and the best of it is contained
in the will to capture these manifestations of a new
awakening and to set them reverberating.   And it
is perhaps not an accident that the belief in the
myths of our time links itself to the belief in the
myths of the ancients, as the really new is always
strongly linked to the really old (or tradition).

" Problems of the theatre are problems of the time. It will, therefore, be interesting to mention some which naturally arise from the new form of the stage. Of course, this form is not yet finally fixed, and impressions gained from rehearsals and productions, so far, lead more often to questions than to answers. Moreover, only those who care to look deeply will discover beneath these questions, which on the surface appear to be related merely to the theatre, a relation to the important tendencies of our time. Perhaps it is because in the essence of all these questions lies a desire to create a new and intenser relationship between the spectator and the work of art (the public and spirit of the artist).

" The first law of the new theatre is utmost simplicity. Apart from the consideration that there is no time for complicated changes, the vast space demands the simplest of forms, and strong, big, severe lines. All accessories are superfluous ; they cannot possibly be noticed, or, if they are, they are a source of distraction. At the most, scenic decoration can only be frame, not function. The elaboration of details, the emphasising of nuances disappear ; the actor and the actor's voice are truly essential, while lighting becomes the real source of decoration, its single aim being to bring the important into the light, and to leave the unimportant in the shadow.]

" Thus the effects are simplified and heightened according to the need of monumentality. Under the influence of these mighty spaces, these big, severe lines, all that is small and petty disappears, and it becomes a matter of course to appeal to the hearts of great audiences with the strongest and deepest elements. The petty and unimportant —elements that are not eternal in us—cease to have effect. This theatre can only express the great eternal elemental passions and the problems of humanity. In it spectators cease to be mere spectators ; they become the people ; their emotions are simple and primitive, but great and powerful, as becomes the eternal human race.

" Many things that appear to most people to be inseparable from the theatre are being discarded. No curtain separates stage and auditorium. On entering the theatre the spectator feels and is impressed by the possibilities of space, and the essential mood is created in him to be preserved after the piece has begun. No small, strongly circumscribed, impassable frame separates the world of the play from the outer world, and the action flows freely through the whole of the theatre. The peep-show character of the "scene," which was known neither to the stage of the ancients, to the Shakespearean stage, nor to the Molièrean stage, and which to people of a conservative frame of mind is still the highest point of theatrical art, simply because they are not aware that they merely worship a fossilised fragment of Italian Opera and Ballet tradition, has vanished. The chorus arises and moves in the midst of the audience ; the characters meet each other amid the spectators; from all sides the hearer is being impressed, so that gradually he becomes part of the whole, and is rapidly absorbed in the action, a member of the chorus, so to speak. This close contact (intimacy) is the chief feature of the new form of the stage. It makes the spectator a part of the action, secures his entire interest, and intensifies the effect upon him.

" Big spaces compel the unfolding of personality. It is in these that men develop their best and final power. Though separated by great distances, men still face each other, and inevitably the conflicting feeling arises as to who is the stronger personality. Here strength and passion become the predominating qualities, the quintessence of tragedy, the conflict of personalities, the two dramatic elements contained in and transmitted by space. It is thus possible to rediscover a feeling which has been lost to us, but without losing that process of greater intimacy which seems to me the most useful result of the late naturalistic movement in the theatre. For through the close contact with the spectator, who, metaphorically speaking, can feel the warm breath of dramatic art, the actor will be compelled to draw from the well of his deepest experience. There is no better proof of the genuineness of power and feeling exerted than to come successfully through this ordeal in this space before the said spectator.

" Of course, it will come easiest to actors who possess a musical temperament, for music is inherent in human beings, and by music we may reach the heart of the vastest crowds. In the midst of the strongest accents of human passions, and the powerful logic of the dramatic struggle, which will always form the most important part

of this side of theatrical art, pauses are imperative.
It is the function of music to fill them in, either
alone or in the form of the rhythmic chorus.
By means of music this theatre will retain its dual
character of the festive and the solemn.

"The foregoing experiences marked the productions of *Œdipus* and the *Orestes*; but as we do
not believe that the big theatre lends itself solely
to one kind of effect—the heroic—the next experiment will be made with an entirely different sort
of work, which has nothing in common with the
other two, except a broad humanity, and which
differs from them in being extremely simple, idyllic,
and popular. I refer to the old morality *Everyman*."

From the foregoing article it will be gathered
that Max Reinhardt has in view a theatre wherein
the drama can emerge from an effete culture, from
sterilising and clogging traditions, and re-establish
itself on a basis that is in harmony with man's
primitive nature. He seeks to bring back into
the theatre the greater, profounder internal and
eternal elements of human nature in the drama
which have been banished by a long period of
mere intellectuality. Such elements are not always
to be expressed in words. Hence the application
of music. But they may always be trusted to find
a response in the playgoer of no matter what age
—and in every member of the greatest audience.
Such elements are to be expressed simply and
unostentatiously. They do not require splendid
and impossible realistic effects, nor elaborate devices
of staging. They require but the mystery and
immensity of space.

In regard to other points, I believe that Herr Kahane refers to " the time " in the sense of the contemporary or modern spirit. I believe, too, that when he speaks of modern scientific inventions, he is referring to them rather as modern myths, just as the Greeks deified the elements and dealt with them in mythological form. He asks, in fact, for a new mythology containing the essentials of a new form of drama adapted to the form of theatre, called the Theatre of the Five Thousand. One of these essentials is the spirit of the time, possibly the morality of the time which modern science has bred. The old forms of drama and comedy must either be buried or revitalised by being brought up to date. Playwrights and producers must sound the note of modern tragedy or comedy. Otherwise the theatre will lose its audience. Theatre managers who, like artists, are out of touch with life, persist in giving the public the old and the obsolete. And the public, or that section of it which has developed along the new or scientific lines, will have none of it. There are playwrights who are aware of this. They have their fingers on the public pulse, and they hold their audiences by giving them crude and commonplace everyday materials. Mr Shaw brings a motor car on the stage. Messrs Henry Hamilton and Cecil Raleigh dramatise current events powdered with " Science Siftings." Herr Kahane asks for something more imaginative—something that goes even beyond the Irish plays, with their combination of the old and the new, but not beyond those of Ibsen. Ibsen alone, among modernists, dressed the eternal man in modern dress. The eternal man must always be in modern dress ; but big-souled and adventurous.

Contained in the article are the ideas springing from Max Reinhardt's latest development. To him the theatre is the first ideal : everything, in fact. He lives in it, thinks in it, and has made it a part of himself. If he loves the theatre, then others must love it, or leave it. In pursuit of this ideal he has so shaped the Deutsches Theater that it shall give only to those who have something to give it. " Serve the theatre and it will serve you " is his motto. Then he reverses its common attitude. Instead of putting questions to the spectator, it must set the spectator questioning himself. Again, he asks that it shall not express the so-called real problems, but the fundamental issues of life. In this he has discovered the difference between old methods and new. Further, he is occupied with bringing the actor and the audience together and making the latter a part of the action through an appeal to the elemental and vital passions. Intimacy is to be attained through external simplicity appealing to internal simplicity. Thus we are led by Herr Kahane to see how Reinhardt has progressed in his idea of intimacy since his " Brille " days ; how he has replaced the one-man intimacy, so prevalent in England, by the ensemble intimacy, till it has grown to the proportions of *Sumurûn* and *Œdipus*. In England we have had a long line of actors, including Macready, Kemble, Kean, Irving, Toole, Hare, Edward Terry, Forbes - Robertson, Tree, seeking to bring audiences solely under their own spell, as if some power went forth immediately they entered the "scene" and disappeared the moment they left it, leaving the audience to fill up the gap with large yawns. The desire to appeal direct to the public through the Will of the Theatre has never been awakened or it might have led to a conception, similar to Reinhardt's, of a huge intimate theatre to hold five thousand spectators, where space and the elemental passions and feelings, the subconscious memory which lies dormant in every creature, are to serve the desired purpose of attaining the big unified effect. Under Reinhardt, the theatre is to play the part of a dynamo containing magnetic currents that are received by everybody. By this means the cosmic memory within each auditor will be stirred, and each will be brought within the action of the play. The process is described in Whitman's lines :—

> A noiseless, patient spider
> I marked where on a little promontory it stood isolated,
> Marked how to explore the vacant vast surrounding
> It launched forth filament, filament, filament out of itself,
> Ever unreeling them, ever tirelessly speeding them.
> And you, O my soul, where you stand
> Surrounded, detached in measureless oceans of space,
> Ceaselessly musing, venturing, throwing,
> Seeking the sphere to connect them,
> Till the bridge you will need be formed,
> Till the ductile anchor hold,
> Till the gossamer threads mingling
> Catch somewhere—O my Soul.

Of course the analogy does not hold good throughout. A theatre can scarcely be compared with a spider, but its function of enabling the

drama to spin invisible threads whereby to secure
the soul of the audience is, figuratively speaking,
the same.   We have only to imagine the collective
mind of all concerned in a production, projecting
itself towards an audience sensitive to vibrations
and atmosphere, to understand what intimacy really
is.   It will be found that there is no clue in Herr
Kahane's article to Max Reinhardt's idea of extracting drama.   We are not told how he seizes
on each classical play in turn, and introduces
the essential modern spirit, or how with a sure
instinct he seizes the essential drama from the
modern play ; how he pours the classic play into
the crucible of his personality and changes it
into the desired element, from which important
details of the original element have been eliminated.
Distilling the dramatic essence of the play in this
way, he is apt to call forth the opinion that the
spirit and essence of it all is false.   History in
modern language is very often falsehood.   But
the article conveys the impression that Reinhardt
is an impressionist.   His aim in the big theatre is
certainly that of creating impressionist sensations
by the use of simple, big outlines, colour, and the
use of light as the predominant factor in a scene,
not as an accessory to it.   Apparently he is con-
structing a huge shell to contain the voice of the
infinite.   But there are contradictions, as will be
seen elsewhere.   His " properties " are not impres-
sionistic.   We find that Reinhardt has also discovered impulse as well as the significance of lyricism and of rhythmic vitality in their relation to the
theatre and drama.   In pauses are contained the

greatest dramatic moments of the drama. The use of music is to fill in these pauses so as to preserve the contact with the spectator. Music is thus the subconscious element that runs and feels with the drama, now rising, now falling, as the dominant rhythm of the action demands. This rhythm has an answering rhythm in ourselves, which it is the function of the drama to find. It is a cosmic rhythm which never responds to local stimuli. The sort of rhythmic unity we want the drama of the theatre to express is contained in these lines from Whitman's " Song of the Open Road " :

> The earth expanding right hand and left hand,
> The picture alive, every part in its best light,
> The music falling in where it is wanted and
> Stopping where it is not wanted.

Read the last line figuratively, and the idea is complete. The music ought not to stop, but should follow the example of African divers, who, M. Verneuil tells us, swim singing round a vessel ; at the eighth bar they all plunge together, mentally following the air while under water ; at the twelfth bar they all push the vessel at once, and at the sixteenth come to the surface. Acting thus in rhythmic unity, none of their efforts is lost. Max Reinhardt is now working towards a big rhythmic unity.

HIS MATERIALS

WE have seen that for Reinhardt the drama has only one meaning, to be of the theatre. ♭ He allows nothing to interfere with this view, neither literature, philosophy, nor morals. It may be said that he has a dramatic twist, and we may recognise him by his dramatic expresssion. We need not go far for evidence. If Herr Kahane's article reveals him to us as re-introducing the theatre to the theatre, there is a very valuable piece of Reinhardt literature which suggests that Reinhardt seeks in the Deutsches Theater to rebuild the culture drama of the world. I refer to Siegfried Jacobsohn's *Max Reinhardt*, published by Erich Reiss, Berlin, which first appeared in serial form. In this illustrated volume Herr Jacobsohn has taken thirty plays, and by means of them traced Reinhardt's progress as a producer. The author says in his introduction that his aim is to present a picture of Reinhardt's development and art. He will prove, as far as a critic can, by thirty different productions, that Reinhardt, like no other German producer, seeks to give every play its individual character and style, its own atmosphere, and its own music. But the author lays stress chiefly on the point that Reinhardt has brought one-half of the plays, the classics, up to date ; while to the other half, the modern plays, he has given extreme modernity ; brought modern life into the one and modern form of art into the other. Thus, in Herr Jacobsohn's view, Reinhardt has created what his critic terms a " half-theatre," wherein to synthesise the old and new. In this way he is organising an unequalled pageant of play and staging. The pageant, however, does not include all the varieties of the stage and drama — Greek, Roman, Renaissance, Puritan, Cavalier, Early Victorian, domestic, economic, the old Italian and French, Molière, Corneille, Racine, etc. It is composed solely of the seven Stages of man : Greek, Oriental, Italian, French, Early English (Miracles, Moralities, and Elizabethan), German (classic and modern), and modern European (English, Russian, etc.). In it are the elements of the old—variety, tragedy, comedy, chivalry, hate, joy, sorrow, success, failure—all the richly coloured threads that were woven into the ancient garment ; and the monotonous element of the new, the failure of life. In short, Reinhardt has not yet discovered a new drama, but is equally balanced between the old and the modern. The original formation and working of these seven stages are worth consideration. Broadly speaking, to-day there are three forms of stage : one derived from the East, one, possessing architectonic qualities, from Greece, and one from the Italian Renaissance. The latter had a foundation in the Greek stage, but early broke away from the architectonic form, and exhibited the disease of painted scenic effects, which has gradually led to the development of the modern framed or pictorial stage. To-day there has sprung up the movement aiming, as described in the preceding chapter, to take up and reinterpret early stages, especially Greek and Shakespearean. The pagan and the Christian stalk the land arm-in-arm, delighted to take up their modern allotment. Of course, the stage has always shown a tendency to determine the form and dimensions of the drama which it shall represent. The Shakespearean stage largely determined the form of the Shakespearean drama. Shakespeare wrote for the theatre of his time, and we are told by many wise heads that if Shakespeare had had the modern theatre with all its resources, he would not only have written his plays differently, but have availed himself of the said resources. So convinced of this are some persons, that they regard the modern rediscovery of the Swan Theatre and the subsequent attempts to reconstruct a Shakespearean stage as the essential preliminary phase of the full development of such resources. In my view, this mania for developing stage mechanics before we know what the new drama is going to be, ought to be taxed. It is the sheerest nonsense to talk about building a new theatre in the belief that a new drama will be born when no one is looking. The drama came first. Some will say the earth came first, then the dancer. I am not concerned with the point here, nor with the current view that if one desires to differentiate the drama of the Renaissance from that of the Middle Ages, or from that of the Restoration, it is necessary to begin by determining the nature of the Renaissance stage, and thereafter estimating the action and reaction its form, size, and working must have had upon structure, representation, and interpretation of these forms of drama. I am only occupied with showing that each great naturalistic reform movement occupied a stage of its own.

The Greek Stage

As many informed persons know, the drama started in a very humble way. I do not propose to deal here with the many theories of the origin of Greek tragedy. The god Dionysus has been dealt with by the optimistic Nietzsche, and Dr Frazer has approached him from a more learned point of view. It will suffice to say that in Greece the mimicry of the savage grew into a highly organised affair. Briefly, the primitive dance, in which the body was used to express emotion too intense for speech, became action, the story became speech, which became song under intense emotion : out of these two grew the drama. The story took the narrative-biographical form and told of great events and the deeds of great heroes, of the struggle between man and Destiny. To the doings of heroic individuals was added the world spirit, or chorus, which expressed the ultimate emotions about great deeds and conveyed them to the great mass of spectators, just as to-day music is being used as a special instrument for expressing those emotions which are too deep for words. To the ancient Greeks the drama must have presented a far different appearance

from what it presents to-day. The infant drama
was nourished on religious ritual and choric
dance, and the newly fledged "cherub" was a
combination of the angelic and satanic, with a
great deal of the child-like. The infant entered
into poetry as a new conception of human expression, and was provided with all the most powerful
adjuncts that the poet could embody in words.
It was brought into the open and encouraged to
invoke the most sympathetic yet festive and
reverent sentiment of the Greek public towards
itself. So nurtured in turn by Æschylus,
Sophocles, and Euripides, it reached full maturity
and fell into decay. But throughout, Greek drama
was never more than a Voice and a Movement.
It was a Voice and a Movement which expressed
themselves to a vast concourse of spectators drawn
together by the religious spirit—the spirit of the
religious festival, and of the Church function. Its
patron was the god Dionysus, at whose festivals
the plays were celebrated. It took the form of
a trilogy, sometimes with a comic tail called a
satyr play. It was a Voice and a Movement which
spoke in a vast open-air theatre, containing at one
end some simple scenic device, a temple or palace
front, and accommodating forty or fifty thousand
spectators. There was no realism in representation or interpretation. The Voice—through the
medium of three or four actors, wearing tragic
masks, with open mouths and glaring eyes, strange
high head-dresses, and stilted and padded and
standing on a high and narrow platform—attained
heights undreamt of to-day. Below, the Move-

ment, expressed by the chorus, fascinated the audience by the beauty of its rhythmic chant, by the dignity of its slow, solemn, and rhythmic pose. Both were united by the all-pervading spell of rhythmic music, in harmony.

THE CHINESE AND JAPANESE STAGES

Drama in China originated in a religious dance, the Bugaku, born 2000 years ago. It took the form of the religious temple dance, which was afterwards introduced into Japan under the name the "Kagura." Apparently the Chinese drama is inaccessible to change. The theatre is exactly where it has been for hundreds of years. Its formation and working remain unaltered. There is a broad naked stage that stretches across one end of a, comparatively speaking, bare interior. It has no wings, flies, or curtain. Gorgeously embroidered banners take the place of scenery ; sometimes symbolic "properties" are used, and sometimes inappropriate "properties" play inappropriate parts, as in the Western Theatre. The centre of the stage is occupied by the orchestra. On either side of the orchestra up stage back is a door. The actors enter the scene by these doors, as well as by means of a long platform running through the centre of the auditorium. In the one case they come from whence the action is taking place ; in the other, from a distance, to take part in the action. The costumes worn are very rich in colour, and their arrangement displays a sense of the harmony of pure fresh colours. Pure colour is put against pure colour, and there is no lowering of tones for the sake of harmony. This is the primitive sense of colour. Nowhere is the glory of colour seen more than in the masses of barbaric Chinese colour. In China men impersonate women and are so carefully prepared for the purpose, even to the crushed feet and mincing walk, that the illusion is complete. The Japanese stage has developed from the Shinto temple stage, a primitive affair erected for the performance of the " Kagura," one of the religious temple dances introduced from China. Here we have a stage, and later the theatre, determined by the drama-dance. The dance, in fact, came first, and without it there would have been no stage. The " Kagura " dance was performed in the shrine before the altar, no special decoration or background being necessary. The erection of a stage for this dance soon followed. From the "Kagura" developed the cultured " No " drama. The " No " drama has a special stage, which is described by Sheko Tsubouchi in *The Mask* as follows : " Having developed out of a kind of Bugaku that was played in the shrines, ' No ' drama, like Bugaku, is presented on a stage that has no background and no curtain. There is in the back of the stage a plank-wall, on which are painted large pine trees. This may be called the background of the stage, but this background is never changed, no matter what play may be presented before it. It is, therefore, rather a part of the permanent decoration of the stage. The floor of the stage and its surrounding walls are made of planks of Hinoki tree. The stage is rectangular, and at its four corners stand four posts. These four posts are regarded as the symbols of the four corners of the earth, and the stage itself is a small world. Under the floor are buried four or five large empty vases, which serve as a sort of a resonator to the sound of the footsteps, and of the harps and the flutes that are played on the stage. Towards the left of the stage is what is called Hashigakari. This is a narrow path leading from the dressing room to the stage. It is made of planks and is really a part of the stage. ' No ' actors play on it as they go through it to the stage. Between the stage and the seat of the spectators lies an un-occupied space covered with sand. This space is meant to mark the sacred stage from the vulgar seat of the spectators. It is a kind of proscenium, but its meaning is more religious. In this sandy place, along the Hashigakari, are planted three pine trees. I am not sure what they mean, but I think both they and the pine trees painted on the back wall symbolise purity and piety or some such religious virtues." The writer goes on to show that the " No" drama has resemblances to the Greek drama, in which music, chant, and dance have equal importance. There is a primitive orchestra of five placed in a similar manner to the Chinese orchestra. There are eight persons who form a motionless chorus, which differs from the Greek chorus in that it sometimes explains what the actor is doing and sometimes sings his part when it is too heavy for him. Further, masks are sometimes worn, and the costumes are rich and appropriate.

As there is an interchange of Eastern and

Western ideas taking place at this moment, I may include here an architectural account of a Japanese theatre, which was sent to me by the eminent architect Josiah Conder of Tokio.

"The general appearance of the theatre is that of a broad, squat-looking building of wooden construction, with a wide central roof of flat pitch, a clearstory, and lower lean-to roofs at the sides. The large roof has generally a low continuous lantern running along the top to admit air and light. The walls are constructed of a framing of vertical and horizontal timbers filled in with lathing, clay, and plaster, having weather-boarding nailed upon the outside. The windows are oblong openings, with wooden bars placed either vertically or horizontally, closed, in bad weather only, by sliding shutters, having paper lights, which are placed towards the inside of the reveals.

"A gay appearance is given to the otherwise insignificant façade by means of large placards heavily framed, which are hung in profusion in front, and decorated with large representations of scenes from the play, in bright, harmonious colours. Some of these posters extend from the ground to the eaves; and, in addition, there are often a number of bright flags on poles fixed in the pathway. The theatres of a Japanese town are generally placed together in the same district; and about them are several large tea-houses (hotels), whence it is usual to procure one's ticket and make all arrangements for seats and refreshments.

"With the Japanese, as with the ancient Greeks, the performance of a play is the matter of a whole day, the theatre opening at about six in the morning and closing at dusk. This is broken by frequent and tedious intervals between the acts, when the audience adjourn to the tea-houses, or take their meals in the theatre. The building is entered from the end facing the stage, through a sort of central hall, containing racks for depositing umbrellas, clogs, and generally serving the purpose of a cloakroom. On either side of this entrance are rooms, some of which are devoted to the manager and his officers, and others to the actors. The actors have rooms at both ends of the theatre. There are also private entrances in the front communicating with some of these rooms.

" Between the entrance, with its adjoining rooms, and the auditorium, or main body of the building, is a passage, running from side to side, leading to the staircases and side passages. Direct admission is gained into the pit, across the main passage, by two doorways, between which is a row of small compartments, closed in towards the entrance, but opening on to the theatre, looking towards the stage. These rooms are some of them occupied by dealers in programmes or provisions, and others by police, who attend to preserve order.

" The pit holds by far the greater part of the audience ; for the raised and supported seats at the sides and end, which correspond to European box-seats, are comparatively few in number. The pit-seats consist of a great number of low, box-like divisions, placed upon a floor sloping slightly upwards from the stage end. The incline is scarcely perceptible. The divisions are about four feet square, and are intended each for the seating of five people, squatting upon the mat-covered floor.

"There are two passages through these seats from entrance to stage, one on either side, and these are sometimes used in passing from seat to seat, but access is obtained to any part of the pit by walking along the low divisions between each compartment, the edges being made flat for the purpose. Sometimes, in addition to this simple mode of communication, there are one or two cross passages of a plank's width; these, as well as the principal side passages being always at the level of the top of the seat divisions, and consequently on the same level as the stage, and of the shoulders of the audience seated in the pit.

"The main passages referred to are also used by the actors during the performance, who often approach the stage from the front of the theatre where they have several dressing-rooms. Sometimes an actor will stop to speak or act in this passage in the midst of his audience, addressing his fellow-actors on the stage across the people. The passage on one's left hand as one faces the stage is called the main passage. It is wider than that on the opposite side, and more used. There is also a corresponding underground passage beneath it, and a trap-door to admit of sudden appearances and disappearances. This lower passage communicates with a wide space below the stage, where are appliances for hoisting connected with several trap-doors in the floor of the stage. A magician or ghost can thus disappear quickly from the stage, and appear amidst the audience; or, what often happens, a hero or victim slain upon the stage will rise in a transformed, ghostly apparition in the passage, illumined by a coloured light.

" Some very pleasing scenic effects are obtained by the use of the upper passages ; sometimes a gaily dressed procession, or an armed suite of attendants, approach the stage in a long line, with all the slow ceremonial and etiquette which belong to the customs of old Japan. At other times an exit will be made imposing by a large train of followers ; a farewell parting will be lengthened out by lingerings and looking back ; or, may be, some favourite low comedian will give full play to his comic strut, action, or grimace, as he makes his entrance or his exit across the long passage. This peculiarity has seemed worth dwelling upon, as, by reason of it, certain representations can be obtained which decidedly improve the effect of the play, and which are more or less impossible in European theatres, where approaches must be sudden, and a slow arrival or far-off action can be suggested only by distant sounds behind the stage from invisible supernumeraries, or by exaggerated expressions of expectation and alarm on the part of the actors upon the stage. To assist this conventionality, and to carry out still further the idea of the all-pervading nature of the scene in a Japanese theatre, strips of painted canvas, continuing the stage scenery, are often hung to the fronts of the upper boxes and galleries running all round the theatre.

" An example of this may be given by reference to a portion of a favourite play, in which is repre-

sented the embarkation of a prince from his own
castle town.

" When the scene opens, a boat lies in the foreground, the floor of the stage being covered with
painted canvas, representing a sandy beach in front
and water touching the prow of the boat, and
extending behind to the back of the stage. The
prince and his suite having entered the boat, it
is moved by means of the turn-tables of the stage,
and at the same time the canvas representing the
water is drawn forward, the sandy beach disappears,
and the whole stage represents sea. Then, gradually
along the sides of the upper boxes strips of canvas
painted as water are drawn by cords, until at
length on the further gallery-front facing the stage
is seen the representation of the distant shore and
castle town. This forms a fitting and expressive
accompaniment to a long farewell soliloquy from
the boat, the prince addressing his native home
which he is leaving behind him. Thus a vivid
reality is given to a change in the scene of action.
The idea which it seems to suggest to the audience
is, that they have in reality followed their hero
to his next abode, leaving with him the last scene
behind, and not that he has left them in the for-
saken town to be transported mysteriously to the
next scene of action. The two or three outermost
rows of pit compartments slope considerably upwards on either side and at the back. Outside
these seats are more spacious compartments running
all round the theatre in a single row. These are
the lower box-seats, and at their front are occasional
wooden posts supporting the floor of the upper tier

above them. They are closed in, and entered by doors at the back. Some height above this upper tier of boxes, and just beneath the long, low clear-story windows, is a light and narrow gallery supported from the wall on brackets.

" This gallery appears to be used only for attending to the windows, being approached by a ladder staircase, and being too frail to support a number of people. At the back of the boxes on either side are the two outer passages for communication with these box-seats, and corresponding passages above for the upper seats. One of the lower passages has a central screen dividing it longitudinally into two, the portion nearer the outside being used by those actors who wish to pass unnoticed from end to end of the theatre. The back portion of the pit opposite to the stage is covered by an upper gallery, on a level with the upper boxes, which extends back over the hall and rooms round the entrance. At the two extremities of this gallery are several small rooms for stores, and a sort of oratory, with a shrine, where it is usual for the proprietors and actors to supplicate success from some deity.

" The appearance of the whole inside of the theatre is extremely plain, and devoid of finish or ornament. The large tie-beams of the roof, of heavy, unsquared timber, are generally visible below a rough boarded ceiling. In some cases, the boarding is placed below the tie-beams, and is slightly ornamented with thin ribs. The heavy timbers of the roof contrast greatly with the frail posts and filling-in which form the walls of support.

The fronts of the upper seats and the gallery front have sometimes a moulded hand-rail, with moulded or carved supports, but in other respects the interior has few embellishments, except in the scenery and hangings of the stage.

" Considerable room is taken up by the stage, which occupies nearly the whole of the further end of the building. In addition, there are a few actors' dressing-rooms, bath-rooms, and small staircases leading to the principal rooms above. These upper rooms are larger, and occupy a portion of the space which below is given to the stage for the purpose of moving the scenery and working the turn-tables. The principal actors have separate dressing-rooms—a hairdresser, and quite a number of attendants ; there is a larger room common to inferior actors. These rooms at the back of the stage are in some cases arranged in three low stories.

" The staircases of approach from one floor to another consist of two strings with treads, and no risers or handrail, placed to a steep slope.

" The height of the stage opening is about 16 feet from the stage floor, which is about 18 inches below the eye of those seated in the front of the pit. The platform of the stage, which has no inclination, comes well forward beyond the curtain opening, forming a wide passage in front communicating with the passages through the pit. The stage is provided with one or two concentric turn-tables coming out to the front, and by the revolution of these the scene is sometimes quickly changed. The front scene will hide the scene behind, which is prepared in readiness, and then the whole is moved round.

" The representation of an interior scene upon the stage as we should make it, namely, by converting the whole stage into a single room by means of side and back scenes, is never attempted, and is scarcely necessary on account of the facility of representing exterior and interior together. A Japanese house has low rooms, is often only of one story, and is mostly thrown entirely open in the front.

" Even in the cold weather it is quite common to see the whole front of a house thrown quite open by removing or sliding back the light paper slides (*shojis*), of which nearly the whole front consists. In stormy weather, either cane blinds are hung outside of the paper slides, or else the whole is closed in by wooden shutters called *amados* (rain shutters) placed outside, keeping out light and air, a small quantity of light being admitted from some small side windows, or by a small portion in front not being quite shut in.

" In palaces or the residences of men of rank, the rooms are grouped together and the block surrounded on all four sides by a wide boarded passage reached by a flight of wooden steps from the grounds. This passage is sometimes double the outer and narrower portion, having a balustrade corresponding to the handrail of the steps, and the inner portions bounded by posts filled in above with plaster, and supporting the eaves of the roof. The spaces between these posts are often entirely open, but they can be filled in with *shojis* and *amados*.

" The internal posts of the passage forming the walls of the rooms can also be filled in or left open according to the weather, so that on a fine summer's day the whole interior can be thrown open, presenting a vista of matted rooms, and groups of posts.

" It is such a view as this that is given to the audience in a theatre. The whole front or end of a house is represented on the stage from ground to ceiling line by means of a light wooden construction somewhat smaller in scale than an actual building. The front thrown open will present to view the interior rooms in which the acting takes place, prolonged sometimes into the semblance of a vista of rooms, by means of painted scenes at the back.

" The perspective of such painted scenes is mostly correct, erring rather in being too sudden. The turn-tables upon which such constructions are placed enables them to be quickly moved to the back by a half revolution, revealing the next scene, which will have been meanwhile prepared behind it. On the front part of the stage, side-scenes, shrubs, or flowers will be placed to form a foreground. The stage-curtain, generally having some simple conventional device in colour upon it, is drawn forward by attendants at the close of the scene.

" At the left-hand side of the stage is a space for the orchestra, who play drums, flutes, and stringed instruments, and who partly explain the acting, and comment upon it, after the manner of the Greek chorus.

" In addition to this orchestra there is a little gallery on the right-hand side of the stage, some 10 feet from the ground, in which two musicians are seated, who accompany the performance. One of these men plays a stringed instrument (*samisen*), and the other accompanies the music at intervals with singing and intoned exclamations. They are sometimes visible to the audience, and sometimes screened by cane blinds, through which they can see without being seen ; for it is necessary for them to watch the movement of actors upon the stage.

" An ordinary theatre has no proper provision for artificial lighting, for the performance generally takes place only during the daytime, when the place is lighted by side and end windows just below the eaves.

" In case of a play being prolonged till after dark, a miserably inefficient light is obtained by a row of candles placed in front of the stage ; besides which a candle fixed to a rod is carried about by an attendant, and held in front of the particular actor who is speaking, in order better to illuminate him.

" Another peculiarity is the presence on the stage of sundry boys dressed in black, with loose black caps, indicating that they are to be supposed invisible. They crouch about behind the actors to remove from the stage anything that is to be dispensed with, or to place a low seat or support under an actor who has to take up a position for any length of time. Most of the plays enacted are taken from Japanese history, and a visit to the

theatre is now the best opportunity of realising the
customs, habits, etiquette, and costumes of ancient
times.

" It is said that the representations may be relied
upon as correct.   With the profession of an actor,
as with other professions in this country, the
business has hitherto been hereditary, and instruction has been personally given or handed down in
manuscript.   This accounts to a great extent for
the want of really good and exhaustive treatises
upon the dramatic and other arts, in which the
people have shown at times remarkable skill.   The
dramatic art of Japan may be said to hold the same
comparison with our modern European drama as
mediæval decorative painting does with the highly
naturalistic picture of to-day.   The story is told
forcibly ;   the action of body and of feature is
what we should call exaggerated ;   the impression of
sorrow or despair is aided by weird, doleful music,
and by the sympathetic wailing of the chorus ;
and sometimes acute feminine grief is pictured by
a dance in which the hands are wrung and the
body writhes in painful action, accompanied by
sobs and snatches of wild song.

"There are dances expressive of grace and
beauty, of humour, or of grief ; unnatural perhaps,
but unmistakably highly effective in drawing the
sympathy of the spectators and conventionally
assisting the effect of the play.   So forcible is the
effect produced that a foreigner, unable to follow
much that is said, will find himself worked into
sad or pleasurable excitement fully in sympathy
with the action of the play."

A fact in Professor Conder's description, worthy of notice, is the use of the revolving stage, an appliance over which Europe is now going crazy. The Japanese set this turn-table stage with portable screens capable of suggesting a variety of effects. Another noticeable fact is that the "No" drama is mystical and mediæval and has always been the drama of the *élite*. With regard to the drama-dance, it should be explained that it is different from that of Western nations. It is not only pantomimic, but every movement means something. The Japanese have, in fact, invented an exclusive and eloquent language of gesture, which it would take Western peoples centuries to learn. Indeed, it is doubtful whether the Japanese theatre form of representation and interpretation can ever be exported.

The "Miracle" and "Morality" Stages

The drama in England is said to have begun with the Miracle Play. Thus in its early stage the drama was a powerful instrument in the hands of the clergy for promoting religious ideals. Later it became laicised in the Moralities and took the form of a School of Virtue. In the Paris Opera House museum there is a model of the stage of a Miracle Play. This particular stage is composed of three stages arranged side by side. The centre is occupied by God in Heaven, seated on the throne of judgment and surrounded by an angelic host. To the right is Earth, and to the left is the Mouth of Hell, into which the Devil is shooting the unregenerate. The Miracle stage varies, and sometimes

the triple bill is represented on three separate plat-
forms, with Heaven above, Earth below, and Hell
underneath. This simultaneous arrangement of the
whole religious drama, with its set pieces enabling
one to tour the whole world of space at once, was
in full view throughout the entire action, each
scene playing its part in turn. Thus the Deity
first appeared on the top shelf or in the centre
compartment, and explained the working and
purpose of Heaven. Then came the Devil setting
forth the advantages of Hell. Thirdly came Adam
and Eve and the Deity expatiating on the creation
and beauties of Paradise. So, in this fashion, the
chief events recorded in the Bible were related in
more or less lively dialogue. In short, the Mystery
Play was the Bible epic played with a cinemato-
graphic background. It was history brought up
to date, and thereby it derived its great vitality.
Like the Commedia dell' Arte it was imbued
with the spirit of the time, which enabled it to
persist for two or three centuries, influencing the
" Moralities " and inspiring such lasting productions as *Everyman*. The Morality Play followed.
It was born of the new sceptical adjustment. The
Heaven of the Miracle Play got mislaid, and men
grew uncertain where Paradise was. The age of
the Morality Play was, in fact, the age of *Paradise
Lost*. With the new moral awakening came a
change of symbols, and the sacred and profane
figures of the Miracle Play were replaced by the
abstract figures, Truth, Virtue, Justice, and so forth.
The vitality of the Morality Play was even greater
than that of the Miracle Play, for if we examine

modern melodrama we shall still find "The Morality" in our midst. What difference is there, indeed, between the old moralities with their personifications and the personifications to be found in modern melodrama. The latter is not even a morality disguised. Both are equally unreal, and modern melodrama would be far more interesting if only it would recognise this and present its characters clothed in the fancies of antiquity. Thus it might give us a mixture of miracle and morality, the heroine (Virtue) with wings and a nimbus, the hero (Good) clothed in shining armour, the villain (Evil) with horns and a tail, his chief assistant (Intemperance) as a dragon pasturing upon the hero's estates, and "Little Willie" (Innocence) as a fat cherub who dies and is taken up aloft by an angelic choir. For local colour there would be red fire, the smell of brimstone, and all the rest of the devilry. The Morality Play was represented on a crude stage similar to the Miracle stage. The Moralities were mostly played in front of or inside a public building, a church or place of worship, where the scenes from cathedral windows and sculptured porches had an appropriate background. They were also hawked about from place to place on a barrow, so to speak, and set up in Elizabethan interiors wherever there was room and a request for them. It is contended that in the crude but in most cases beautiful decorations of the Miracle and Morality stages, and in the costumes worn by the players is to be found the beginning of an Art of the Theatre in England. The

contention is doubtless true, for the Miracles
and Moralities were contemporaries with the great
Art and Craft period of our history.

In some countries the Mystery Play stage was
usually a very long platform with a building,
such as a church, for background. The spectators
were seated in front of this platform. This long
stage was divided into many compartments, providing a gradual transition from heaven to hell.
Evidences of this performance are to be found
in the dramatic altar screens still preserved in
Continental cities.

The Early Italian Stage

The most interesting period of the Italian stage
is that of the Commedia dell' Arte renaissance,
which comes between the Moralities and Mysteries
and the Elizabethan stages. It was the great
period of the drama of Harlequin, Pantaloon, and
Columbine. The Commedia dell' Arte was the
beginning of the great Folk drama, just as the
Greek, Indian, Chinese, and Japanese drama-dance
was the beginning of the Religious drama.
Materials for a brief but interesting chapter on
the history of this stage are to be found in
recent numbers of *The Mask*. Let me quote some
of the principal points. The Commedia dell' Arte
was a break away from the conventional drama in
answer to a demand for a representation of contemporary life. " It was the name given to the
improvised performances of the professional actors
and stage-managers." " It was a theatre which
appealed to the ordinary public, to the man of

culture, and to the actors themselves." "These actors were so excellent, so intelligent, perceived so well the advantage of communicating directly with their public instead of through the medium of a material foreign to themselves." "Instead of one actor playing many parts he played but one." A list of parts is given, from which it appears that Punch or any other part may be played in a dozen different ways according to its many and varied moods. Here was the beginning of the Repertory Theatre. Imagine all the interpretations of *Hamlet* — mad, sane, philosophic, philosophic-humorous, and so forth—being given by one man, a sort of modern Frigoli who changes his part with his dress, and there you have it. The actors "were free to say what they liked ; they were free to do what they liked ; they had only to let their feelings escape at the right moment, and *to obey the stage-manager*." Their freedom was limited by the stage-manager. Their intentions were given direction by "a piece of paper pinned up at each side of the stage. The actor had only to study this paper carefully after the stage-manager had composed it carefully. If this master of the ceremonies had genius, he composed it so that the performance became natural, the passion weaving these foolish and profound figures into a pattern." The stage-manager was the pattern-director of Mr Craig's dreams. One of the greatest of the Commedia dell' Arte scenario constructors was Gozzi. His *Turandot*, upon which the hand of Schiller fell heavily, was revived by Max Reinhardt, while an entire number of the

Blätter des Deutschen Theaters was devoted to its exposition. The first article opens with the significant words, " Gozzi's work is dead." Says Philippe Monnier : " The Italian Comedy dell' Arte, the Italian Comedy of improvisation, of masks, of plots and incidents (taken from novels) developed along parallel lines with the Italian Comedy written in the study. It died with the *ancien régime.*" Then in a vivid passage he describes its origin, " stage," and methods : " To set it in its proper frame, we must reconstruct for ourselves an Italian fair with all its wild excitement. . . . A gibbet was outlined against the sky. Strings of onions hung from pedlars' stalls. Boys and dogs and hedge-priests, servants and wandering merchants mixed upon the stage. Cripples of every kind drawled out their prayers. Men in plumed hats stood, hand in pocket, spitting upon the ground ; few had the good taste to step aside. . . . In the glare and hubbub of these orgies, to the accompaniment of blows given by insulted servant-girls, amid cries and stinks, among cheats and swindlers, that strange, monstrous, savage growth burst forth, with the gestures of an artist, and the soul of a child. Starting from some such fair of the Impruneta, Italian comedy spread through all the land. A yoke of oxen dragged round its chariot with its canvas awning. Beneath the canvas Isabella suckled her child. At each rise in the road the actors got down and pushed against the wheels. They knew chance resting - places, and strange hostelries, all the hazards of the great roads."

The passage proceeds to relate how these wandering sons " of night and mud " found " the great gates of the palaces opened to them and entered in." Everywhere they were received by royal personages with open arms. Thus they travelled across Europe, influencing the great dramatists, Shakespeare, Molière, and the rest, partly rose again through Goldoni, and finally died.

THE SHAKESPEAREAN STAGE

It is not necessary to dwell upon the influence exerted by the Commedia dell' Arte on Shakespeare, nor upon the resemblances between the two. Like the Commedia, Shakespeare drew his plots from all sources. There is a resemblance between some of his types and those of the Commedia ; he drew his inspiration from the time ; his drama was national, and in a sense a break away from a more conventionalised form ; many of his characters were spontaneous and life-like, so life-like, in fact, that it was difficult to believe they had not been transferred from the street to the stage. To-day the exponents of characters are practically transferred from the street to the stage, as anyone that produces ultra-realistic plays will tell you. Furthermore, there was the Commedia element of broad humanity in Shakespeare's plays, and the plays themselves appealed to the ordinary public, man of culture, and to the actor. The point of chief interest here is the form and working of the Shakespeare stage. The theories surrounding this point are innumerable. Was the stage a make-shift one ? Was it a stage for all time, whose

possibilities have never yet been fully realised?
Did Shakespeare write for a peculiar form of stage
with a forced method of staging constantly before
him? Or was invention busy devising a new
and more suitable playhouse for him? Opinion is
divided on these questions. It may or may not
be true that Shakespeare did not bother about a
theatre, but had a platform, and that was all that
was necessary. It may or may not be true that
Shakespeare considered every condition under which
his plays were to be produced, and made every
allowance for the open platform with the curtained recess at the back, and a balcony, and for
the effects of direct sunlight, as his theatre was
open to the sky. And it may be true that Shakespeare was only concerned with his verse, knowing
that the spectator came to hear, not to see. There
are at least three facts which should determine the
answer. The first is that Shakespeare thoroughly
knew his theatre. Like Max Reinhardt, he began
as a call-boy, from thence progressed to actor.
He took shares in theatres and founded the first
theatrical trust, in order to prevent the church
party opposing him in places of public worship.
In time he acquired property and became one of
those banes of the economic socialist, a bloated
capitalist and monopolist. We have no record of
what the Elizabethan "socialists" thought of
Shakespeare, but it is probable they blessed him
with a curse, as a certain section of socialists are
now blessing the capitalist dramatist, George
Bernard Shaw. If Shakespeare were alive to-day,
he would doubtless be a great admirer of Frohman,

the American octopus. Another fact is that the Shakespearean theatre was not a fixed affair. The Globe, for instance, was a new invention containing innovations of which Shakespeare availed himself, just as the Elizabethan age was a new age of drugging. Tea arrived with the Dutch East India Company, tobacco with Raleigh, and the intimate drama with Shakespeare. A third fact is that Shakespeare was not the literary director obsessed by the belief that he has a vision. Though it is true that his chief contacts are literary, and he has drunk at all sources, Sophocles, Euripides, Seneca, Plautus, Cicero, Horace, Catullus, Virgil, Ovid, Lucretius, Tibullus, Pliny, Plato, and Montaigne ; though, too, he " lifted " plays bodily, took characters and dialogues from old tales and sagas, and was greatly influenced by this great man and that, by Marlowe, whose spell of scepticism and rhythm is over some of his later plays ; yet he poured forth plays that were neither literary nor moral, but a compound of his own distilled for his own theatre. To-day the Elizabethan stage is being approached from all sides, and diverse opinions are being expressed concerning its form and utility. The latest re-interpretation of the stage comes from architect Zeh of Munich, who is convinced that though the Elizabethan stage was so admirably proportioned, apparently it was only primitive, and its advantage lay in the variety of its scenic possibilities. It has all along been misinterpreted. In this architectural view we see a tendency not to create but to improve on earlier forms. The archæological view is divided. Scholars and critics believe that on the one hand the Elizabethan stage was perfect and it should not be re-adapted. Others believe it was primitive and should be brought up to date. Hence the many new Shakespearean stages at Munich, Buda-Pesth, and elsewhere. A very excellent description of the actual stage is given in the following notes by Mr F. J. Harvey Darton, who is writing about a model of the stage designed according to the knowledge of Mr W. Poel.

"The stage used is designed according to the theories of Mr William Poel and other scholars as to what an Elizabethan stage really was like ; it is only fair to say that different opinions are strongly held. The view here taken is that the 'traverse,' or curtain in the middle of the stage, stretched between two solid fixed pillars, was meant to give the actors and the playwright a chance of using different scenes for different places ; there was no painted scenery to guide the audience, and no front curtain to lower to show the lapse of time or change of scene ; the audience stood or were seated on three sides of the stage.

"On this theory there were three possible scenes : (i.) in front of the 'traverse,' when the curtain was closed. This might be a road, a plain, a forest glade, or any more or less open scene. (ii.) In front and behind the line of the traverse, the curtain being open, so that the whole stage up to the back wall could be used. This would be employed for interiors, or large important scenes. (iii.) There was also a gallery or balcony at the back, in which apparently musicians sat, or possibly even spectators. Probably this was used wherever a high scene was needed, *e.g.*, Juliet's balcony, or the walls of Angiers.

" With these three possible scenes, the actor could give the audience the idea of a change of place without difficulty. He could, for instance, in Scene (i.) say, ' I'll to the king at Pontefract,' and go off ; the traverse curtain would then open, and create Scene (ii.), and the king would be seen in an obviously different place—which it would not require much imagination to consider Pontefract ; presently the first actor would come in, and he would clearly have come from somewhere else—from Scene (i.). Thus scene after scene could be played on alternate stages, or, if the place was supposed to be the same for several scenes (as in *As You Like It*, for example), on the same portion of the stage. There would be no need to wait for scenery to be moved, and the whole play could be acted without an interval.

" It may be mentioned, perhaps, that Shakespeare nearly always makes it clear in the dialogue where the speakers are supposed to be. Orlando, in *As You Like It*, says at once, ' He keeps me rustically *at home*,' and later, to Oliver, ' I am here in your orchard ' ; *King John* begins with the reception of an embassy from France, and the dialogue clearly shows that John is in his own kingdom, and so on. The perfect stagecraft of Shakespeare, and his extraordinary knowledge of what was essential from the audience's point of view, are excellently brought out by acting the plays in accordance with this theory of the Elizabethan stage.

"There were several theatres in Shakespeare's London. Those whose site is most easily identified now were the 'Curtain' and 'The Theater,' both close to the present Curtain Road, Shoreditch, and the 'Globe,' on Bankside, which is commemorated by a tablet in the wall of Barclay's Brewery, Park Street, Southwark (on the southeast side of Southwark Bridge). Other theatres of Shakespeare's day or a little later were at Newington Butts, Cripplegate (the 'Fortune'), Bankside (the 'Rose,' the 'Hope,' and the 'Swan'), Blackfriars, Clerkenwell (the 'Red Bull'), and Drury Lane (the 'Cockpit')."

The Red Bull Playhouse was originally an inn-yard theatre with an open-air platform or stage, of which the inn formed the back and sides. There was a resemblance between this open-air theatre and the house-yard theatres of Spain.

In De Witt's description of the Elizabethan playhouse there are some interesting facts on dimensions. Thus we learn that the stage of the Fortune Theatre was 43 feet long, and in breadth extended to the middle of the " yard "—that is, 43 feet long and $27\frac{1}{2}$ feet deep. The proscenium opening of the modern theatre is from 30 to 40 feet. Mr John Corbin, to whom I am indebted for a copy of his article " Shakespeare and the Plastic Stage," published in the *Atlantic Monthly*, is of the opinion that playhouses like the Swan, the Fortune, and the Globe, were built on a radically different plan from the other existing theatres. "The stage was a platform, extending, as an apron, to the middle of the pit, so that the spectators viewed it from all points of the compass, except only the narrow surface separating the stage from the tiring-house—and even this, at least after 1600, was at times invaded by the public. No proscenium arch was possible, no wings, and no flies—and consequently no properly pictorial illusion. Opinions on the question of Shakespeare and scenery are also greatly at variance. There are those who believe that Shakespeare used no scenery—George Brandes, Sir Sidney Lee, William Poel — and those who believe otherwise — Professor Dowden, John Addington Symonds, and others. Then there are the advocates of spectacle—Sir Herbert Tree, for instance—who endeavour to prove that Shakespeare himself would have employed the modern developments of scenic appliances. Others go so far as to say that Shakespeare justified them. Then there are those who say that Shakespeare's verse was sufficient to rivet the attention of the audience, and scenery would only have distracted the mind of the spectator from the jumble of unconnected incidents of the earlier plays. In fact, his verbal scene-painting was sufficient. Beyond these there are some who refer to the enormous influence of Shakespeare himself as a reformer in stage-management. In regard to naturalness and unity of scheme and the arrangement of his play or stage-production he was far ahead of his period ; while the red-hot Shakespearean maintains that as stage-craftsman he was far ahead not only of his day but of ours. What he has done and what he is going to do for Germany is too stupendous for words. True, Shakespeare knew nothing about the modern unity in variety of stage-setting. He did not use a revolving stage, but he used alternate stages, which, combined with the rapidly spoken scenic descriptions, solved the problem of quick changes. But, after all, mechanical stage devices are as old as the stage itself ; they were employed by the Greeks ; and the man who was the first to string together a vast quantity of incoherent, unconnected scenes was no doubt ingenious enough to set them moving with a rapidity quite out of question with a succession of realistic scenes. So why worry over Shakespeare in this or other directions ? We have but one question to ask Shakespeare and the rest of the Old Masters : " What is your individual value to us ? Have you anything to contribute towards the reform movement in our theatre ? " If they say " No," then the proper comment is " Get out ! " Probably the truth is that they have nothing but a few suggestions to offer. Three of the present suggestions are towards : (1) doing away with the proscenium (or picture-frame), thus making the stage and auditorium one, so that the audience may move in the same world as the actors ; (2) the devising of means of a more rapid change of scene ; and (3) the development of the simplified stage.

THE MOLIÈREAN STAGE

The stage of Molière, the classical dramatist of France, stood to French drama in much the same relation as the Elizabethan stage stood to English drama. There was the same scenic austerity, and the same absence of spectacle. There was no music during the performance. The spectators sat on the stage and probably behaved as badly as the Elizabethans, who ate and drank quite regardless of the acting. The noteworthy fact of the Commedia dell' Arte, the Elizabethan and Molière stages, was the intimacy between the actors and the audience. The intimacy of the first two was of the rough and tumble fair order. The simplicity of the Molière stage also recalled that of the Commedia dell' Arte, many of whose conventions Molière is said to have borrowed. Some historians go so far as to charge him with building his theatre out of the materials supplied by the Italian Comedy. Without the Commedia dell' Arte there would have been no Molière. But whether " the theatre of Molière was the most exquisite fruit of the Commedia " is doubtful. It is highly probable that Molière's comic genius would have found an outlet even if the Italians had never existed. Molière, like his contemporary wits of the Court of Louis XIV., punctured the vanity of pedantry even to the point of threatening sound learning. The repudiation of the artificial and superficial in French tradition was his main theme, which he expressed in comedy, and he is charged with using the machinery of the Commedia synopses, scenes, episodes, and types for the purpose of " manufacturing " such plays as *Tartuffe*, *George Dandin*, *Scapin*, *le Malade Imaginaire*, etc. I think it would be safer to say that what Molière did copy was the attempt of both Elizabethan and Italian comedy to break away from stilted artificiality and to adopt a more natural manner of representation. Indeed, naturalism appears to be at the root of all the creative epochs of the drama. As the ancient and superficial manner of representation became apparent to live minds, so they discarded it for a more natural manner. Thus creative drama has ever been inspired by " the time." The vehemence of life which Molière put into his valets was in Molière himself and of his time, or it would not have appeared as vehemence of life. You cannot copy the vehemence of life of one age and make it appear the vehemence of life of your age. It is sheer stupidity to say you can.

An idea of the formation and working of the Molière stage may be gathered from the following passage taken from Karl Mantzius' notable work :—

" Whether this development of stage decoration has been a reform of dramatic art, and whether we may be certain that the modern theatre, with all its perfection in the way of picturesque effects, ingenious mechanisms, and magnificent light, idealises the ideal stage, is a great question. Who knows whether we shall not some day prefer to return to a stage which affords the best conditions for seeing and hearing the art of the author naked and undisguised rather than to go on developing a decorative scenery which seems more calculated to throw a veil over the defects of both. . . ." It was during the Italian age of complicated scenery that the stage took the shape which it has nowadays. "It was no longer a projecting platform surrounded by the audience on three sides. It was a separate space, an enormous square box, the first wall of which had been removed, and in the inside of which the plays were presented to the spectators like pictures against a background. . . . France soon adopted the Italian system, which supplanted both the French platform stage and *lé décor simultané*; even plays which seemed written and calculated for the latter form of stage were now performed with the simple, regular, and invariably recurring scenes: 'a street,' 'a public place,' or 'a classical colonnade' and 'a forest'; and in addition to these a room with five doors symmetrically placed—one in the background, two 'upper entrances' and two 'lower entrances,'—a scene which is still used in several of Molière's comedies, such as *Tartuffe*, *le Misanthrope*, *l'Avare*, etc. These plays, indeed, are so completely adapted to this scene that they cannot be performed with any others."

It should be mentioned that the stage here referred to is the later one employed by Molière. His first acquaintance with the theatre was as a strolling player and manager of the Théâtre Illustre. This theatre travelled about the country in a lumbering cart, erecting its stage in tennis courts. Perrault tells us what the arrangements of this theatre were in Molière's early time. Tapestries were hung round the stage, and entrances

and exits were made by struggling through the
heavy curtains, which often knocked off the hat of
a comedian, or gave a strange cock to the helmet of
a warrior or a god. The lights were candles stuck
in tin sconces at the back and sides, but luxury
sometimes went so far that a chandelier of four
candles was suspended from the roof. At intervals
the candles were let down by a rope and pulley,
and anyone within easy reach snuffed them with
his fingers. A flute and tambour, or two fiddles,
supplied the music. The highest prices were paid
for seats in the dedan (cost of admission fivepence) ;
for the privilege of standing up in the pit two-
pence-halfpenny was the charge. The doors
opened at one o'clock ; the curtain rose at two.

Goethe's Stage

The later stage of Goethe represents another
break with tradition in favour of naturalism. In
this direction Goethe derived a great deal from
Shakespeare. He was very old when he received
his legacy. He was, in fact, in his seventy-seventh
year when the true nature of Elizabethan stagecraft became apparent to him and revolutionised
his conception of the stage. The quarto which
came to his notice revealed that the stage directions of the play indicated neither locality nor
decorations, and was innocent of act and scene
division. Thus Goethe saw that the imagination
of the spectator was left unfettered to follow the
full course of the author's imagination. Though
a newer edition of the quarto in which the play was
divided into acts and scenes, and its localities and

decorations were indicated, came into Goethe's hands, he ignored the alterations, and decided to follow the first quarto, and considered that the plain Elizabethan stage was the right thing. Had he come into contact earlier with the actual Shakespearean stage, he would have left dramas in place of autobiographies which, like *Faust*, took him the greater part of his life to write. Thus through an acquaintance with Shakespearean stagecraft Goethe conceived the modern idea of intimacy which he, together with Schiller, applied to the theatre with a view to reforming it. They believed that a return to the extreme naturalism and simplicity of representation of earlier times was necessary to the life of the drama. One of the conditions of the reform was that the spectator and player should be brought as closely together as possible. Accordingly, under the direction of Goethe, an architect, Schenkel, planned a theatre containing new features, or rather features based upon disused conventions. One of the latter was the revival in a modified form of the curved or " apron " stage, which projected into the auditorium, after the manner of that of the old Globe Theatre. By such means the spectator and actor were to be brought together and the receptivity of the former increased by contact and simplicity, instead of being decreased by distance and over-elaboration of detail. The Goethe-Schenkel theatre was built at Weimar.

THE WAGNERIAN STAGE

Next we find Wagner and his music-drama theory feeding on the unceasing diet of revolt, and

striving to set music free of its shackles. Wagner
accepted Goethe's idea and expressed it in his own
way. He agreed that the reality of the drama
needed a stage as near the spectator as possible.
But he felt that it is different with opera,
which, being designed to produce illusion—to be
attained by a voluptuous mingling of all forms of art,
under whose spell men would reach an emotional
union—requires that the stage picture should be
removed as far from the spectator as possible.
With this idea in his mind he called in the aid of
an architect, and together they set to work to construct a new theatre. The problem which Wagner
sought to solve in this theatre was intimacy. The
exterior was designed to conform to the interior,
which was constructed solely to preserve in the
spectator the mood created by the music-drama.
The structure of the interior had several innovations. The orchestra was sunk beneath the level
of the stage. There were no circles, as in our
theatres, the tiers of seats, circles, and galleries, one
above the other, were abolished, and the newer
amphitheatre, consisting of rows of seats rising
from the sunken orchestra to the single row of
boxes at the back, was established. Each seat in
this amphitheatre was self-contained, so as to allow
each spectator to live in his own world of imagination. A second proscenium was introduced—a
front one, unlighted, and designed to divide the
stage from the audience and to create the desired
effect of distance. Wagner named it the " Mystischer
Abgrund." To him it separated the real from the
ideal and added mystery to the scene and acting. To

break the monotony of the wall space in the auditorium columnar projections were added. But on the whole the architectural features were not beautiful. They have been greatly modified in other theatres built according to the Semper-Wagner model. Both the Wagnerian and the Shakespearean stages are greatly influencing Germany at present. The Wagnerian auditorium is springing up everywhere. Professor Max Littmann is busy embodying its principles in his theatres, as may be seen at the Künstler Theater, Munich, and the Schiller Theater, Charlottenburg.

The following note on the structure of Wagner's theatre, by Mr Edwin O. Sachs, is of interest. "The theatre, which stands on a height a little under a mile from the town, is built from the plans of Gustav Semper, the idea of the design being Wagner's own, an experiment indeed, but one which succeeded beyond all expectation. The seats are arranged on a kind of sloping wedge in such a manner that everyone has an almost equally good view of the stage, for there are no boxes, and the only galleries are quite at the back, one, the Fürstenloge, being reserved for distinguished guests, the other, above it, for the townspeople. Immediately in front of the foremost row of seats a hood or sloping screen of wood covers a part of the orchestra, and another hood of similar shape starts from the front of the stage at a slightly lower level. Thus, there is left a space between the two hoods through which the sound of the orchestra ascends with wonderful blended effect."

The Moscow and Wyspianski Stages

There is very little to be said about either of these stages. The Moscow stage is of the conventional type. It is very large, well equipped with the latest mechanical devices, and has a revolving section. The revolving stage was invented by the Japanese, and the idea made its way to Munich, where it was realised by Lautenschläger. In the pursuit of artistic expression in the Moscow Theatre, there is no entre-act music, the audience does not applaud, and there are no calls before the curtain. The original theatre of Wyspianski had an illusion stage, which was decorated with the symbolic scenery designed and painted by Wyspianski. The theatre of Wyspianski, which the Polish painter aimed to make the theatre of the Polish conscience, has disseminated the seeds of the new plastic stage, some of which have flown to Moscow.

Ibsen and Contemporary Stages

The contemporary stage is an offshoot of the Italian Renaissance stage, which has culminated in the peep-show or picture stage. It is used for every kind of drama, old and new, both with and without form, drama all technique (Pinero), and drama which has no technique to speak of, no plot, no strong dramatic crises, no construction, a formless drama nurtured by the Court Theatre, London, and of which Mr Bernard Shaw's later go-as-you-please discussion-demonstrations are the most extravagant development. A discontent with this present-day form of stage has led reformers into an age of experiment. Ibsen might have been in the van of these reformers by devising a circular stage to give effect to his conception of sculptured figures, or figures seen in the round and not in the flat, as most dramatists see them ; but he preferred to transfer the centre of his theatrical life from the theatre to the library. Hence, the Ibsen stage has yet to be born. When it is, the conception of dramatic action laid entirely within the characters, aided by the revelation of music and the plastic forms of art, will carry the action of the drama and its representation as much beyond Wagner as Wagner carried them beyond the Greeks, when he sought the aid of modern forms of art and music in order to conceive a new dramatic form.

The said age of experiment has given birth to various reform stages which Dr Carl Hagemann classifies under the head of revolving stage, idealistic stage, illusion stage, relief stage (Munich), picture stage, sunken stage, moving stage, Wagner stage, etc.

Max Reinhardt is among those who are actively searching for a new stage. His search has carried him in many directions, into many countries. He is testing in turn the old and new reform stages, from the Greek stage in its final form under Sophocles and Euripides to the Shakespearean stage in its newest form as developed by Drs Kilian and Klein from the primitive reactionary stage devised by Jacza Savits. In doing so he is gradually evolving a form of stage suited to his idea that " the theatre belongs to the theatre."

HIS RESOURCES

MAX REINHARDT has two theatres, the Deutsches Theater and the adjoining Kammerspielhaus. These theatres have three points of general interest. They are examples of theatres run on a very successful commercial and artistic basis, perfectly equipped and organised, and efficiently worked on the repertory system.

HISTORY AND PHYSIQUE

Although the Deutsches Theater is comparatively an old-established theatre, its present history, like that of the Kammerspielhaus, begins with Reinhardt. For years it was under the direction of Josef Kainz, the classicist Adolf L'Arronge, and of Otto Brahm. But it was Reinhardt who applied to it the revolutionary doctrine that the theatre is neither a literary nor a moral institution, that its function is not to educate nor guide human conduct, nor to uphold mere scribbling for scribbling's sake.

But the chief historical importance of the Deutsches Theater is that it is a private theatre, not a subsidised one. It is a convincing proof that it is possible to conduct a theatre on artistic lines, and it gives the lie to the hide-bound Court and other endowed theatres on the one hand, and the ginger-bread commercial theatres on the other, which are run solely for money, and which Froh-mania has elevated to a superstition in our midst. The Deutsches is really the intermediate theatre, demonstrating that it is possible to conduct a paying theatre on artistic lines. Maybe it is a stepping-stone to the purely artistic theatre. The physique of this theatre commands a great deal of attention. Generally speaking, it is a spacious and well-appointed house. Its Greek exterior would appear to symbolise Reinhardt's search for simplicity and proportion. It is built upon an inexpensive site out of the main thoroughfare. But the position does not matter, seeing that the theatre does not cast its net to catch stray fish. The dimensions and form of the theatre are determined by function. As a repertory theatre on a large scale, and one, moreover, worked on the newest principles, it requires plenty of stage and store-room for machinery, scenery, properties, and costumes, and more especially as each play is given an entirely new outfit, and is not faked up with old stock scenery and costumes, as used to be the custom of stock theatres and is now sometimes that of English repertory theatres, and always of that bright particular flower, the Stage Society. One of the first innovations in the Deutsches Theater to take one's notice is the revolving stage with its endless possibilities, and its call upon the inventiveness of the scenic artist for limit-less novel effects. Another outstanding feature is the ingenious mechanical contrivances by which electricity is extensively drawn upon in a well-organised lighting system. To-day the most marked efforts in the reform theatre lie in the search for a solution to the problem of lighting. Years ago Adolphe Appia came forward with his scheme for reforming the lighting of Wagner's operas, which was subsequently embodied in his notable work *Die Musik und die Inscenierung*. The work has been freely cited and its influence exerted in many directions. Then came Fortuny's invention, aiming to do away with sky-borders and to substitute a pure white light for the tinted light in use. Colour is obtained by the light being thrown first upon reflectors prepared to receive it, and thereafter upon the scene in such a way that the tinted light is diffused instead of being focussed upon certain points, say the backcloth, or the bald head of the leading man. Forming part of this system of lighting is a hooded background of white concrete upon which Fortuny throws his light in order to obtain vast and very impressive sky effects. I believe that this hooded horizon, which covers the back and the part of the stage where the flies usually are, can be made of a portable material, that may be closed up out of the way when not in use. But when I was in Berlin I was only shown the model made of concrete. This method of solving the lighting problems has also exerted an influence here and there. The Deutsches Theater is provided with a round horizon. As in the Fortuny system, there is a vast horizon or heaven which passes round the back and side of the stage. It has a slight dome, but not nearly so marked as the Fortuny one. This huge segment of a circle is a light iron structure covered with plaster. On either side nearest the audience this wall is supported on columns to allow of the passage of the scenery on to the "Vorbühne," or stage proper. When not hidden by built scenery, these columns are hidden from the auditorium by curtains of the same colour as the plaster. Thus horizon effects can be obtained at any corner or portion of the stage. This heaven is lighted by an enormous " Oberlicht " (overlight), placed above the centre of the stage and so constructed as to throw its rays of light horizontally and not *vertically*. In addition there are two large arc lamps placed on either side of the large light. The purpose of these lamps is to light the space immediately in front of the heaven, as the " Oberlicht " is meant to light the round horizon, and not the stage.

The construction and working of the overlight is a profound secret, almost as deep indeed as was once the structure and application of the great grey screen of Mr Gordon Craig. It was devised by some one connected with the theatre, and many persons and some journalists are after its past. Of course, the journalists will win. The new conditions of lighting do not preclude the use of conventions. Thus there are battens which, however, are rarely used, except for getting light at awkward angles. There is also the usual equipment of movable lamps and footlights. Reinhardt's use of footlights is interesting. He never uses them for exterior scenes if he can avoid it. He thus gains greatly in natural effect, and kills the fallacy that intense light is always needed for outdoor scenes. Thus his use of foot-lights is almost confined to the lighting of interiors, where he finds such lighting necessary to modify the effect of the ceiling on the faces of the actors. The entire illumination of the scene is worked by an operator on the stage, and not under it, as at the Künstler Theater. The arc lamps can be used on resistance, to speak technically, and thus all kinds of sky effects are obtained. The Deutsches Theater system of lighting has found its way to England, and may be trusted to undergo some development at the capable hands of Mr Basil Dean of the Liverpool Repertory Theatre. The lighting at this theatre is already attracting attention, and is admitted to be the best in the provinces. Birming-ham has followed Liverpool's lead, having engaged Mr Dean to apply his practical theory to its new Repertory Theatre. There will be no further excuse for Birmingham to grope in theatrical darkness.

THE REPERTORY SYSTEM

The history of this system has already been discussed. The Meiningers revised it, added the ensemble, and we have seen how Brahm placed it in Reinhardt's hands to be launched on a prosperous career. The repertory system is composed of two parts : players and the pieces they play in. A repertory theatre may be likened to a wardrobe to which a fresh set of costumes is added each day. The wearers of these costumes must be of such adaptable proportions that each can take down any costume and wear it becomingly. Thus if to-day one wears a livery of green silk, with yellow roses as large as spring cabbages stamped all over it, to-morrow he must put on the vastly important knee-deep waistcoats, Mechlin ruffles, the sword, sweat, and other patents of nobility. Metaphorically speaking, this is what the Deutsches Theater players, like those in other German repertory theatres, have long been accustomed to do, and as a result the Deutsches Theater acting is remarkable for its modernity, resource, versatility, and spontaneity.

The repertory system is not new. But the modern form of this system is not the same as the old or "stock" one. The stock company system succeeded the circuit or strolling players system which had been in existence from pre-Restoration times. From the Restoration till late in the nineteenth century most of the great towns of this country contained an established theatre in which stock companies played for a season at a time; while the smaller towns provided centres for strollers from whose ranks the stock companies were recruited, just as the stock companies provided a source to which the London patent theatres went for their supply of talent. The stock company was usually composed of twelve or more stationary types of players. Each player assumed one line of business and took no other. Thus there was the "leading" man, the "heavy" man, the "juvenile" man, the "light" and "low" comedians,

the " walking " gent, the " first " and " general "
utility men, the " leading " lady, the " heavy "
woman, the " old " woman, the " utility " and
" walking " ladies, the " chambermaid," and so on.
The " bill " was changed three or more times a week.
Plays were put on at a moment's notice, thus leaving very little time for study. As a result, the
performances were usually of the go-as-you-please
order, the parts being played by actors of the rant
and furious school, whose movements were afflicted
with a stage stalk, who spoke with strange accents
and seldom knew their parts. Under the stock
system the scenery, costumes, and appointments also
assumed the go-as-you-please manner, being amaz-
ingly inappropriate, as well as adaptable to all sorts
and conditions of plays and players. Needless to
say, such a system could only have one result. The
performances were always rough and unfinished ;
while the players seldom had the opportunity, even
if they had the inclination, to become absorbed
in their work. With the growth of travelling
facilities the stock system gradually died out. It
was replaced by the touring system, according to
which London successes were sent on tour. The
companies presenting these successes were, and are
still, composed of a " star," supported by minor
players, who, instead of having constant practice in
a great number of parts, are only expected to play
one part each for months together. The company
are drilled into their parts in London, and here
their concern with the play ends, unless we except
understudying parts, which is, as a rule, merely a
process of photographing the principal players.

That this is a bad system for the player is incontestible. It simply reduces him to a wooden automaton. The modern repertory system has a great advantage over the aforementioned systems in being better organised, and in providing a response to the demand by dramatic societies in large centres for an appropriate expression of the life and customs of such centres. Thus it has had not only the effect of establishing repertory theatres with highly efficient resident companies playing the "legitimate" repertory, but of calling forth local dramatists well equipped to produce a local form of drama. Perhaps its chief good consists in affording players constant practice in a great number and variety of characters, thus opening up a valuable training ground to them, and thereby developing many remarkable talents ; and beyond this in developing ensemble acting in the country, whereby the player is enabled so to project his part into the play as to become part of a whole, and yet so to project himself into the character which he is interpreting that his own individuality becomes merged in the interpretation. In short, the new repertory system is essentially one for students of the drama.

ACTING AND ACTORS

Reinhardt's company, besides being cosmopolitan, contains some extraordinarily clever players. Despite the gloomy opinion of a certain class of cheap critic, they can do something more than they are told. Not only can they think out their parts, but they can invest them with life and passion. Brahm, it will be remembered, gave birth to the ultra-

GERTRUD EYSOLDT

modern type of player—educated, cultured, talented, highly restrained, understanding rather than feeling "the part," the offspring, in fact, of modern intellectual drama. Reinhardt went beyond the new tradition, and promoted Brahm's moderns to ultra-moderns by affording an opening to impulse. These may be divided into types. The first type is represented by Gertrud Eysoldt, an actress of the ultra-modern movement. She expresses the emotions through the intellect — the intellect, indeed, fashions the emotion. In fact, she is the extreme type of the intellectual actress, in whom the intellect is a fine instrument for shaping the feelings. She is the present type of actress—not the type that the new theatre and new drama will evolve. She is the actress who *knows*, is always on the level of consciousness, like Bernard Shaw. In this respect she recalls one or two English players whom Ibsen has created in England. William Archer once saw Gertrud Eysoldt in the part of Lulu in Wedekind's *Earth-Spirit*. His impressions are stated in these words : " The extraordinary skill with which Frau Gertrud Eysoldt plays Lulu is the only thing that to British nerves could render this assemblage of horrors endurable on the stage. Frau Eysoldt has the gift of being recklessly realistic without offence. She is in this part the incarnation of soulless femininity, without a suggestion of anything that exceeds the limits of art. It was this actress, by the way, who played both Oscar Wilde's Salome and Bernard Shaw's Cleopatra. . . . Frau Eysoldt's performance was the most remarkable thing I saw in Berlin." The second type

is found in the cosmopolitan and versatile actor
Alexander Moissi. This actor plays an extraordinary wide range of parts, among these being
Romeo, Franz Moor (Schiller's *Robbers*), Faust
and Mephisto, Hamlet and Œdipus Rex, Oswald
Alving (*Ghosts*), and Dubedat (*The Doctor's Dilemma*).
His achievement is all the more astounding when we
consider that he is an Italian, and has learnt from
forty to fifty parts in a foreign language. Possessing
the fiery Italian temperament, he is able to invest
his work with that rare element, passion, while a
voice of exceptional cello-like quality enables him
to charm and hold the spectator much as Bernhardt does. Herr Moissi is an example of Reinhardt's
extreme loyalty to the members of his company,
and especially to the new-comer. At first he encountered a great deal of opposition, but Reinhardt
stuck by him till he had carried him through.
An English actor-manager would have seen his
own position threatened by Herr Moissi's success
and would have got rid of him as soon as possible.
Under the star-system in England small-part people
are never given a chance. It is the most selfish
system in existence. A third Deutsches Theater
type is represented by Friedrich Kayssler, who last
season left the Deutsches Theater for the Deutsches
Schauspielhaus. This third type—differing from
the other two, the highly intellectual one of
Gertrud Eysoldt and the excessively emotional one
of Moissi—is of a strong, silent, self-contained
character firmly disciplined by an artistic will.
Herr Kayssler aims always and truthfully to express himself or his personality as he conceives it

and desires it to be realised. That is, he believes
he has a value and endeavours to make it fully felt
by everybody. He never changes, and thus reveals
the impenetrable characteristics of the unmistakably
North-German type. Broadly speaking, he is a
mixture of Mr Norman McKinnel and Mr Forbes
Robertson.

Another type is found in the old traditional
actor, Rudolf Schildkraut, whose methods have
the aroma of a full-bodied wine that has been in
the cellar many years. Both the actors and their
acting are the outcome of thoroughness and a reverence for the theatre. They exist for the play ;
they are never exploited as " stars " ; each is a part
of the whole, and each is rehearsed as a part of
the whole, and not as a sapless and voiceless entity
designed to prop up the darling of the gods.

School of Acting and Promotion

The promotion of the Deutsches Theater player is
also an organised affair. Understudies are not treated
as mechanical appliances. They are not only kept
prepared to go on for certain parts, but they are
allowed to appear in parts as vacancies occur, which
they frequently do owing to the constant change
of programme both at the Deutsches Theater and
the Kammerspielhaus. By this means a cast three
deep is built up, which has the advantage of enabling
pieces to be played by their original cast throughout their entire run, or for two or three seasons at
least. The Deutsches Theater method of promotion
resembles that of the Moscow Theatre, with the
exception that it is not bound by the co-operative

system of the latter theatre, whereby everybody employed in the theatre becomes a shareholder. Another point of resemblance is found in the school of acting attached to both theatres in which the players are prepared. In both schools the Jaques-Dalcroze system of rhythmic dancing is taught. By this system it is hoped that the music of physical movements will be restored, and actions and gestures will once more express thoughts and feelings that lie too deep for words. There are many supporters of the school of acting. Sir Herbert Tree is one, Sarah Bernhardt is another, a third appears in Miss Gertrude Kingston, while a fourth is Mr Gordon Craig. What others have conceived in theory, Max Reinhardt has given birth to in practice. Reinhardt is aware that the haphazard education of the actor is responsible for the inanities of acting. This may or may not be true. Personally, I believe that instinct plays as great a part in acting as in other forms of art, and given instinct there is little or no need of education. However, Max Reinhardt thinks differently, and he is in good company. So when he became director of the Deutsches Theater, his first step was to inaugurate a school wherein budding Eysoldts, Moissis, and Kaysslers might be turned out by the score. Here pupils are put through their preliminary paces, and taken carefully through all the departments of a player's career. A notable feature of Reinhardt's school is that it reproduces in miniature his idea of co-directorship. According to this idea there is an organiser and a number of intelligences who together form a collective will, and who separately and together impose this will, though not tyrannically, on the student. Thus the student in his journey round the circle passes from master-mind to master-mind, gathering the finest principles of speech and action in elocution, posture, dance, gesture, and grace, till the circle of his adventures is complete. It is said that Reinhardt's policy is to discover talent. He prefers the raw to the finished material. And out of the raw he weaves a piece of fine tapestry which falls harmoniously within his general design.

The Repertory Bill

As a clue to a normal week's working of the Reinhardt theatres and the source whence the actor's opportunity springs, let me quote a list of plays mentioned by Mr Granville Barker, in a contribution to the *Fortnightly Review*, as well as his concise comments thereon :—

	Deutsches Theater.	Kammerspielhaus.
Tuesday, Oct. 25	*Faust*	*A Comedy of Errors.*
		Le Mariage Forcé.
Wednesday, Oct. 26	*Sumurûn.*	*Der Graf von Gleichen.*
Thursday, Oct. 27	*Judith*	*A Comedy of Errors.*
		Le Mariage Forcé.
Friday, Oct. 28	*A Midsummer Night's Dream*	*The Doctor's Dilemma.*
Saturday, Oct. 29	*Herr und Diener*	*A Comedy of Errors.*
		Le Mariage Forcé.
Sunday, Oct. 30	*Herr und Diener*	*A Comedy of Errors.*
		Le Mariage Forcé.
Monday, Oct. 31	*Sumurûn.*	*Gawan.*

" Let me analyse this programme. The production of *Faust* dates from 25th March 1909.

It has been given many times this year, and this
was its hundred and fourteenth performance altogether. I saw it; it was excellent, and the house
(which is rather smaller than His Majesty's, rather
bigger than the Haymarket) was very well filled.
Sumurûn is a pantomime play with music, built
upon the famous 'Tale of the Hunchback' and two
or three other stories from the *Arabian Nights*. It
is a brilliant romp, remarkable, too, for the individual excellence of some of the acting, but above
all for the ingenuity and inventiveness of the production; quite one of Reinhardt's triumphs. It
was one of the spring season's successes and is still
popular, having reached perhaps its fiftieth performance. Hebbel's *Judith* was first produced here
on 25th February of this year, and has been played
fifty-three times. *A Midsummer Night's Dream* was
Reinhardt's first big Shakespearean success. It
has been played over five hundred times and is
never long out of the bill. This is probably the
theatre's record, and, indeed, too long a life for
any production. The playing it in repertory,
and the constant changes of cast (at this performance only one of the original actors appeared),
have kept it as fresh as may be, and the meaning
and spirit of the production survive well enough;
moreover, to the connoisseur in these things there
is a certain charm in the easy, well-worn way it
all goes. Still, it would be the sounder really
for a drastic readjustment and retuning. *Herr
und Diener* is a new play of Ludwig Fulda's,
something, as Bottom would say, 'in Ercles
vein,' and played very much so. These were

its first two performances. On Monday came *Sumurûn* again.

"Now for the Kammerspielhaus. The *Comedy of Errors* with *Le Mariage Forcé* is the latest production, a few weeks old only, and a great success, as appears by its being in the bill four times in one week. I fancy that no play may be done oftener. That this has been given twenty-three times in six weeks is at least a record.

"*Der Graf von Gleichen*, by Wilhelm Schmidt-bonn, one of the younger of the Rhineland school of dramatists, is a play drawn from a mediæval saga. It was produced in December 1908, and holds its place.

"*The Doctor's Dilemma* was produced here in November 1908. It has now a hundred and thirty-two performances to its credit, and is never out of the bill for very long. It steadily attracts its congregations. *Gawan*, by Eduard Stucken, is one of a cycle of plays dealing with the Arthurian legend ; one might call its author, not quite inappropriately, a sort of dramatic Burne-Jones. It was produced in the spring and has achieved about thirty performances."

THE PRODUCING STAFF

Reinhardt's power of organisation is further demonstrated in the extreme ability with which he selects and handles his producing staff. Here again we find the idea of co-directorship applied. Here again there is an organiser of great ability (Reinhardt) and a number of fine intelligences who together form a corporate whole, and together express the Will of the Theatre. Composing the circle are the producer (Reinhardt), the literary director (Arthur Kahane), the musical director, the interpretative body of players, the art director (Ernst Stern), the technical director, and so forth. These and others are the heads of the departments. Each directs and controls his own department, while working according to a general design. Generally speaking, the English Theatre is lacking in such a collective method of interpretation.

Financial and Public Support

Although it is maintained that in this commercial age theatres of the Deutsches Theater class cannot flourish without financial aid, I find no proof that Reinhardt's theatre does not pay its way as a successful private venture. Evidence has been produced in some quarters in the attempt to show that some of the private theatres in Germany are heavily endowed and are not expected to pay their way. It is said they are private only inasmuch as they do not publish balance-sheets. But persons who talk in this fashion usually confuse a private theatre with an endowed one. The Düsseldorf Theater is spoken of as a private theatre ; yet, as I have pointed out elsewhere, it receives municipal aid—the same assistance, in fact, as a municipal theatre. It is private, then, only in the sense that it is not public property. The Deutsches Theater is a private theatre, but that is no ground for assuming it is an endowed one. It is extremely doubtful whether Reinhardt is in need of financial assistance. Judging by his equipment and methods, I should say not. He is an unusual blend of business man and artist, and his grasp of business qualities has enabled him to put both his houses on a paying basis. Some persons confirm this by saying that Reinhardt's principal object in cultivating drama is to earn an honest living. If so, he has a good precedent in Shakespeare, who managed his own theatre, kept an eye on the box-office, was more careful of his money investments than his play construction, and was so successful in the theatrical business that he retired at an early age to live upon his profits. Reinhardt has been very successful throughout. Long runs and crowded houses have marked his progress. The secret of it is that he confined himself entirely to one thing—the theatre. He has lived for nothing else, and has received adequate support for this reason. I imagine that if Mr Granville Barker had adopted the same course there would be no need for him to deplore the absence of financial and public support. But, unfortunately, he has divided his strength between the theatre and political and socialistic propaganda, has permitted himself to be diverted by G. B. Shaw from the theatre to the exploitation of socialistic theory and Fabian socialism. Like Reinhardt, he should have recognised that the theatre is a jealous goddess who accepts no votive offerings but those belonging to the theatre. Such strange goods as economic theory and the wage system and guild socialism do not belong to the theatre. The political dust-heap is the proper place for them. When Mr Barker has been weaned from Mr G. B. Shaw and economic theory, and educated to regard the theatre and drama from an art standpoint, he will be ready for a successful start. The Moscow Art Theatre is another example of an undertaking whose commercial success is due to concentration on the things that belong to the theatre. For several years after it was established it had a large yearly deficit. But to-day it earns yearly between £8000 and £10,000 clear profit.

The public support of Reinhardt is and always has been fully assured. And I believe it would have been just as great even if public taste in Germany had not undergone so long a course of preparation. And this simply because on his business side Reinhardt has always had his finger on the public pulse, a policy which Mr Henry Arthur Jones used to follow during his most successful period. If the public demanded this, that, or the other form of contemporary drama, there was Mr Henry Arthur Jones with a sample. Mr Jones was always careful to remember that we are still a race of shopkeepers.

The record of the resources of the theatre would not be complete without mention of its propaganda sheet, *Blätter des Deutschen Theaters*, which is written by the heads of the departments, and to which attention has already been drawn.

HIS PRODUCTIONS

OF the plays produced by Reinhardt a list is included in the appendices, which attests that his theatre is in the true sense an international one. Plays of various periods and countries, by dramatists of different degrees of greatness, are selected for the purpose of having their essential spirit of comedy or drama extracted, brought up to date, and thereafter administered to the spectator in the form of a spell that acts upon him and by whose mesmeric power his own spirit is brought into the action of the play.

PRODUCTIONS IN GERMANY

What of Reinhardt's German productions? There is a great deal to admire in them, and they contain much that is of value to the English stage. During my visits to Germany I have seen several pieces in Berlin, as well as in Munich where Reinhardt usually spends his summer vacation producing festival plays at the Künstler Theater. On one occasion the anniversary of the amazing Kleist, the German Shakespeare, brought forth a production of *Penthesilea*. It was treated in an exceedingly simple way. All the top and side hamper of the stage was done away with, and the action of the play, which was condensed into four acts, took place at different points of the plain in front of Troy. The revolving stage was set accordingly with one tall cypress tree, which changed its position as the stage revolved. The white round horizon served as a background, being tinted to represent the desired sky effects. On another occasion the *Orestie* led me into the circus and gave me my first glimpse of Reinhardt's intimacy idea grown to gigantic proportions making its bow to a vast audience. Here, indeed, was " the colossal proportions which befit the monumental style." I fancy I must have had J. R. Lowell's *My Study Windows* in my pocket, for at the moment I did really believe that " things do really gain in greatness " by being done on a great scale, and it is wise " to act on a great stage," because " there is inspiration in the thronged audience." But when I left the building my belief was modified, for Moissi played Orestes, and though he has a voice that a Greek would have envied, his proportions were not by any means monumental. Since that time my belief in the resurrection of the circus as an aid to drama, in being suited to huge dramatic spectacle and having a seating capacity for from 6000 to 10,000 persons, has changed. I now believe in an age of the little theatre. The little theatre has an entrance for the public, but none for sensation, and if properly constructed and worked it will have no emergency exits. On another occasion *Oedipus Rex* gave me an insight into Reinhardt's methods of handling a Greek chorus and crowd. *Oedipus* also took me into the circus, where again the intimacy idea was fully exploited. I noticed one thing in particular, that the circus construction was far better suited to the production than the Covent Garden Opera House. The floor of the building was quite free, and the passages between the seats, which rose tier upon tier, as in the Greek amphitheatre, facilitated the movements of all the players. Thus I felt a kinship for the " crowd " more keenly than I did in the London production, to which I shall refer presently. As a contrast there came later, still in the circus, that fine old morality *Everyman*. It gave one a new emotion to find this piece of immortality scoring a triumph in a building so utterly different from the places it had visited in England under Mr William Poel's guidance. It appeared in the German dress that Hugo von Hofmannsthal had given it, in adapting it from the Nuremberg version of Hans Sachs. But I am still at a loss to know why Reinhardt considered the circus indispensable to the production of *Everyman*. There were no crowds, no chorus, and the quaint three-tiered stage, the only thing requiring room, would have gained in artistic proportions in a smaller building. Except in the Banqueting Scene, where Death appears invisible to all the revellers, save Everyman, the stage is not occupied by more than two or three characters at a time. Perhaps Reinhardt believed that only in space could its very simple, child-like character be felt. Apart from this consideration, it was one of Reinhardt's finest achievements. It was a Gothic contribution to the stage. Everything was Gothic except the circus, not that this mattered, for *Everyman* is not a piece of architecture; it is simply players mouthing the metaphysics of the Middle Ages. The entire scheme of line and colour and movement had the Gothic feeling. The production had, in fact, the uniform, homogeneous character of a style. The angular gestures made so familiar to us by the early primitive paintings and woodcuts were delightfully reproduced, though one or two of the actors appeared to tire of them in the course of the play and returned occasionally to the meaningless, conventionalised roundness of everyday acting. I liked the banqueting scene in Everyman's house. The burial scene was very effective, though it bordered on the archæologically correct. It had for background a carefully staged copy of the mediæval triptych, with the well-known angels upholding a scroll before a Gothic screen. The skill with which Moissi played Everyman added largely to the simple effectiveness of the production. His quiet, reverent repetition of an old Hans Sachs' prayer familiar to all German students, and most ingeniously introduced before Everyman goes to confession, was perhaps the most telling part of the whole performance. By Goethe's *Faust II.* I was introduced to Reinhardt's wonderfully ingenious use of the revolving stage used in conjunction with a part of the auditorium. The staging of this impossible " drama " is fully described in my volume *The New Spirit in Drama and Art.* I imagine that Max Reinhardt went wandering after this strange god only because it offered him an unequalled opportunity of demonstrating his remarkable talent as a producer. This piece has always been the despair of German

producers. How were they to get this metaphysical exposition staged within reasonable time.
It is true that the eminent writer Eckermann
adapted it in 1830 for the stage under Goethe's
supervision. It is true also that here and there
a daring producer has presented it in scraps during
the nineteenth century, and that Ernst von Possart,
the Shakespearean tragedian, almost got the whole
of it on the stage in Munich in 1895. But how
to stage it entire so as to preserve its magnitude, as
well as the patience of the audience, that was the
question.

Although the problem was not so bad as that of
Götz von Berlichingen, with its fifty-five scenes, it
was bad enough. The latter part of Goethe's specu-
lation on his journey to Hell and back again to
Heaven makes an immoderate call on the drop curtain and the scene-shifter. It is indeed a tough
problem. But Reinhardt's Shakespearean experience and his new conception of the stage and
stagecraft helped him to solve it. By erecting a
false proscenium level with the tiers of private
boxes and using the space between this and the
back of the stage to form alternate stages, he
overcame the play's reckless demand for scene-
shifting and long waits. In this way he got the
bigness of the work across the footlights, and its
sombre metaphysical character also. Thus presented, the latter half of Goethe's masterpiece gave
me the impression of one of Watt's great gloomy
figures seated on a ponderous globe chewing the
cud of contemplation. It will be gathered that
Reinhardt's success in galvanising *Faust* into up-

to-date life was due to his knowledge of Shake-speare's stagecraft. If Goethe had had this knowledge when he began to write *Faust* (which took him over half a century to complete) probably there would have been no triumph for Reinhardt. As a contrast to the black-and-white metaphysical treatment of *Faust II.* there is the colour treatment of Shakespeare. I think that Reinhardt appears at his best in his productions of Shakespearean comedy. Here he has full scope for his belief that the scene should appeal to the eye, that Shakespeare should be played in the festival spirit, that you cannot give him too much colour, brilliant colour being, in fact, the most appropriate setting to the mood in which the poet conceived his plays. Besides this, Reinhardt finds in Shakespeare full scope for the childlike vision which he possesses, and which is really in-dispensable in a producer of Shakespearean comedy. Thus his production of *Much Ado about Nothing* fully revealed that he has the gift of seeing things in a mass, as a child sees them, and that he considers the lighter plays of Shakespeare to be the best medium for exercising this spirit. *Much Ado* was really the child's Shakespeare. It contained just the big, simple masses, the colours, lines, sounds, and movements a child would enjoy and remember. There was nothing academical or literary about it. Its fourteen scenes were set at the same time on the revolving stage, thereby solving the problems of act division and quick changes of scene, and abolishing localities. The only locality mentioned on the programme was "The Scene is Messina." The scenes were, accordingly, simple and impressive — a mere suggestion of a lofty hall, or two box-trees and an infinite blue or blue-black horizon, or a double row of old-gold walls seen in perspective running out to a thin streak of blue sky. From the colour arrangement it was apparent that Herr Ernst Stern had also felt the festival spirit and was expressing it in fresh and delirious colour. His colour was full and rich in tone. Harmonious golds, blues, and reds composed the backgrounds for a wide range of very effective colour to move against. Some of the settings were skilfully adapted to serve two or three scenes. For example, an exterior would be suggested by a row of columns. Next, the exterior would be changed to an interior by the simple device of dropping a curtain in front of the columns. Further evidence of Reinhardt's childlike vision of Shakespeare will be found elsewhere in the extract from Mr William Archer's contribution to a symposium on the Deutsches Theater. Among Reinhardt's most recent productions was *The Blue Bird*, to which he gave the simple character of a German fairy tale, thus avoiding the pantomime and ballet characters of the London and Paris productions respectively.

PRODUCTIONS IN ENGLAND—" SUMURÛN "

When Reinhardt came to London he had immense difficulties to contend with. There was no suitable theatre for him, no up-to-date lighting system, and no intelligent organisation of the theatre staff, no one in the theatre

who, from reform - education, or pursuit, or
inclination, could greatly help him. He was regarded as a purveyor of sensation, and he was taken
by the nation on trial, so to speak, for a few weeks
at one of its principal music-halls. Thus pieces
which he had produced in Berlin under the new
and enlightened conditions had to be reproduced
here under old and obsolete ones. He made his
appearance modestly with a condensed version of
a play under his arm, and proceeded with it to the
Coliseum Theatre in the spring of 1911 as being
a place that possessed a revolving stage and some
possibilities of lighting. The piece was *Sumurûn*.
This play, which was of a mimetic character, a
combination of appropriate gesture and music, had
already appeared in Germany, where it created a
great deal of attention as being Max Reinhardt's
first attempt to apply the language of gesture.
Of course the experiment was not new. At an
early period in the world's history man was accustomed to express himself—his thoughts and feelings
—by action. Articulate speech is an encroach-
ment on the domain of human action, and in some
persons' opinion it is not an improvement. [Per-
haps in producing wordless plays Reinhardt is
expressing a growing feeling that it is time the
closure was put on articulate sounds, especially in
the theatre and parliament, and full scope be given
to man's desire to express his definite thoughts and
emotions by gesture.] In pursuit of his mimetic
idea that every possible human emotion should be
expressed by action, he cast *Sumurûn* with his most
distinguished actors and actresses, players who had

indeed been appearing in his biggest productions. To these he gave the task of removing the modern reproach created by the back-to-talk and the Shaw dramas, that nowadays some players can talk and cannot act, while other players can do neither.

The Coliseum cast of *Sumurûn*, although not the original one, fully vindicated the acting reputation of a part of the profession at least. And the production, scrappy though it was, revealed the fact that in Reinhardt a new force, working for the reform of the theatre, was in our midst. Judging from the reception given to the piece, and the demand of a certain section of the press for further samples of this class of goods, it is conceivable that Max Reinhardt returned to Germany with a lighter heart, and perhaps a heavier purse, than when he left it. If so, he was extremely fortunate, for the Coliseum production of *Sumurûn* was not a good one from a strictly critical point of view. The play was presented piecemeal; the Coliseum stock scenery was faked for the occasion, and the auditorium was too vast for the element of intimacy. The lighting, however, was good, and quickened the really beautiful colours as they moved across the scenes. A few months later the complete play, as given at the Deutsches Theater, was given at the Savoy Theatre. The exchange from the variety theatre to the legitimate stage was good, with the exception of the lighting. The Savoy stage was badly lit, and there was no dome focus light, such as had been used so effectively at the Coliseum, to concentrate the passions. This apart, the play was more together, the dimensions of the stage were more suited to it, and the action was closer to the audience

The Story

Sumurûn is a story without words that comes from the East. It is partly derived from the *Tales of the Arabian Nights,* by Friedrich Freska. It tells a story of Eastern passion, of love, hate, and revenge, the chief emotional characteristics of a race that has always been accustomed to give expression to its strongest emotions. It is the story of a well-conditioned, handsome merchant named Nur-al-din, who is in love with Sumurûn, the fascinating wife of an old Sheik. It is the old, old dramatic theme of a lover and his beloved and an obstacle, and a means to remove the obstacle. Nur-al-din, besides being a merchant, is a dreamer. Long before the play opens he has been dreaming of the perfect woman. One day, at the opening of the play, she arrives, and with her coming Nur-al-din's dream is realised. Their glances meet and the action of the play begins. Nur-al-din is now in love with the Sheik's wife, and she with him. He has felt the fascination of this seductive Eastern woman, and she has responded to the allurements of the handsome dreamer. But there is an obstacle to their happiness. The Sheik has to be removed. Nur-al-din's neighbour is a hunchback showman, who has a troupe of performers, including a beautiful dancer, an old woman who charms snakes, and a huge negro. The Hunchback also has his romance : he is in love with the beautiful Dancer. When the Sheik arrives with Sumurûn he is accompanied by his son, who, being a love adventurer, is willing and anxious to bestow his favours on the first promising object. So we see him trying to flirt with one of Sumurûn's maids, and, being defeated in his aim by Sumurûn herself, he turns and bestows his attention upon the Hunchback's dancer. The Hunchback, though poor and humble, is not the man to be trifled with. He has poured all his passion into this love for the Dancer, and though there is a great division between his position and that of the Sheik's son, nothing can restrain his intense jealousy and the frenzy of his anger. All the primitive savage in him rises to the surface and flings him upon his rival. But it is of no avail; for the rival is quickly rescued by the intervention of the officials of the Bazaar. The Hunchback, half killed, turns to Sumurûn and begs her to restore peace between him and his powerful adversary. Sumurûn gracefully promises. Now comes the scene to carry on the action. The scene between the Hunchback and the son has ended, and people begin to return. Among them is the Sheik in search of his wife. It happens that his eyes, like those of Eastern potentates, have the bad habit of going astray. The Dancer is about, and the sight of her is too much for him. Thereupon follows a scene of attempted barter. The Hunchback will not sell, but the old woman snake-charmer is quite willing to do the business for him; and she prepares to negotiate with the Slave Dealer, who is acting on behalf

of the Sheik. The Hunchback depicts in vivid
gestures his horror at this cold-blooded plot to rob
him of his pearl of great price. Scene II. carries
the action into the interior of the Hunchback's
theatre. The performance is proceeding ; the
Hunchback shows nothing of the passions raging
within him. The Sheik's son is still making
approaches to the Dancer, while the Sheik himself
is present hoping to secure the Dancer. By this
time the Hunchback is in a more conciliatory
mood. He sees a way to revenge himself on the
son, by disposing of the Dancer to his father. So
the deal is concluded. A scene in which the
power of colour to communicate magnetic action
is demonstrated, follows. The Dancer arranges
her gorgeous wardrobe and packs her trunk, so
to speak. In doing so she turns her back on the
Hunchback, who, driven to despair, attempts to
commit suicide by swallowing a piece of poisonous
food called Bhang. The Bhang, however, oblig-
ingly sticks in his throat in order to help the
action. For, as subsequent events prove, it is
necessary that the Hunchback shall make his way
to the Sheik's palace, and this by a devious route.
A pathway is opened by the old snake-charmer and
the son. The former returns with the gold which
she has obtained for the Dancer, and, finding that
the Hunchback is to all appearances dead, flings
him on a couch, covers him with draperies, and
departs. The son returns and discovers the hidden
body, which at first he takes to be the Dancer
asleep, but on learning the truth he bundles the
body unceremoniously into a sack belonging to the

merchant. The Hunchback is thus assured a safe journey to the merchant's instead of to heaven. The curtain falls on the rapid exit of the son as the merchant's slaves enter and bear the sack away. Scene III. reveals the Hunchback passing to his ultimate destination and receiving many unkind buffets on the way. A sack is not a comfortable form of transit, and it does not inspire reverence in those who handle it. In this scene before the Sheik's Palace, the sack and its contents play but a subordinate part, and perhaps for this reason its occupier deserves the punishment he receives. He is caught up in the tangled threads of the scene, and flung hither and thither, bobbing up and down like wreckage making its way across the Atlantic. The scene then is not the Hunchback's but Nur-al-din's, who is brought from the market-place in order to carry on the love interest and to reveal the cunning of Sumurûn and the fair slaves in evading the orders of the old Sheik. We learn that in this comedy intrigue against the Sheik, the women are for Nur-al-din. The Sheik's suspicions are aroused, and the son's pursuit of the Dancer is quickened. So the action is carried to Nur-al-din's shop in Scene IV. The Hunchback arrives in his sack considerably more damaged than when he first started. The secret of the sack is discovered by the merchant's servants, who, paralysed by fear, throw it into a box and fly.

Then follows a scene between Nur-al-din and Sumurûn, who has come with her ladies, presumably to buy, but really to make love. By this time the action is moving rapidly in the direction of the Palace, where both the Hunchback and Nur-al-din are due. How to get them there, that is the question ? The Hunchback is in the box where the servants have transferred him. The old snake-charmer comes and localises him for future purposes, and when Sumurûn returns to the shop after a brief absence, what is more natural than that she should conceive the idea of smuggling her lover into the Palace in a box, unconsciously using the very box where the ill-used Hunchback has been deposited amid perfumed draperies. The Hunchback makes no protest. Why should he ? What does it matter to him now that a human being is added to the weight of his sorrows ? Is he not now fully adjusted to stand any pressure ? Then as a sort of summary comes the famous silhouette scene, where the characters of this fantasy pass before us in review, as it were, on their way, and marking a further stage towards the Sheik's Palace. There they all pass, these comedy and tragedy puppets, these human marionettes dancing on the strings of love, hate, jealousy, and revenge. At the tail of the procession is the basket containing the lover and his liberator. The Hunchback is the symbol of destiny. The action next passes before the Palace. The atmosphere of suspense is cleverly maintained. How will the two smuggled men get into the Palace. Nothing easier. The Sheik's servants come out to search Nur-al-din's baskets, and very ingeniously Sumurûn's maid contrives to transfer the merchant to a basket which has been inspected, leaving the Hunchback to be discovered

by the peripatetic old woman. What happens next
is obvious. She discovers the piece of Bhang blocking the entrance to the alimentary canal, and forthwith proceeds to extract it. With this obstacle out
of the way the Hunchback is once more a man of
action. He becomes witness of the son's renewed
effort to possess the Dancer ; he sees that the son is
playing a dangerous game in which the loss of a
trick would prove fatal. So when the old Sheik
draws the daring Dancer into the Palace, having
discovered her intrigue with his son, and the son
follows at the Dancer's beckoning, he too enters,
creeping in unobserved. At last we are in the
harem with the *dénouement* within sight. It is an
Eastern scene of voluptuousness, where the wife and
her ladies hold carnival while the master is absent.

Nur-al-din is released from the basket by the
women, who proceed to make the most of his
company. The spirit of dance is set free, and
rapidly succeeding emotions are expressed in
rhythmical gesture and motion. The Sheik enters
unexpectedly. But they dance away his suspicions.
Sumurûn even communicates her love for him
through her dance, or so it seems to the Sheik.
But he is mistaken, for when he approaches
Sumurûn she repels him, and in his anger he calls
for his new slave, with whom he departs in sight
of Sumurûn and her women. Sumurûn turns to
console herself with Nur-al-din. As the curtain
falls the figures of the son and the Hunchback are
seen following the direction the Sheik has taken.
Scene VIII. carries the action to the Sheik's bedroom, where it begins to reach a climax. The Sheik

and the Dancer are asleep. The Hunchback enters, showing conclusively by his actions that he is there for a fixed purpose. He conceals himself within the drapery at the back of the bed. Then comes the son of the Sheik. He signals to the Dancer. She responds and they embrace. They are pledged to each other, they will fly together, but first there is one thing to be done. The Sheik must be effaced. The son hesitates. She urges him. Time is flying. The Sheik may awake. He yields. He steps forward. A form suddenly appears. To the Dancer it is the ghost of the Hunchback. She shrieks. The Sheik awakens. He drives his dagger into the body of his treacherous son, and flings aside the creature who would betray him. But the end is not yet. The Hunchback has not yet fulfilled his dramatic purpose. The lovers have to be united. But the obstacle still remains. As the scene closes the dying son leads his father to the harem where the action in Scene IX. passes. Here, during the tragedy in the bedroom, Sumurûn and her women and lover, wearied of their love-making and dancing, have fallen asleep. Danger suddenly touches them. They awake and hurriedly conceal Nur-al-din. The Sheik searches for him, while the women, seeking to abstract his attention, dance madly round him. Suddenly he catches sight of the white face of the Hunchback in the gallery above. He swiftly drags him down. The women make one more appeal. Sumurûn stoically invites him to kill her. Thereupon Nur-al-din steps from his hiding-place, in order to die for Sumurûn. There

is a fierce fight between him and the Sheik.
But the strength of the old man prevails.   Nur-al-
din is about to be killed when the battered figure
of the Hunchback moves rapidly forward and
plunges a knife into the back of the Sheik.   So
destiny in the person of the Hunchback plays its
part and the lovers are united.

Scenery, Decoration, Music, and Acting

The scenery was noticeable for its almost austere
simplicity.   The background was indeed little more
than a whitewashed wall against which the vivid
colours moved.   This gave the representation the
appearance of a number of set scenes, rather than
scenes unified and continuous.   They were scenes
carefully composed in the way they would look
best, in which the light will fall on the draperies
and create a fantasy of colours, will bring out the
lines in bold relief and strengthen the general
design, and fall in a less important way on the
actors, in which everything has a place in the
general design, and nothing shall be accidental.
There was no attempt to build up architectural
uniformity and coherence.   In fact, there was very
little of the Arab characteristics in the background.
The lines of the smuggling scene should have been
alive with inquietude and eccentricity.   The lines of
the very impressive silhouette scene, with one simple
mass against another, black against blue, did not
harmonise with the quaint rhythm of the figures
moving against the white base.   There is no quietness in the Arab character, and there should be no
quietness in its widest expression.   There was an

indication of fiery impulsiveness in the bedroom
scene. And that big and attractive harem scene
should have been ringing with the symbols of
imaginative excitability, arches buckling and bend-
ing in all directions, lines curved, filiated, and twisted
into innumerable designs, the whole forming one
big rhythmic design. Still, though the background
was lacking in the essential movement, the colours
were full of it. There were slaves dressed in riotous
patterns, there were gorgeous draperies that strewed
the floor and decorated the walls, and appropriately
took up their harmonious cues. When a red
drapery entered you knew there was a blue to
keep it company. In the scene before the Palace
there were the whitewashed walls, the deep black
exits, the row of red men before the main entrance,
and above them at the casement window the bevy
of fair women in scintillating colours—reds, yellows,
greens, blues, and so forth. So they went dancing
joyfully across the play.

The music, by Victor Hollaender, was composed
to tell the story. It was rather an accompaniment
than supplementary, rather the conscious element
of the play than the subconscious. For instance,
at one part Sumurûn taps the box in which the
merchant is concealed. The music taps also, thus
giving the impression of two persons doing the
same thing at one time.

Pantomimic acting is not new to London. Jane
May revealed some of its great possibilities in
L'Enfant Prodigue. With this standard in mind I
can still say that the pantomimic acting of *Sumurûn*
was exceedingly good, seeing that modern players

are only accustomed to elocutionary acting.   In
fact, the conventional stage mode of expression is
speech, and for one player who can express by a
gesture, a pose, a movement, a dance step or two,
a thought or emotion, there are nine hundred and
ninety-nine who can only express them by so many
words.   The best test of pantomimic acting is the
cinematograph.   In England acting will not stand
the test of this medium.   The public crowd to the
cinematograph theatre to see acting, where the best
examples of Italian, French, and American acting
are alone to be found. Take our leading players.
Sir Herbert Tree is a failure on the cinematograph.
So is Mr Gerald du Maurier. So would be the
"stars" of the discussion drama.   In Germany the
acting is good, and it is significant that there are,
comparatively speaking, but few cinematograph
theatres.   The public frequent the playhouse
instead.   Some details of the staging of *Sumurûn*,
which are new to London, are worth mention.
One was the Eastern idea of the players crossing
the floor of the auditorium by means of a "flower
path," as though coming from a distance, while
another was the arrangement of entrances and exits
to suggest the coming of persons from nowhere
in particular.

"OEDIPUS REX"

The production of this tragedy by Sophocles
marked another step in Reinhardt's development
towards the vast spectacle. It was also an experiment in elocutionary acting of the Greek order.
Beyond this, it had the element of daring with

which Reinhardt is associated in Germany, and which some persons maintain will be his downfall. Therefore, when he announced his intention of producing *Oedipus* in a circus, all sorts and conditions of people arose and shrieked, "This is, indeed, the limit!" But the manufacturers of pessimism were disappointed. In point of fact, there never was any cause for serious apprehension. In the matter of the conquest of all sorts and conditions of "stages," Reinhardt had already shown his skill, and having succeeded so often there was every likelihood of his doing so again. So from a predicted sensational extravagance ending in disaster, he passed to a success on his own lines. Why he played *Oedipus Rex* in a circus is best stated in his own words: "I played it in a circus because that form of building is best suited to my requirements. The actors do really move among the audience, there playing out their little drama in the midst of their fellow-men, just as the great drama is played every day of our life on earth." Later, with this cosmic idea in his mind, he regarded the Albert Hall as the most suitable place in London for the production of *Oedipus*. "It is circus-shaped, dignified, and large enough to accommodate such an audience of five thousand as was present at my Berlin *Oedipus* production." Apparently this change of scene meant that Max Reinhardt was experimenting with the Greek idea of intimacy. But, strictly speaking, this would not be correct, because he was not experimenting under Greek conditions. *Oedipus* was, in fact, a renewed try for Reinhardt's con-

ception of intimacy. At Frankfürt the tragedy
took possession of the Albert Schumann Circus,
wherein was seated the five thousand spectators,
rising tier on tier to the roof. Being somewhat
of an intimate character itself, the circus did what
it could for its own credit to secure and preserve
the desired element. It offered the whole (not a
part) of its arena to the principals, chorus, and
crowd, who entered some through the door of the
Greek façade erected at one end, and others by
the steps and entrances leading to the arena. The
ring thus provided allowed the action to take
place at the feet of the audience as well as among
them. In fact, it took place so directly before the
eyes of the audience and got so close to them,
especially that part of the action carried on by the
plague-stricken mob, that it may be reasonably
believed that the desired sensation was transmitted
complete, and every man and woman left the circus
with the sense of the mystery of patriotics, of the
struggle of man with Fate, as revealed in the Laocoön,
deeply upon them. After *Oedipus* had stirred the
Germans, it went, in response to much clamour-
ing, to other countries, and eventually came to
London, and this mainly through the praiseworthy
enterprise of Mr Martin Harvey.

The Story

In London *Oedipus* made its way to Covent
Garden Theatre — of all places in the mighty
metropolis. Probably this was the only available
theatre. If it had been possible to produce it at
the Albert Hall, whose form, size, and acoustical

properties are better suited to its proportions and
dimensions, I believe far better effects would have
been obtained, and some of the critics would have
ceased from complaining that " Reinhardtism has
no message for England, artistic or otherwise " ;
and that " Reinhardtism has always allied itself
to religion or the horrible." Having, however,
arrived at Covent Garden Theatre, it was obliged
to live up to the limitations of the place.
Here it had to tell its full story, to move and to
bring the spectator into its action within the hour
and a half allotted to its existence. That it did
so in a highly impressive way argues much for
the skill of the producer and of those who were
associated with him in the work of representation
and interpretation. The story of *Oedipus* runs
that during the reign of Laïus and Jocasta, Thebes
was terrorised by a mysterious and murderous
Sphinx known as the " She-Wolf of the Woven
Song." Apparently no one was able to stop the
deadly work or to answer the riddle of the Sphinx.
Laïus, thinking to gain the assistance of the Oracle
at Delphi, sets out to consult it, but is murdered
on the way. Shortly after there arrived at Thebes
a certain young prince, Oedipus by name. Oedipus
believes that he is the son of Polybus, King of
Corinth, and has left that city in order to escape
a terrible position in which the Oracle has placed
him. Arriving at Thebes, he reads the riddle of
the murderous Sphinx, who thereupon destroys
itself, and forthwith Oedipus is offered the throne
of Laïus, and Jocasta for consort. For ten years
he rules wisely and peacefully. At the end of

this period a pestilence breaks out and devastates Thebes. The action of the play now begins, and we are introduced to the silent spectacle of the eager throng of pestilent-smitten supplicants at the palace gates. To them the King appears with royal condescension and public zeal. The priest expresses their heartfelt loyalty, describes the distress of Thebes, and, praising the past services of Oedipus, implores him to exercise his power and wisdom on behalf of the relief of his people. In his reply the King discloses his solicitude for his subjects and a means of awakening their hope. He mentions that he has sent " Creon, my own wife's brother, forth alone to Apollo's house in Delphi, there to ask what word, what deed of mine, what bitter task, may save the city." Just at this moment Creon is seen approaching. He is crowned with Apollo's wreath ; his look is triumphant. What has Phoebus said ? Creon tells them that he has returned with the news that the murderer of King Laïus is harboured in the land of Thebes. He must be discovered and banished. The country must be purged of his crime. Then follows the dramatic scene between Oedipus and the blind seer Tiresias, whom Oedipus, in his anxiety to do the Oracle's bidding, forces to tell the truth. Tiresias declares that Oedipus is the man. Oedipus, however, sees nothing in Tiresias's words but a conspiracy between him and Creon to seize his throne. As an immediate consequence he quarrels with the Leader of the Chorus, who seeks to reason with him, and with Creon, whose replies to his questions only inflame him still more. By this means the interest of the audience is roused for the entrance of the Queen. With Jocasta's entrance begins the unravelling of the mystery of Oedipus's past. Accordingly we learn that before the opening of the play the Oracle had decreed that Laïus should be murdered by his son, and that the son should marry his own mother. In order to defeat this decree Jocasta, it seems, ordered it to be given out that her child was killed. This revelation partly removes Oedipus's fears, who confesses in turn that he fled from Corinth to escape a fate similar to the one to which Jocasta's son was doomed. At this point a messenger arrives with the news of the death of Polybus, the supposed father of Oedipus, whom the latter believed he was decreed to kill, and whose death he now believes sets him free from the decree of Fate. But the messenger has not finished ; he bears in addition the news that Oedipus is not the son of Polybus. As he proceeds, the awful truth bursts upon Jocasta, who with words full of tragic meaning turns and enters the palace. It now only remains for an old shepherd to confirm the messenger's story. He tells how he received Jocasta's child and handed it in turn to a stranger from Corinth, whence Oedipus had fled. The chain is complete. Oedipus recognises that Fate has destroyed him. He enters the palace, and, finding that Jocasta has effaced herself, he deprives himself of sight. Bleeding and blinded, he appears before his people, and, sightless and alone, passes forth to serve his self-inflicted term of punishment.

Such, then, is the story told in modern language, and such is the significance it bears to the modern mind. Whether the modern spectator understands its early meaning is open to doubt. The ordinary spectator to-day can scarcely be expected to understand the divine form of the art of the Greeks, the war of the deities, of giants and heroes. To him the vital mythology found in Greek tragedy is a closed book. Ask this modern spectator to enter the marvellous stream of mythic fiction flowing from early Greece and translate these stories upon which the tragedies are based in terms of myths, and he could not do it. He could not, for example, translate the myth of the shipwrecked mariners put to death as related in *Iphigenia*. Neither could he explain the eternal doctrine and myth of *Oedipus*. Given the knowledge to do so, much that is brutal and repellent to his modern mind would disappear. As a clue to my meaning, let me quote from Professor Gilbert Murray's preface to the published edition of *Oedipus*.

" Mythologists tell us that Oedipus was originally a dæmon haunting Mount Kithairon, and Jocasta a form of that Earth-Mother who, as Æschylus puts it, ' bringeth all things to being, and when she hath reared them, receiveth again their seed into her body ' (*Choephori*, 127 : cf. Crusius, *Beiträge z. Gr. Myth*, 21). That stage of the story lies very far behind the consciousness of Sophocles. But there does cling about both his hero and his heroine a great deal of very primitive atmosphere. There are traces in Oedipus of the pre-Hellenic Medicine King, the *Basileus* who is also a *Theos*, and can make rain or blue sky, pestilence or fertility. This explains many things in the Priest's first speech, in the attitude of the chorus, and in Oedipus's own language after the discovery. It partly explains the hostility of Apollo, who is not a mere motiveless Destroyer, but a true Olympian crushing his Earth-born rival. And in the same way the peculiar royalty of Jocasta, which makes Oedipus at times seem not the King but the Consort of the Queen, brings her near to that class of consecrated queens described in Dr Frazer's *Lectures on the Kingship*, who are ' honoured as no woman now living on the earth.'

" The story itself, and the whole spirit in which Sophocles has treated it, belong not to the fifth century, but to that terrible and romantic past from which the fifth-century poets usually drew their material. The atmosphere of brooding dread, the pollution, the curses ; the ' insane and beastlike cruelty,' as an ancient Greek commentator calls it, of piercing the exposed child's feet in order to ensure its death, and yet avoid having actually murdered it (*Schol. Eur. Pheon.*, 26) ; the whole treatment of the parricide and incest, not as moral offences capable of being rationally judged or even excused as unintentional, but as monstrous and inhuman pollutions, the last limit of imaginable horror : all these things take us back to dark regions of pre-classical and even pre-Homeric belief. We have no right to suppose that Sophocles thought of the involuntary parricide and metrogamy as the people in his play do. Indeed, considering the general tone of his con-

temporaries and friends, we may safely assume
that he did not. But at any rate he has allowed
no breath of later enlightenment to disturb the
primæval gloom of his atmosphere."

The origin and nature of the *Oedipus* myth is
here clearly stated, and the fact borne home to us
that as a myth its horrors are also myths. The
extreme difficulty lies in separating the ideal from
the real by preserving the proper Greek associations
of each Greek tragedy represented. The ancient
Greek spectator of a Sophoclean tragedy was able
to preserve these associations. He was invited to
witness the supreme crisis of an individual destiny
and was possessed at the outset with the traditions
of his race. But it must be said that these associations are not preserved by moderns without many
difficulties.

The Scene

For one thing, there is the difficulty of creating
an appropriate Greek atmosphere in a roofed-in
theatre. Better results are, of course, to be attained
in an open-air theatre, say Bradfield College. But
even there the things that favoured the production
of Greek tragedy are lacking. Though the theatre
is open to the sky, though it commands a wide
perspective, and air full of vitality, it has not
the Greek dimensions that would enable it to seat
50,000 spectators. At Covent Garden Theatre,
therefore, a compromise had to be effected. It
was skilfully done, and no doubt it served Max
Reinhardt's purpose. As at Berlin and Frankfürt,
the whole of the interior of the theatre was made

to serve the "scene," the entire proscenium was fitted with a black screen representing the front of the palace of Oedipus. The centre of this screen was occupied by high, impressive brass doors, on either side of which were three massive black columns supporting a grim portico. The orchestra well was covered by a black platform, with a piece projecting from the centre upon which the altar was placed. On either side of this "apron" flights of steps led to the arena, or ball-floor of the theatre. This floor formed a lower stage, and was built up in order to enable the spectator to realise that he was participating in the scene before him. In pursuit of the intimacy idea, a space was cleared in front of the stage by removing rows of stalls, for the chorus and crowd to act in and mix with the spectators. The front row of the stalls was, in fact, in touch with the outer fringe of the crowd, while all the players made their entrances and exits through the audience at various points of the arena. The scene was lit from all points of the theatre according to the new methods, whereby coloured limes are thrown on neutral surfaces, and the desired effects obtained by mixing the coloured rays as they fall on each object. The principal aim of the lighting was, however, to keep a blinding white light beating upon the palace, and to break it up with vivid bits of colour. The general conception of colour was black and white, great masses of white, sometimes tinted with yellow, moving against the dense blue background which occasionally deepened to violet. Perhaps the most artistic effect was that attained by the crowd and Oedipus. Oedipus stood on the rostrum calm and self-possessed. Beneath him surged the infuriated mob, with outstretched arms, swelling up to him like a sea of angry emotions, and returning thence to the Leader of the Chorus in response to his call. There on one side Oedipus stood like an intellectual pinnacle islanded in the billowing ocean of human beings ; and there on the other side the Leader stood like the Spirit of the Infinite swayed to and fro by elemental passions.

The Acting

The acting was contemporary. There was no attempt to go back to tradition, but everything was brought up to date. The cothurnus, the mask, and other aids to Greek interpretations were absent. Still, the chief object of the Greek poet, that of obtaining the utmost beauty from his only instrument, language, was not overlooked. Rhythm, which is one of the chief components of Greek verse, was there. In more than one instance the words were bound rhythmically together, and fell pleasantly on the sensitive ear. Greek immobility was also successfully attained, especially in the acting of Mr Martin Harvey and Miss Lillah M'Carthy. The handling of the crowd revealed Max Reinhardt's methods at their best. It was an up-to-date crowd composed of individual speakers, a human crowd formed of living elements. and far more natural than the crowd composed of undergraduates in the Frankfürt production. To me it was even a more wonderful crowd than the individual one in *Lysistrata*, which is considered by many persons as the high-water mark of Reinhardt's stagecraft. The latter crowd appears at the end of the play and manifests the many and varied emotions of the inhabitants of the delivered city, which has been handed back to Eros. Colours race all over the scene, lines (formed of dancers) advance and recede, entwine, break, and joyously melt away. There are shouts of laughter, singing, and every expression of pent-up emotion. In the background, at a distance, are seen the lights of the condemned town ; from afar come cries and murmurs, mixed with laughter and shouting, which gradually increase until they merge with the others in one mighty climax of joy, and the curtain falls on one of the finest pantomimic climaxes provided by Reinhardt. Reinhardt's main object in arranging his crowd is to bring the latter into active unity with the actor ; his handling of the chorus is no less unified and harmonious. The production of *Oedipus*—the English version of which was prepared by Professor Gilbert Murray and Mr W. L. Courtney—afforded an excellent example of this.

It may be asked, if Reinhardt is not giving us Greek drama, what is he giving us ? The reply is Reinhardtism—an essence of drama of his own distilling. Max Reinhardt may or may not know that all the great dramatists have no common standard for dramatic action and what is suited to the stage, that Sophocles, Shakespeare, Racine, Molière, Goethe, Ibsen, have only names in com-

mon, that each had a value for his own times, and
may have one for us, and, if so, it must be made
apparent to everybody.   In any case, he sees each
author with the Reinhardt eye, and uses each as
an expression of the Reinhardt value, namely, a
dramatic one.   Thus to Shakespeare, Goethe,
Sophocles, Kleist, and others, he gives his own
reading, and that of his co-operators, thereby
rousing the resentment of certain critics who complain that Reinhardt is not Sophocles.   This was
the objection raised to the production of *Oedipus*.
Reinhardt was told his work was " not Greek,"
and charged with having degraded a classical play.
The charge was met by Professor Gilbert Murray,
who, writing to the *Times*, said :

" By ' Greek ' we normally mean classical or
fifth-century Greek.   Now the *Oedipus* story itself is not Greek in that sense.   It is pre-Greek ;
it belongs to the dark regions of pre-Hellenic
barbarism.   It struck one of the ancient Greek
commentators, for instance, by its ' senseless and
bestial cruelty.'   Oedipus is pre-Hellenic ; Sophocles is Greek.   In the production ought we to
represent the age of Sophocles or that of Oedipus ?
The point is arguable, and I have my own view
about a middle course ; but he who insists on
keeping to the age and style of Sophocles must
also insist on dressing Macbeth in Elizabethan
ruffles.

" Professor Reinhardt was frankly pre-Hellenic,
partly Cretan and Mycenæan, partly Oriental,
partly—to my great admiration—merely savage.
The half-naked torchbearers with loin-cloths and

long black hair made my heart leap with joy. There was real early Greece about them, not the Greece of the schoolroom or the conventional art studio.

"The general colouring, then, was pre-Hellenic. But Professor Reinhardt makes no profession of treating the play with archæological reverence. He simply takes the text and says : 'There is drama in this, and I will bring out that drama by every means that modern stagecraft puts in my power.' This is obviously a legitimate line of action. It must stand or fall by its general result. At certain times, for instance, he beats a gong. I think the result very effective ; some people hate it. In any case it is the result that must be judged. There is nothing inherently sinful, nor yet admirable, in beating a gong. And, in general, what is the result ? I do not think there can be the smallest doubt that it is—to use the bluntest and simplest word—successful. Vast audiences come to hear the *Oedipus*—audiences at any rate far larger than Mr Granville Barker and I have ever gathered, except perhaps once; they sit enthralled for two hours of sheer tragedy, and I do not think many of them will forget the experience. That is one test of a good production. Another is the effect it has on the actors. And it seems to me that practically every performer in the *Oedipus* is at the very top of his powers. Certainly Mr Harvey's superb performance has been a revelation to many even of his admirers. How I should like to see him as Hippolytus ! "

"THE MIRACLE"

The Miracle was Max Reinhardt's Gothic contribution to the pantomimic spectacular drama. It was distinguished by structural bigness, and the quality of strength in action. The whole conception and realisation was full of tremendous energy. It was the last word in a synthesis of music, song, dance, colour, and line on a gigantic scale. Its official aim is expressed in the following extract from printed matter supplied to me by Mr C. B. Cochran : " *The Miracle* is meant to be something more than a spectacle. It aims at reaching the highest pinnacle in the great range of dramatic endeavour. It is not to be a pageant, yet it is of pageantry. It is not a play or a drama in any ordinary sense, yet it will be the greatest dramatic play of all. It is a simple story set forth simply, yet with all that vigour, delicacy, power, and immensity which the mind of Reinhardt alone can give to it. It is meant to make the mark of an epoch. *The Miracle* will be produced from a scenario prepared by Dr Karl Vollmoeller, a scenario whose power of appeal must be vastly enhanced by the wonderful music which has been wedded to it by Professor Engelbert Humperdinck, the composer of *Hänsel and Gretel*. For the interpretation of *The Miracle* two thousand players will be employed, and under the direction of an eminent conductor, an orchestra of two hundred, and an invisible choir of five hundred, will be utilised in the rendering of Humperdinck's music."

From this we gather that *The Miracle* was the

greatest undertaking Reinhardt had attempted. It went beyond *Oedipus* and transformed *Sumurûn*, so to speak, to the proportions of a vast amphitheatrical wordless play. The play itself was variously described by the terms drama, mystery, miracle, and so forth. It was even compared with the Oberammergau Passion Play. But I am convinced that it does not fall under these heads. To me it had a character of its own. It was Gothic pantomime brought up to date. Here we had a scenario based on an old Rhine legend fitted in with modern music, song, dance, pantomime conception of decoration, and electrical and mechanical effects.

The Story

The story has made its appearance under various disguises. For instance, it is the theme of Maeterlinck's miracle play *Sister Beatrice*. Sister Beatrice is a young nun who is wooed and after a struggle won by a prince. As soon as she leaves the convent the figure of the Virgin is re-incarnated and takes the erring nun's place. The action of the Virgin is regarded by the other nuns as a miracle, and it is believed she has come to life in order to confer some high spiritual distinction on Sister Beatrice. A period of years elapse, and Beatrice returns to the convent, having tasted the bitters of a worldly experience. Abandoned by the Prince, she passes through vicissitude after vicissitude, until, with health, beauty, and purity gone, she seeks her old sanctuary. Upon her return, the Virgin, having completed her task, assumes her former position. Beatrice confesses her sins to the nuns, who, however, still believe her holy and worship her as she dies. In this scenario is the element of mystery which great drama demands, as well as that of silence which is one of the requirements of great dramatic pantomime. It is, in a word, a cosmic theme, the importance of which words cannot adequately convey. We enter the action and pass in silence through a process of disillusionment or enlightenment. We are under cloistral restraint. We are suddenly offered a vision of the world and its temptations. We yield to temptation and go forth to indulge the physical side of us at the expense of the spiritual. We pass from disillusionment to disillusionment till hell is reached. And finally, we return to the spiritual fold to exchange the impurity of our recent experience for a purity to which it should inevitably lead. In *The Miracle* the theme is treated on a broad temporal basis. As the curtain rises we are present at a festival. We join the great procession winding slowly across the mountain, and making its way gradually towards the stately Cathedral. Enshrined herein is the statue of "Our Lady," before whom all kneel in adoration, whilst a miracle is performed. From among the halt, and sick, and blind there comes a lame man, who is carried forth within the magic, luminous glow of the radiant statue. There is a moment of great silence while we are initiated into the vital mystery of his cure. This done, we move with the great crowd, solemnly and splendidly as it sweeps with a song of thanksgiving over the mountain, and fringes the violet ribbon of the Rhine. In the Cathedral there is now no one save the Nun. She is alone with her new experience and the statue. She has seen the doors of the Church open upon the world and she dreams of its pleasures. Now comes the Spielmann symbolising the Devil, and with the sound of his piping is heard the joy of children's voices. The Nun feels the stimulus of the outer world and responds by joining in the dancing. Thereafter we become part of an action similar to that already described in the story of "Sister Beatrice." A Knight appears; the Nun struggles to repel him. For a moment she succeeds. She closes the great doors of the world upon the Knight and seeks the Madonna's aid. But there is no response. A knocking at the Cathedral doors is heard. The door opens and the Knight appears. He advances; the Nun yields, and together they go forth accompanied by the Spielmann piping the lay of passionate love. The Madonna comes to life and takes the place of the fugitive Nun. The Abbess and Nuns enter, and, discovering the loss of the Madonna, are about to scourge the kneeling figure, whom they believe to have been the cause of the disappearance of the Madonna, when they discover her divine nature. Then follows the intermezzo, and we pass through the process of worldly enlightenment. The events follow each other rapidly and are everyday incidents clothed in mediæval costume. There are the adventures of the Nun and Knight, the death of the Knight, the capture of the Nun by the Robber Count, the death of the latter and the transferring

of the Nun to the King's Son, the death of the
latter, leaving the Nun under the protection of the
King.   There is the burning of the royal palace,
the charge of witchcraft against the Nun, her
rescue by the crowd, and her re-appearance as a
camp-follower carrying a baby.   And there is the
Nun's return to the Cathedral seeking grace.   On
top of this disillusionment by means of seduction,
murder, suicide, the Inquisition, battle, maternity,
comes the final atonement and restoration to divine
favour.

In the second act we re-enter the Cathedral with
the Nun just after the Madonna has resumed her
position as the Miraculous Image.   Then follows
the discovery by the Nuns of the restored image
and of the prodigal Nun.   *The Miracle* ends differently from that of *Sister Beatrice*.   Beatrice dies,
while the Nun, after passing the night in the
darkened Cathedral, rises from before the Image
and passes through the great doors to toll the
Matins.   Her renewed spiritual life is symbolised
by the rising sun which greets her.

The Production and Representation

The ideas influencing the production of *The
Miracle* were similar to those affecting the production of *Oedipus* and perhaps *Everyman*.   There
can be no doubt that Reinhardt was seeking
for a means to break away altogether from the
picture stage, to develop the idea of producing a
drama that can be acted within the auditorium
instead of within the picture-frame, and to afford
a still further illustration of what a play gains in

intimacy when its characters become part of the audience. It may be thought by some persons that in thus converting the auditorium into a stage, Reinhardt was merely making a departure in one direction in order to make a return in another, that he was breaking away from the tyranny imposed upon the modern stage by the Italian theatre of the sixteenth century, in order to expand the innovation introduced to the English stage about the same period. If he sought the vastest ground area for his stage, it was merely in order to carry on the expansion of the Elizabethan " apron " stage, an expansion which he had long contemplated and undertaken. But there is no evidence forthcoming to show that Reinhardt had any such idea. On the contrary, there is much to show that he was strongly influenced by Greek tradition, upon which his theatre of the five thousand undoubtedly rests. It is more probable, indeed, that Reinhardt regards the Shakespearean " apron " as an atrophied form of the Greek arena. However, let that be as it may, Reinhardt was bent on finding the largest stage for his " drama," and though Berlin from a geographical and national standpoint would have been in his view more suitable than London as an experimental centre, London offered him the best building for his dramatic purpose. He came and saw Olympia, and at once his production became realisable. In the vast Exhibition Hall, having nearly four times the floor space of the Albert Hall, he felt it was possible to subordinate the setting to the panto-mimic drama. The scene he had in mind was that of the huge nave of a Gothic cathedral as being most suitable for preserving the religious mood created by the interpretation. Herein the spectator could be seated and led to think of the central theme, the Madonna and the Nun, or the Church and the World, with less risk of being led to think of Max Reinhardt than in other productions. The scene itself arose as he had conceived it. A small circle of efficient co-operators—Hermann Dernburg, Rudolph Dworsky, and Ernst Stern—directed the work, which was carried out on the broad general lines of Reinhardt's scenic policy, according to which everything of a solid and up-to-date nature is utilised. Doors, windows, walls, roof, columns, properties, all are real ; the lighting system is the completest that can be employed ; every advantage being taken of the latest advances made in electrical engineering. This actuality was one of the chief features of the cathedral scene of *The Miracle*. There is no need to enter here upon the technical details of construction, nor to mention the quantity, weight, dimensions, and cost of the materials used. It is sufficient to note that the Olympia was transformed into a cathedral interior on the solid basis of an actual building, that appeared to be constructed to stand till the cement dissolved. Apparently the Gothic builders enjoyed their task of converting a structure resembling the largest railway terminus into one containing a likeness to architectural style. They handled every expedient and stratagem involved in this kind of struggle with skill, and contrived, in an open way to conceal the original features as much as possible behind sham columns, arches, architraves, springs, vaults, mouldings, and other Gothic details, thus forming a fabric of one solid lump of concrete. They endeavoured, indeed, in composition, and in detail down to the designs of the stained-glass windows, to preserve the Gothic motive. If they did not altogether succeed, it was not their fault. The cement veil could not be drawn over every part of the standing structure. There were gaps. The quality of energy was missing, and the lines throughout were anything but light and sinewy. This was a pity, seeing that an elastic and vigorous framework was so necessary to serve the function for which the setting had been designed, namely, to contribute to the action of the play and convey the sense of motion. It should be mentioned, however, that the Gothic builders were largely hampered by the peculiar requirements of the Reinhardt staging of *The Miracle*. It appeared that the nave of the cathedral was meant to serve not only as an interior scene, but as an exterior. Thus, when the Church had finished with it, the World entered by a very simple contrivance. The vast Gothic doors at one end were opened, and a huge mound crested with trees was wheeled in. By means of this and another contrivance the characters were enabled to step from actuality to actuality. The second contrivance was a huge sinking stage placed in the centre of the arena. This platform was made to sink, so that each time it rose it could bring a complete change of environment. By this means the action was carried uninterruptedly from banqueting hall to bed-chamber, to inquisition chamber, and so forth. This sinking platform was indeed an example of Reinhardt's ingenuity, and appeared uncommonly like an up-to-date variation of the Shakespearean principle of alternate staging.

Along with the erection of the structure went the laying down of the electric light installation. Here again every department was in efficient hands, and every angle and inch of necessary space was utilised for the purpose of attaining desired effects. The lighting system plays a most important part in Reinhardt's productions. Indeed, it may be said that without light a greater part of the emotional language of his scenes would be lacking. The bigness of the system at Olympia may be gathered from the fact that over ten miles of lighting cable was laid down for a special electric installation for the spectacle. This, when compared with the simplicity of the stage lighting in Shakespeare's day, takes one's breath away. Just beneath and spanning the roof of the " nave " a bridge was constructed, having three lime bridges or islands of lights each containing forty searchlights or prisms. These lights were thrown down upon the scenes and players. Powerful arcs working from various points of the auditorium were focussed on the stage. Hundreds of lights were used to illuminate the Gothic windows, their rays pouring down from all points, north, east, south, and west. For lighting the horizon on Reinhardt's own principle electric battens were employed. And not only were the lofty roof and the galleries and loft of the cathedral " wired " to their fullest extent, but the "crypt" was also turned into a bewildering maze of elaborate, electric mechanism.

When I visited Olympia at the invitation of Baron von Gersdorff, Reinhardt's stage-director, I had a full opportunity of examining the nature and working of the mechanism. I was handed over to the chief mechanician, under whose guidance I explored the underground arrangements. We passed down a narrow, sloping passage, which, unlike the entrance way to the real cathedral crypt, had no smells, earthy or unearthly, to recall memories of priest and monk and of incensed procession marching in step with the sound of funeral dirge. Such smells were replaced by the commonplace one of beams and newly constructed brick walls forming rooms and recesses running beneath the vast arena. As we proceeded, the low roof and the projecting beams kept our heads ducking like the movable noddles of toy china-men. Big broad pipes laid along the brick walls, for carrying steam, tripped us up. Weird objects glared at us from the huge pit into which we descended. Out of its centre came a heavy elaborate mass of cogs and iron wheels, raising aloft the platform that took the centre of the vast arena. Turning, we saw streams of coloured light, yellow, blue, and white, flaming through the latticed surface of square black boxes or prisms posed on stork-like legs. Forty-seven electric fans drove up the yellow silken ribbons upon which the light from the forty arc lamps beat. The shrieks of the revellers filled up the intervals of the fiery effects as they made themselves felt in the conflagration overhead.

For some moments we stood in the midst of blinding lights, flashing flames, and crashing winds. Then the bell rang and there was the silence and darkness of death. The platform descended, and with it the resurrected dancers, moving round what was once the banqueting hall.

In the matter of rehearsals of the players, it is needless to say that the actor-director in Max Reinhardt dominated everything. He saw in the production its acting possibilities, knew precisely the value of each part, how it should be played, and who should play it. In order to understand his methods of selecting the cast and rehearsing it, it is necessary to bear the fact in mind that he has the actor's nature and approaches both play and players from this side. This fact largely accounts for his choice of the right people to interpret *The Miracle*. He certainly found an ideal " Madonna " in Maria Carmi (Frau Voll-moeller), an exceptionally clever " Nun " in the distinguished dancer, Mme Natacha Trouhanowa, and a consistent " Spielmann " in Max Pallenberg. The same correctness of choice marked his selection of the elements of the crowd and led him to form an assemblage of persons that fully expressed the drama of this particular crowd—its joys, sorrows, horrors, superstitions, and so forth. As an actor he is also able to feel the audience and to compose the scenes and arrange the situations so as to have the greatest effect upon it. That is, he knows how to get every effect across the footlights. But if Reinhardt is fully equipped to rehearse a large company himself, he also understands the value of intelligent co-operation, both as a time- and temper-saving device. Accordingly, though he conceives the work in bulk, he leaves it to be carried out in detail by efficient co-operators. Thus, if anyone had visited Olympia during the rehearsals of *The Miracle*, he would have found groups rehearsing in every corner of the building and everything proceeding according to an intelligently conceived and well-ordered plan. He would have found the dancers being rehearsed in one part of the building, the singers in another, the crowd in another, the music in another, and so on. And he would have seen this continued day after day, till finally everything was reduced and placed under the control of the single instrument of the stage-director—the switch-board. His inference would be that Max Reinhardt himself really did very little in the actual work of rehearsal, beyond seeing that effect after effect was tried till the appropriate ones were arrived at. He did not rush furiously round the arena in a huge motor-car, as predicted by one press agent ; he made no breathless charges upon stupid groups of " supers," whose only desire is to handle their weekly salary. On the contrary, he took things quite calmly, and even came to the theatre without a preconceived idea of what the many details composing the whole should be. He was content to deliver the details over to the charge of his co-directors, and to remain watching the clay as it passed through their hands. The advantages of this co-operative method of company rehearsing are many. The chief of them is the immense gain in time. As an instance I may quote the experience of Mr Louis Calvert, who once told me that it took him, single-handed, six weeks to rehearse the *Julius Cæsar* crowd at His Majesty's Theatre, and that as a contrast he produced the Convention scene in the last act of *Robespierre* in three rehearsals, owing to the fact that he had the co-operation of several persons who had worked with him in *Julius Cæsar*. He said, " to each of these I gave a squad of men " (a section of the crowd). Both Louis Calvert and Max Reinhardt know the value of concerted action.

The Decorations and Lighting Effects

Coming to the decorations and lighting effects, we find they were carried out under the direction of the art co-operator, who aimed always to express his own individuality while interpreting the spirit of *The Miracle*. Ernst Stern is the gifted art-director to whom Reinhardt entrusted the designing of the scene, costumes, properties, and the general arrangement of line and colour. It was from Herr Stern himself at the Deutsches Theater, Berlin, that I learnt the principles and methods which he applies to a play. From his words to me, it appears that he is accustomed to meet Max Reinhardt prior to the production of each play for the purpose of determining its general character or spirit. Thereafter he, the decorator, retires to his studio to develop his portion of the work. He begins by getting the basis of his structure, a line in character with the motive. If the motive is Gothic the line will have the Gothic energy and flexibility. By the use of this line he anchors everything in the scene ;

costumes and accessories become part of a design.
Next, he selects his colour, harmonising with the
line and expressing the general conception of the
motive. Thus, for example, if energy is a dominant note, he would use cadmium, as in *The Miracle*,
or if irritation is predominant, he uses red ; but if
tranquillity is sought for, then he uses blue-greens.
But the colours have to be used very intelligently
in order to obtain the desired sensations. Next,
he selects materials having the essential colours and
design. Then he selects his characters to reflect
his line and colour as being part of the whole. If
he is using a revolving stage he next works out
his ground plan, using a model of the stage for the
purpose. Then follow sketches—suggestions for
the parts of the whole. After this he constructs
a working model of scene and figures, and adds life
to his line and colour. Finally, he attends rehearsals and commences to get his chiaroscuro.
By this time the scene has assumed the form of
a chess-board, upon which he moves his figures
singly and in masses, till he has obtained the
variations that go to create the atmosphere of the
original motive. All this is a method of pattern-
making which has been adopted by theatre decorators on the Continent, and which was fully
applied by Herr Stern to *The Miracle*. Here the
form, line, and colour of the scene, costumes,
accessories, and the lights to be thrown upon them,
were determined by the twelfth-century Gothic
motive. The result was not altogether satisfactory.
But this was rather the fault of the size of the
structure than of the decorator. For one thing,

the huge proportions of the interior dwarfed the figures and destroyed the slow dignity of movement. The gigantic scarlet doors symbolising the world were magnificent, but artistically they had no relation to the rest of the play. The scenes were lacking in unity. They were all well done, but though pictures were obviously aimed at, in no single case would it have been possible to put a frame and found the essentials for making a picture. The play of colour was amazing, but owing to the fragmentary character of the scenes it could only be seen as a brilliant shower of confetti. In *The Miracle* it was noticeable that Herr Stern obtained his colour effects chiefly from lighting. He works by a system according to which rays of light are thrown upon neutral or coloured surfaces. The effects are got by a single ray of white or coloured light, and by two or more coloured rays mixing. In the latter case the colours are mixed by the electricians, who work the prisms according to a very old colour theory. First a blue is thrown upon the white or neutral screen ; then a note of yellow mixes with the blue and produces green, or it may be blue and red producing violet. There are endless developments in this colour mixing. Exceedingly fine effects were by this means obtained from the misty vault of many coloured lights at Olympia, the most beautiful being that attained by the mixing of colours with the gorgeous robe of the " Madonna." Herr Stern follows Max Reinhardt's example in preferring solid to canvas scenery, and uses plastic materials whenever it is possible.

The Music

The music by Humperdinck, though failing to
represent throughout the subconscious element of
the audience, told the story intelligently and greatly
added to the emotional colour of the play.   By its
aid alone one was able, generally speaking, to follow
the dramatic action.   Thus the sustained note of
the intonation brought in the great surging crowd
swinging over the mountain.   The Nun's dance
contained the note of temporal awakening, while
succeeding the dance came the shakes and twirls
on the flute indicating the torture of the Nun's
mind.   Then came the subsequent note of
indecision in the music, changing to the call of
duty in the decisive notes of the trombone and
oboe, and the succeeding love motive on the
stringed instruments.   The virile movement of
the triumph of the world yields to a sort of
incarnation as the Madonna takes the place of
the departed Nun.   Upon the disappearance of
the Nun the drums assume the note of consterna-
tion and alarm, and so the music-action progresses
to the point where it ends with a sort of variation
upon " Sun of my Soul."   In this way it moved
from act to act, occasionally missing its cue, as in
the conflagration scene, where it refused to catch
fire, and in the march past of the army, where
it forgot to give out the donkey motive.   The
donkeys, by the way, were very intelligent actors.
Generally speaking, the music succeeded in bits
rather than as a whole.   It appeared as though
the largeness of the cosmic theme was too big for

Humperdinck's genius. Like Herr Stern, he was overwhelmed by the proportions of his undertaking. In consequence, weird and fascinating bits of composition bulged from the body of the interpretative music, and stuck like burrs. And one remembered afterwards, the quaint Spielmann motive given out on a very high clarionet, a sharp twirl reminding one of the secret motive in the opening of the second act of *Siegfried*. The diabolical motive of death given out on the trombone and harp was also persistent. The wonderful rhythm of the Hungarian dance, and the quaint rhythm of the grotesque old German dance in the banqueting scene, the bedroom love music, the opening of the grim inquisition scene announced by a fanfare, and the martial roll of drums, such outstanding features of music that sought to run and dance with the drama, made a deep impression. Another noticeable thing was that the composer had introduced a number of old English carols and other foreign material. In the concluding scene, for instance, the notes of supplication, with touches of love, followed by anguish as the Nun's child dies, were succeeded by the Sicilian Mariner's hymn as the Virgin takes the dead child, and the music-scene is brought to a close with a well-known carol as the crowd enters and bears off the Madonna in triumph.

The following figures, taken from the *Pall Mall Magazine*, show the financial cost of the enterprise :—

"*The Cost of the Production*

" The cost of the production and of the eight weeks' run that is contemplated will amount to seventy thousand pounds. Some of the principal sums of expenditure may be enumerated :

Costumes	£12,500
Scenery and properties	8,000 .
Movable mountain	800
Excavation for the Trap	1,690
Iron framework for cathedral doors . . .	1,250
Electric installation apparatus	3,000
Electric wiring and fixing	1,500
Use of the organ	1,000
Artists' salaries per week, including :	
Principals	800
Chorus of 500	1,200 .
1000 minor players	1,725 .
Orchestra of 200	950
Boys and girls	115
Girl dancers	175
Approximately (for 8 weeks' run), £40,000."	

The following notes on the size of Olympia are worth adding :—

Dimensions of the Great Hall	440 ft. × 250 ft.
Height to crown of roof	about 100 ft.
The span of the roof	170 ft.
The main ribs of the roof	34 ft. apart.

The roof is an example of large span roof.

" A VENETIAN NIGHT "

A Venetian Night was by Karl Vollmoeller, with music by Dr Friedrich Bermann. It was a species of drama-comedy-pantomime having some of the characteristics of *The Miracle*. Like the latter

Stage Setting for Queen's Room (Hamlet)

[Julius V. Klein

spectacular wordless play, it was designed to
lend itself to the newest and widest methods of
Reinhardt production, being provided with a
scenario plot to be filled in by the producer with
all the resources at his command. Such design, however, was defeated here in England by one or two
circumstances. For one thing, the play was presented on a stage not fully adapted to its requirements; for another, it fared badly in a conflict
with the Lord Chamberlain, which necessitated
alterations affecting its harmony of composition.
The Lord Chamberlain found it at the last
moment too dangerous to public morals to be
permitted to be played as it stood, and removed
his ban only after it had been altered. The in-
cident gave rise to the usual newspaper controversy,
during which Mr Granville Barker and Mr H.
Hamilton Fyfe exchanged compliments in the
Daily Mail. But no boom resulted. The play
was unsuccessful from the start; and all attempts
to make it appeal by hacking it about failed. At
the end of three weeks it came off.

The Story

The story consisted of two sets of events,—the
waking and the dream ones. The former occurred
in the first, second, eleventh, twelfth, and thirteenth
scenes; and the latter took place in the third,
fourth, fifth, sixth, seventh, eighth, ninth, and
tenth scenes. The argument is that The Young
Stranger wandering through Italy in 1860 in
search of adventure arrives, in his gondola, at an
hotel in Venice. His arrival coincides with that

of a wedding party. The Bride, who has been forced into a marriage by her father, has arranged to meet the man she loves for the last time. She leaves the party to give her lover a sign agreed upon. The Young Stranger sees the sign, and believing that it is intended for him follows The Bride into the hotel. At the wedding feast and dance that follow The Bride again signs to her lover and points to her room. The sign is seen and misinterpreted as before. The action next takes us to the bedroom of The Stranger, who falls asleep, and the succeeding incidents are the outcome of his dream. The scene changes to the bedroom of The Bride, in which the events take place that called for the intervention of the official censor. While the bridegroom is intoxicated downstairs the lover comes to the room and a passionate scene ensues which is interrupted by the appearance of the bridegroom. The latter, however, is persuaded by The Bride to leave, and the scene is resumed and ends by the lover being killed by a thief who enters unexpectedly. The Young Stranger, who meanwhile has dreamt that he has been specially chosen to play the part of hero and lover to The Bride, now enters prepared to do as The Bride bids, and even undertakes to dispose of the dead body. The remaining scenes are taken up with The Young Stranger's amusing attempts to get rid of the corpse and of the equally amusing objection of the corpse to be got rid of. This removal of the dead gives rise to a long and somewhat farcical chase, during which The Young Stranger is pursued from " garret to cellar," so to speak, by various odds and ends of hotel humanity. Beggars, waiters, the landlord, soldiers, and public, all take up the chase. The morning comes, and The Young Stranger is disillusioned. He watches the wedding party depart accompanied by the lover who has been introduced to the bridegroom, and as he does so, he quietly drops—a rose.

The Staging (Decorations and Lighting)

This thin story provided the outline with which Max Reinhardt and his collaborators had to work. In the endeavour to give it proper proportions and effectiveness at the Palace Theatre, many things had to be done. One of them was the construction of a revolving stage, without which the play would have been utterly impracticable owing to the rapid action demanding an equally rapid change of scene. Indeed, it seemed as though the play itself had been designed to test the quick-change capacity of the revolving stage and sets. The Reinhardt method of using the revolving stage is described in one of the Appendices. A similar method was adopted in the production of *A Venetian Night*. The stage was set with all the scenes before the rise of the curtain. It was divided into four almost equal parts,—hotel exterior and interior, the rooms of The Bride and The Young Stranger. Thus the curtain rose on a section of the stage set with the canal scene—a typical Venetian scene of canal, gondolas, flight of bridges in middle distance, and hotel to the left. By one quarter turn of the stage the colour atmosphere and movement of the canal scene was exchanged for those of the hotel interior. Another turn and a bedroom appears, and so on. With regard to the colour arrangements not much can be said. Herr Stern did his best, but the bad lighting killed his efforts. It was evident that efforts had been made to put the stage lighting to its new use, but without success. For instance, the Reinhardt frontal and horizon lighting were missing, with the result that the back of the stage was mostly in darkness, and the scenes had the appearance of falling to pieces. All this destroyed the one great thing for which Reinhardt always aims, viz., intimacy. As we have seen, intimacy is the result of the collective mind of all concerned in a production projecting itself towards an audience sensitive to vibration and atmosphere. But this mind must be fully tuned up, complete in all details—reaching its highest force of will-power. That is, every member of the company and staff must be able to will in harmony, or the said collective mind will lose in projecting force. Thus there must be a harmony of, or equal vibrative force exerted through the coloured lights, coloured music, and coloured movement. If one expresses an emotion registering 40,000 vibrations, the others must do likewise. Otherwise, if the vibrative force of the lighting does not equal that of the music or of the movement, there will be a discord and the feeling of intimacy will not be attained. There is a physical connection between colour, sound, and movement. This is the basis of a new search for unity. By changing lights, and by colour mixes in the lime boxes, not only is change of time indicated, but emotional unity of setting and emotional effects are realised. It is in this attempt to get unity throughout, unity not only of setting but of vibrative force, that Reinhardt is advancing both beyond the Greeks and Shakespeare. The one had limited unity—in voice and movement—without variety ; the other variety without unity. Reinhardt makes for unity with variety, and harmony of vibrative force.

" Turandot "

Carlo Gozzi's *Turandot* was first produced in Berlin in October 1911. A special number of the *Blatter des Deutschen Theaters* was devoted to the exposition of its characteristics and to an explanation of the Commedia dell' Arte. Among the contributors were Karl Vollmoeller, who revised the plot ; Ferruccio Busoni, the Italian composer-pianist, who took the comedy as the basis for an Oriental Suite, which was adapted to the Vollmoeller play by Johann Wijsman ; and Ernst Stern, who designed the scenery and costumes. Sir George Alexander was present at the first production, and secured the English rights of the play. Hence its appearance at the St James's Theatre, London, in an English dress provided by Mr Jethro Bithell for the occasion. As to the origin and character of the play : historically, it represents the final struggle to preserve the traditions of the extemporaneous form of drama which began with the improvised comedy known as Commedia dell' Arte. Gozzi (1722–1806) was a member of the Granelleschi Society which aimed to preserve the Tuscan literature free from impure influences. Pietro Chiari (1700–1788) and Carlo Goldoni (1707–1795) were displacing the old Italian comedy by plays based on French models. Gozzi came to the rescue with a comedy which was represented by the Sacchi Company of players who had been thrown out of work by Carlo Goldoni. Subsequently Gozzi produced a number of pieces based on fairy tales, but after the breaking up of the Sacchi Company they were disregarded. The decline of the Commedia dell' Arte is explained in the following notes derived from the *Encyclopædia Britannica* :—Italian comedy in the seventeenth and eighteenth centuries had fallen into decay, when its reform was undertaken by the wonderful theatrical genius of Carlo Goldoni. One of the most fertile and rapid of playwrights (of his one hundred and fifty comedies, sixteen were written and acted in a single year), he at the same time pursued definite aims as a dramatist. Disgusted with the conventional buffoonery and ashamed of the rampant immorality of the Italian comic stage he drew his characters from real life, whether of his native city (Venice) or of society at large. . . . Goldoni met with a severe critic and a temporary successful rival in Count C. Gozzi, who sought to rescue the comic drama from its association with the actual life of the middle classes, and to infuse a new spirit into the figures of the old masked comedy by the invention of a new species. His themes were taken from Neapolitan and Oriental fairy tales, to which he accommodated some of the standing figures upon which Goldoni had made war. With regard to the origin of the masked comedy (four conventional figures of which were introduced by Gozzi into *Turandot*), it may be noted that the improvised comedy (commedia a soggetto) was after a time, as a rule, performed by professional actors, members of a craft, and was thence called the Commedia dell' Arte, which is said to have been invented by Francesco (called Terenziano) Cherea, the favourite player of Leo X. Its scenes, still unwritten except in skeleton (scenario), were connected together by the ancient Roman Sannio (whence our Zany). Harlequin's summit of glory was probably reached early in the seventeenth century, when he was ennobled in the person of Cecchino by the Emperor Matthias ; of Cecchino's successors, Zaccagnino and Truffaldino, we read that " they shut the door in Italy to good harlequins." Distinct from this growth is the masked comedy, the action of which was chiefly carried on by certain typical figures in masks, speaking in broad dialects, but which was not improvised, and, indeed, from the nature of the case, hardly could have been. Its inventor was A. Beolco of Padua, who called himself Ruzzanti (joker), and is memorable under that name as the first actor-playwright—a combination of extreme significance for the history of the modern stage. He published six comedies in various dialects, including the Greek of the day (1530). This was the masked comedy to which the Italians so tenaciously clung, and in which, as all their own and imitable by no other nation, they took so great a pride that even Goldoni was unable to overthrow it. Improvisation and burlesque were inseparable from the species. The masked characters, each of which spoke the dialect of the place he represented, were (according to Baretti) Pantalone, a Venetian merchant; Brighella, a Ferrarese pimp; Arlecchino, a blundering servant of Bergama. The four masked comedians in *Turandot* were Brighella (face painted with a red mask), Tartaglia (face painted with a white mask), Truffaldino (face painted with a yellow mask), Pantalone (face painted white and red).

The Story

Gozzi then took these four stock characters from the Venetian masked comedy and added them to those of the five-act fantastic fairy play *Turandotte Principesse Cinese*, the plot of which he based upon the Persian story of the cruel Princess Turandot and the handsome Prince Calaf, as related in *The Thousand and One Nights*. This play was used by Schiller, who translated it for his theatre at Weimar; and, in spite of his heavy handling, it survived in Germany for close upon a century. And what is the story? It is simply that of the taming of a primitive feminist. There was once a beautiful Princess of China named Turandot who had set her mind on not getting wed. Now Turandot was wooed by many of the marriageable princes of her day. But so resolved was she not to share her life with a man, that she surrounded herself by what she imagined to be an impassable barrier. She said to the Emperor her father, "You must issue an edict setting forth that if any prince desires me in marriage he must answer three riddles to be set by me ; and should he fail to answer the riddles then he must die." This the old Emperor, for the sake of peace, consented to do.

It will be seen that the edict offers a great scope for executions ; and it is not surprising, therefore, that the curtain rises upon a scene that suggests a riot in head-lopping. It is called the Gate of Pekin. Above this Chinese Temple Bar is a row of heads with shaven pates, that once belonged to infatuated men who, having failed to answer the royal riddles, have risen to this height in succession. In order that we may see how the mind of one of these unsuccessful suitors works when confronted with execution, we are first of all introduced to a prince who is being led away to his doom by four Chinese. At this moment there comes the Prince of Astrakan, who, as Calaf, is travelling in search of love and adventure. Almost the first person the prince meets is his old tutor, Barak, whom he has not seen for years. Barak is, of course, overjoyed to see his pupil, and agrees upon hearing the latter's story to keep his identity secret. Then, in answer to Calaf's inquiry, Barak explains the cause of the commotion as well as the meaning of the heads that adorn the gate. But though Calaf is aghast at the cruelty of this princess who, like her prototype in *Alice in Wonderland*, is always exclaiming, "Off with his head !" and has no mercy on men who cannot answer her riddles, no sooner does he see her portrait than he falls madly in love with her and swears to win her or die. It makes no difference that one after the other the principal characters seek to turn him from his purpose. To one and all he turns a deaf ear ; to Barak, to the three comic officials, Pantalone, Tartaglia, and Brighella, even to the Emperor himself. It matters not to him that the Emperor is growing tired of royal executions and the international complications that continually arise therefrom. Turandot is his game, and Turandot he means to have—even though she were the Sphinx. So, with a light heart, he enters upon the guessing competition planned on such novel, if dangerous lines. He sees no cause for fear. Why should he ? If some men are not good at riddles, there are others who are adept at guessing them. And might he not be one of the latter ? At least he has a sporting chance. Well, the great moment comes, and in the Emperor's divan the princess asks her riddles and, strangely enough, Calaf answers them correctly at once. Apparently he has a large stock-in-trade of the requisite goods on hand, for he names the abstract qualities of which the answers consist without turning a hair. You would think that the princess would be overwhelmed with this display of mental proficiency. But no, it would seem that she regards it as an unwarrantable insult that any man should dare to answer her riddles, and bursting with rage she demands to be allowed to put three more questions. If this is not playing the game, it is not her fault ; she maintains that she was taken unawares and was not ready for deep thinking, but, given another opportunity, she will ask such riddles that shall not fail to make Calaf lose his head. Her imperial father does not agree. He has had enough of her riddle-making business, and desires to see her better employed—wedded to the prince who has fairly won her. The prince, however, touched by her angry annoyance, proposes to give her another chance ; and he does so by asking her a question which she has to answer correctly the next day. If she fails to answer it then she must marry him ; if she answers it then he will die. Turandot consents, and Calaf sets her to guess his name and that of his father.

It will be seen in a moment that it is a question giving rise to endless intrigue, and with the opening of the second act Turandot is in this dilemma : either she must discover the two names and thus uphold her wild feminist head, or she, the unconquered, must consent to further defeat and humiliation at the hand of one of the hated sex. How to get the names, that is the question ? Does anyone know Calaf ? Yes, Barak's wife does. Then let Barak's wife be sent for, and sent for she is. Barak's wife, however, does not know ; but she knows that her husband knows. So Barak is sent for, and from him Turandot subtly endeavours to draw the secret. But Barak is dumb, and torture has no terror for Calaf's faithful tutor. Then, just as Turandot is about to put him to torture, her fatuous old father arrives. It seems that the latter has learnt the fateful names, and not wishing to see his daughter further humiliated, and wishing to be of service to Calaf at the same time,

offers to reveal the names if she will stop her
nonsense and give way to Calaf. But Turandot
refuses. Meanwhile Calaf, who has been locked
up in the palace by the orders of the Emperor, is
having the time of his life. One after the other
the principal characters come to him seeking to
pierce his identity. First there are three of the
comedians. Then Zelima, Turandot's gentle slave,
tries her hand and fails. Finally Adelma, her
favourite slave, comes in and tries to frighten
Calaf into running away with her. She tells him
that she is a princess in her own right, and if they
fly together they will live, on the whole, in a
happier state. Calaf believes her, but does not
quite see how it bears upon the question, because
whatever happiness there may be in other countries,
it is not so much as it will be in this ; for he
loves the princess. Unfortunately, however, in
his desire to put the matter as clearly as possible
before Adelma he inadvertently reveals his identity.

Of course, after this, Turandot is ready in the
third act with her answer. Calaf is so disturbed to
hear it that he attempts to stab himself ; but Turandot, who has been touched by his magnificence,
arrests his hand. Exclaiming, " You shall live for
me," she withdraws her ban on men. On hearing
these words the jealous Adelma tries to fall on
Calaf's dagger. Calaf prevents her doing so, and
Turandot, now magnanimous where she was once
heartlessly cruel, petitions her father to restore
Adelma to freedom. The old Emperor, who is
now thinking of wedding gifts, does so, adding by
way of " conscience money " the kingdom which

he has taken from Adelma's noble father, whose royal head doubtless adorns one of the Gates of Pekin.

Decorations and Lighting

Needless to say, a story such as this, somewhat poor and commonplace though it be, offers infinite possibilities to the imaginative decorator with a feeling for strong Oriental colour. It found in Herr Stern the imagination it required. Ernst Stern belongs to the new era of stage reform on the Continent, which has brought forward an entirely different class of scenic-artist who has sought to apply the principles of art—not mechanics and hydraulics—to the scene. Artists of this class are not required to turn out painted flats with impossible shadows, and back-cloths with stupid perspectives, but to design and give unity, due proportion, and harmony to the scene and all that it contains. To this class Herr Stern belongs; and his work represents all the difference between the English scene-painter like Harker or Telbin who contracts to build a scene to order, fill in the stage space with a miscellaneous collection of painted flats, cloths, borders, etc., and the German scenic-artist who co-operates with the director in producing decorations that express the spirit of the play. Herr Stern is indeed one of the strongest, best equipped, and most brilliant of the said class of scenic-artists, and he marks the advance of Germany not only in scenery designing but in the designing of everything in a production. In Germany he takes his place as art-director; in

England he would be regarded as a tradesman.
For it cannot be emphasised too often, that here,
in this country, the theatre is still in the hands of
the scene manufacturer whose business it is to turn
out serviceable stuff to order, much as a house
furnisher supplies manufactured goods for a desirable residence. Such scenic stuff may be exported
or reserved for home use, being readily adaptable to
any play. As a matter of fact, the English scenic-
painter is a practical mechanic. He has a
thorough knowledge of the requirements of the
stage and a factory wherein he is, at all times,
prepared to meet such requirements. When he is
asked to provide an interior with so many doors
and windows, and an exterior with so many garden
rows and lengths of hanging creeper and a rostrum on which the leading gentleman may make
his last dying speech and confession, he forthwith
supplies them. Still, bad as things are in the
theatre in this country, more than one thoughtful
person has remarked a change for the better ; and
what with the fine pioneering work of Gordon
Craig and the visits of Ernst Stern, there has arisen
a greater disposition to make the representation of
plays less dull and tedious. Herr Stern's methods
of work have already been examined in the account
of *The Miracle*, and therefore there is no need to go
into them here. *Turandot* afforded him the widest
scope for the display of his immense abilities ; and
one gathered from such slender evidence as the production of the play at the St James's Theatre offered,
that he had made a far more important thing of it
even than *The Miracle*. The evidence was slender,

owing to the restrictions put upon the production by the St James's Theatre, to which I shall refer presently. Whatever pleasing results were attained at this theatre, I think far better ones were attained at the Deutsches Theater, where everything was prepared to receive the play and to give it the widest expression.

In the official organ of the Deutsches Theater for 1911, Herr Stern states his conception of the decorative treatment of *Turandot*. He reminds us that Turandot is a child of the Rococo spirit; that this spirit belongs to every period of culture. Thus, it makes out of every culture a delightful play pleasing " to the elegant world from Paris to Venice." Out of the Greek culture a pastoral; out of the Oriental culture a story from *The Thousand and One Nights*; out of the Chinese culture a porcelain fantasy. It is never serious, never real, pedantic, historical, or ethnographical; but always occupied with illusion and joy. Hence it offers unbounded freedom to the artist, and does not fetter him to any one age. A present-day performance of Gozzi's *Turandot*, if seen with the Rococo eye, cannot reconstruct China of to-day, but that of the eighteenth century. So we conjure out of the Emperor's throne-room a Chinese fantastic city with its illuminated houses of papier mâché; Turandot dwelling in her highly-lacquered room; Prince Calaf dreaming his love dreams guarded by two giant vases. But to all this the present-day decorator may add something of his own. Hence *Turandot* is not a Chinoiserie of 1760, but a Chinoiserie of 1911.

Needless to say, such a conception did not call forth archæological correctness, but an amazing display of improvised colour and line. Herr Stern, indeed, let himself go in a world that suited him best ; with the result that he obtained a kaleidoscopic splendour of effects many of which could not fail to dwell in the memory of the spectator. Who does not remember the quaint, gorgeous, and splendid Chinese costumes moving riotously in rich masses or separately against harmonious backgrounds ; the dazzling processions of soldiers, slaves, lamp-bearers, composing themselves against the curtains of the butterflies and the dragon ; the coloured pomp and circumstance ; the sumptuous ceremony ; the embroidered absurdity ; the purple tones of Calaf's bedroom ; the street scene at night with the pagoda houses and their lighted windows ; the rich, final divan scene.

But if the decorator let himself go it was in the face of difficulties over which he had no control. The chief difficulty was perhaps the lighting. It cannot be repeated too often that the appeal to the eye is the essential feature of the Reinhardt dramatic production. In this connection the German producer takes every advantage of the enormous advance in the methods of stage lighting, especially utilising the increased power of illumination by electricity. Of course, the innovation has the fault of its magnitude. The fault of the Reinhardt system of lighting from the front is that a great deal of the apparatus is visible to the audience, and will remain so till Reinhardt employs a system of lighting by means of which the apparatus is entirely hidden from the audience.   It is said that such a system has been devised, and will be seen in use in London shortly.   In spite of this fault, Reinhardt gets immense effects from his lighting, and plans all his productions to utilise his system in full.   As a consequence, he cannot present a play produced under the conditions of lighting at the Deutsches Theater at another theatre not so well equipped without risking a loss of decorative effect.   The loss is significant, for it means that a part of the original design has been seriously affected, and the essential cumulative effect on the audience cannot be attained.   This was the case at the St James's Theatre, where the old method of lighting is still in use, and where the stage is lit from the top with battens, from the bottom with footlights and rows, from the sides with perches and wing ladders, and from the flies, and where the front of the house lighting is not in use.   The effect of this lighting was particularly noticeable in the curtain scenes. The proscenium lights, for instance, fell in patches on the curtains and interfered with their colours and designs.   Then the lighting at the back was sometimes so strong as to make the curtains transparent ; then it was unequal, and thus tended to kill the figures moving against a strongly-lighted patch.   For instance, in the Princess's room, when she and some dancing girls are moving about, the orange-red background is so strong and out of tune that the figures lose all interest.   The lighting of the first scene, " The Gates of Pekin," with its harmony of white gates, blue sky, and red lights, was also far too strong for the colours worn by the characters. Better results were attained in the first harem scene, with its delightful harmonies of purple, blue, and red hanging lamps, and in Calaf's room which, with its purple background, green and purple bed, purple and gold prince and orange lamps, made a simple and very telling composition, the effect of which was heightened by the entrance of the slaves, especially the one dressed in green and carrying a yellow lamp. The three magnificent decorated curtains suffered most from defective lighting, and one could only imagine the full beauty of their colour and design—one with two coloured butterflies on a big simple blue ground, and another with dragons moving against a tremendous mass of orange.

The Music

Busoni's music was cleverly adapted to tell the story. The prelude introduced us to the scene, and the principal characters were given their themes. The entrances were announced, the Emperor's by a fanfare, Turandot's being given out by the 'cellos and basses, and so on; the music thus moving and acting throughout the play. Much of the music is indeed worthy of quotation as an example of its successful application to the needs of the drama.

"THE TAMING OF THE SHREW"

This account of the production of *The Taming of the Shrew* belongs, in most respects, to the Appendix on "Recent Developments in England." If I have decided to place it here, it is because it revealed a more direct application of Max Reinhardt's ideas than was to be found in Mr Granville Barker's two Shakespearean productions. For instance, it was Reinhardt's idea to preserve the " play within a play " illusion throughout, not only by seating the intoxicated Sly where the orchestra well usually is, and from where, partly seen, he can witness the play which he believes is being presented for his special benefit ; but by making all the changes of scene by the use of properties, which appear to be actual properties, either brought on by the players in their waggon or extemporised out of the furniture and effects of the Lord's house. It will be gathered from this that a great deal is left to the imagination of the audience, as in the Chinese play, *The Yellow Jacket*.

I was, unfortunately, not able to attend a performance of the play, and I am therefore indebted to Mr Martin Harvey for his extreme courtesy in placing me in possession of the following facts on the general production. Perhaps the chief point of interest was Mr Harvey's collaboration with Mr William Poel, thus establishing a link with Reinhardt, and completing the circle of modern Shakespearean rediscoverers—from Poel, Savits, Reinhardt, to Harvey and Barker. Mr Poel's ideas were to be traced in the representation of the play in the Elizabethan manner : the uncut text, the continuous performance, the Elizabethan setting with its open stage and the absence of the usual proscenium arch, the absence of modern scenery, and an air of scholarship which distin-

guishes the Poelean from the Reinhardtian Shakespearean production. The ideas were there, though
not always fully expressed. Thus the setting
of *The Taming of the Shrew* used by Mr Harvey
at the Prince of Wales' Theatre was invented
by himself as a result of his personal experience of the open stage and decorative or scenic
economy, which were the basis of Reinhardt's
mounting of *Oedipus*, and of certain conversations
and consultations with Mr Poel. The idea of
placing Sly on the covered-up orchestra well was,
as we have seen, suggested by Max Reinhardt.
But from Mr Poel came much valuable advice,
particularly as to how the mind of a modern
audience, with its strong bent towards overwhelm-
ing realistic detail, would meet the challenge to
its taste and imagination offered by the use of bare
essentials and indications of scenery such as it was
proposed to use in this revival.

The Setting

The setting invented by Mr Harvey was as
follows :—The footlights were removed and the
stage extended a foot or two into an "apron."
From each end a flight of steps led down to a
lower platform which covered in the orchestra
well. In the centre of the platform stood a carved
stone seat with its back to the audience, commanding a view of the stage, and being about four feet
in width. To this seat, after the "Induction," the
bemused Sly and his pseudo-wife were conducted
by the Lord's Majordomo, and here they sat
throughout the play, excepting the few minutes

occupied by the one interval in the action, during which they retired behind the curtain. The stage, the front structure, the steps, and the seat on the platform were painted a subdued grey, against which the colours of the costumes and furniture moved brilliantly. The grey was repeated in a cloth which, reaching to the roof and extending to the edges of the boxes on either side, masked in the ordinary proscenium arch. The opening thus obtained was marked and framed with a bold arch of monster green laurels forming a semicircular arch. In the centre and at the sides were bows of broad gilt ribbon, harmonising with the renaissance style of decoration. The front arch was repeated by three false arches seen in perspective, and set behind each other up the stage. The sides of the arches served as " wings," while their curved tops served as " borders " to limit the sight line of the spectator. The three arches were of black wood with a gold pattern. Thus the entire stage was converted into a large Pavilion or Hall with an outlook at the back on to a broad landscape and a wide road disappearing in the distance. Across the back of the stage ran a terrace with a black stone balustrade both on its outer and its inner edge. In the centre of the terrace a flight of three steps led down on to the stage, and a corresponding opening at the back suggested a similar flight on to the open landscape. The opening at the back was marked by two conventional bay trees clipped circular and festooned with gold. A bold triple festoon of twined laurels and gold hung at the furthest archway across the skyline.

Changes of Scene

First. INDUCTION. The act drop, formed by the two heraldic curtains, was parted disclosing two tapestried curtains depicting an Italianate landscape. This curtain scene served for the scene in which Sly is discovered outside the Alehouse.

Second.—THE LORD'S CHAMBER. Also played in curtains set a few paces further up the stage, and discovered by drawing apart the tapestries. These were of white Roman satin, and each was decorated in the centre with a large medallion painting illustrating the Lord's "wanton pictures."

Third.—The curtains were drawn aside and the stage fully disclosed, thus preparing for the entrance of the players who entered in a waggon which was drawn in on the upper terrace. The waggon was painted scarlet and yellow, in harmony with the motley of the players.

Fourth and succeeding. — Then the business between Katharina and Petruchio began, the various scenes being played in curtains and screens employed to mark succeeding interiors and exteriors. The screens were large pieces of canvas about eight feet high and broad, painted grey, and stencilled with a graceful gold festoon pattern near the top. Each was run into position by a servant dressed in the period, who stood hidden behind his particular section. The pieces, it may be said, were joined to a continuous flat surface or an irregular frontage just as desired. Stage properties, such as chairs, tables, and so on, were placed in position by the said servants, in full view of the audience, while the curtains were being changed.

In the second half of the play a large canopied seat with a table in front occupied the centre of the stage whenever a scene was supposed to be taking place in Petruchio's house. These properties were so arranged that they could be hoisted into the flies while a screen scene was being played. Finally, the banquet was arranged at a long table similar to that used in Leonardo's " Last Supper." The lighting of this scene came from three large candelabra carried on by the servants, Biondello, Grumio, and Tranio, who walked at the head of the procession of guests. The back-cloth was lit with a deep blue Italian night colour.

At the conclusion of the play all the players danced across the stage hand in hand to the air of a jig played by musicians who, during the supper scene, sat on the terrace with their instruments of the period.

It should be mentioned that during the one interval of the play, the drop curtains were raised, disclosing a bower of golden trelliswork entwined with golden bay leaves against a curtain forming a deep blue background. Seated in this bower a trio of musicians played a selection of old English music on the Viola da Gamba and the Viola d'Amore.

FORTHCOMING
REINHARDT PRODUCTIONS

"THE YELLOW JACKET"

AMONG the plays which Reinhardt has marked out for production are *The Yellow Jacket*, and, in co-operation with Mr Martin Harvey, *Hamlet*, on the lines of the Berlin production, and the second play of the *Oedipus* trilogy, *Oedipus at Colonus*, which Professor Gilbert Murray will translate, and which will be given by Mr Harvey as a second part, in continuation of *Oedipus Rex*.

As Max Reinhardt proposes to adapt the London-American version of *The Yellow Jacket*, it may not be out of place to state the main features of this version. *The Yellow Jacket*, then, was produced at the Duke of York's Theatre under the management of Mr Gaston Mayer. It came to London from America, where its novelty had attracted consider-able attention. Though it did not contain all the elements of a pure specimen of the Chinese drama, —its authors, George C. Hazelton and Benrimo, being careful to say so,—nevertheless it revealed sufficient to show the enormous imaginative value of this species of drama, alike from a point of view of

representation and interpretation.   In some ways it
carried the mind of the spectator back to the origin
of the Chinese drama, concerning which I cannot
do better than quote from the account by Dr Lionel
Giles, sent to me by Mr Mayer, for the purpose.

" It seems probable," says Dr Giles, " that the
drama in China, like that of Greece, had its
origin in the sacrificial ceremonies of religion.
We know that in the time of Confucius, 500 B.C.,
it was customary for solemn dances to be performed
in the ancestral temples, at which feathered wands,
battle-axes, and other objects were brandished in
unison by the dancers.   We also hear of pantomimic
displays and representations of ancient historical
events, divided into a number of scenes.   Certain
ceremonies for the expulsion of evil spirits, in
which a house-to-house visitation was made by
villagers dressed in fantastic garb, may also have
some connection with the beginnings of dramatic
art.   Others are inclined to derive the drama from
the puppet shows, which, from time immemorial,
have been a feature of the life of the people, and
they point to the fact that in many parts of China
a theatrical performance is still preceded by a display of marionettes.   However that may be, it is
certain that for the immense period of twelve
hundred years after the time of Confucius no great
development of the drama can have taken place, if
indeed it can be said to have existed at all.   No
record of anything in the nature of a modern stage-
play can be traced until the reign of the Emperor
Ming Huang of the T'ang dynasty, in the first
half of the eighth century A.D.   Being exception-

ally fond of song and dance, this emperor is said to have founded a sort of academy known as the ' Pear-tree Garden,' where a company of three hundred persons was personally trained by him for the production of what, for want of a better name, may be described as operas. Music must have constituted the basis of these performances, but it seems that the slender thread of a story was also introduced between the choral songs ; and to this day actors in China are often called ' Apprentices of the Pear-tree Garden.' " According to Mr A. Corbett-Smith, this " Guild of the Young Folks of the Pear Garden," as he terms it, has a relation to the founding of the historical drama in China—a form of drama which finds greatest favour with the Chinese public. Writing in *The Era*, he mentions that the Emperor Huan Tsung (A.D. 753), being desirous of showing his affection for his wife, asked his Prime Minister to devise a novel form of entertainment. This the latter did by searching the historical records and instructing " some of the noblest and most graceful of the youths about the Court " how to recite the narratives thus unearthed. The entertainment was given in " a gorgeous pavilion amidst blossoming fruit-trees," and " the institution of a Guild or College of Dramatic Art " was the result. With regard to the modern stage-play, Dr Giles tells us that " modern Chinese plays still follow, in external construction, at any rate, the model of the dramas produced under the Mongols. They are usually divided into four acts, with or without a prologue, and are accompanied throughout by an orchestra consisting of gongs, drums, and cymbals, besides string and wind instruments. The words are delivered in a high-pitched recitative, varied by bouts of chanting in passage, where special stress is required for the heightening of emotion or the utterance of moral reflections. There is, as a rule, one particular character who breaks at intervals into songs, and fulfils in some degree the function of a chorus. Few Chinese plays last much over an hour. It is the rule for a number of plays to be performed continuously. This accounts for the widespread notion that Chinese plays are ridiculously long." As to the actors and women on the stage : " A full Chinese theatrical company is made up of fifty-six persons. The various rôles are classified and kept distinct, each actor being expected to play only one particular class of character. The principal classes are : (1) Shêng, including the parts both of hero and walking gentleman ; (2) Ching, the bold and unscrupulous villain ; (3) Tan, the female parts, respectable and otherwise ; (4) Ch'ou, the low comedy man. Contrary to the usual belief, women took part in theatricals throughout the Mongol and Ming dynasties, and a stop was only put to the practice as late as the eighteenth century under the reign of the Emperor Ch'ien Lung, whose mother had herself been an actress. Of recent years the ban has been removed, and an increasing number of women are again performing on the public stage. Chinese actors are notoriously among the finest in the world, those who take female parts showing particular skill and likewise commanding the highest salaries. Gorgeous dresses are worn, and the make-up, if not always realistic, is strikingly effective. The actor's life is often wretched in the extreme. Bought or hired from poverty-stricken parents at an early age, he is subjected to a very rigorous course of both histrionic and acrobatic training. In addition, he has to memorise between a hundred and two hundred parts, so as to be able to appear in them at a moment's notice, without rehearsal or prompter. In spite of his comparatively high intellectual standard, he is, nevertheless, regarded as a social outcast, and all his descendants, to the third generation, are debarred from competing in the public examinations." As to the theatres : " Permanent theatres in the proper sense of the word are to be found only in Peking and Canton and some of the larger treaty ports. Even in these, the accommodation is very simple. There is a pit furnished with benches and a table in front of each, and a balcony divided into a number of separate boxes. The stage, which is built out into the auditorium so as to be commanded on three sides, must on no account face west, this being the inauspicious quarter controlled by the White Tiger. There is no scenery, no curtain, and but few accessories. Two doors at the back serve, one for entrance, the other for exit. The theatre, except where customs have been modified by foreign influence, is free to all, but it is understood that every visitor will pay for some refreshment." As to stage conventions : " Owing to the complete absence of scenic accessories, it is obvious that a great deal has to be left to the imagination of a Chinese audience. As each character enters, he tells you himself, quite in the manner of Bottom, who he is and what part he has to play in the coming drama. The members of the orchestra sit on the stage itself, and footmen wait at the sides ready to carry in screens, chairs, tables and the like, wherewith to represent city-walls and houses, forests and even mountains. An actor will gravely bestraddle a stick and prance about the stage as though on horseback, without the least fear of evoking a smile. Or, if dead, he will contrive to alter his face and then get up and carry himself off, making movements as though acting the part of a bearer. Again, it is quite a usual thing for a player who is getting hoarse to have a cup of tea handed to him by an attendant. A change of scene is indicated by pantomimic action, or by all the dramatis personæ walking rapidly in single file round the stage."

With the foregoing facts before us, it is possible to determine how far *The Yellow Jacket* expressed the real Chinese drama, staging and acting, which doubtless have an important message for us if only we could get at the meaning of it.

The Story

Of the two classes, military and civil, into which Chinese plays are divided, *The Yellow Jacket* belongs to the latter. Judging by its story, the play answers the description of a fairy tale in which cruelty and craft are met by fidelity and self-sacrifice, with poetic justice in the end. This is also a descrip-

tion which may be applied to the English Morality
play. The story is concerned with the adventures
of a certain member of the lordly Wu family.
When the curtain rises Wu Hoo Git—for such is
the name of the hero—is supposed by his wicked
father to have been slain, together with his mother,
in infancy. But it seems that the mother wrote
her child's history with her own blood upon his
clothes, and a peasant and his wife saved him and
brought him up in ignorance of his parentage.
Thus he reaches manhood. Meanwhile his brother
has supplanted him on the throne, and knowing
Wu Hoo Git's identity, employs every means to
bring about his ruin and death, being assisted in
his endeavour by an evil misshapen creature Yin
Suey Gong by name. The latter does his best to
get rid of the hero. For one thing, he induces
him to purchase a love damsel for a large sum,
without, however, attaining any better result than
that of opening the eyes of the hero to the fact
that love of the sort is too expensive a luxury.
Along with a desire for knowledge the hero develops
a Chinese craving for ancestors. Something tells
him that he does not belong to the humble rank
of his foster-parents. Accordingly, he sets out like
Japhet in search of a father, meeting with all sorts
of strange adventures on the way which the crafty
Yin Suey Gong is careful to honeycomb with pit-
falls. When, however, a pitfall appears, there is
the shade of his grandfather to protect the hero.
One of the adventures is the meeting with " Plum
Blossom," Moy Fah Loy, with whom he falls in
love. But there is an obstacle to their union. The

hero has " no name." Then comes the disclosure
by his foster-father of his identity. But this
knowledge does not complete his happiness. There
is still the throne occupied by the usurper to be
won ; and till that is accomplished and he has
placed the coveted distinction, the symbol of
Honour, the gorgeous Yellow Jacket, on his own
shoulders, there can be no peace for him, and his
wanderings may not cease.

Staging

Such is the kind of story which lends itself to
the peculiar Chinese methods of representation and
interpretation. Representation, as we have seen,
is quite a primitive affair. Dr Giles tells us there
is no attempt to stage plays as in the Western
method. The stage is little more than a platform
projecting into the auditorium and designed merely
to accommodate the orchestra and players, and the
scenery a mere device to hide the walls. We
cannot call this revolutionary, though there are
some extremists who would identify it with the
movement towards simplified staging. In the
strict sense it is not revolutionary, seeing that
the present search is for staging that grows out of
the dominant mood of a play, and is not merely
an adjunct to speech and action. At the Duke
of York's Theatre the staging was no more than a
makeshift. Thus the stage was squared up to the
size of a fairly large scene, the scenery consisting of
flats and a little built-up gallery in the centre of
the back of the stage. There was an entrance to
the left at the back of the stage, and an exit to the

right at the back. Between these was an opening nine feet high, forming an alcove containing four Chinese musicians and their instruments. At the back of the alcove, hidden from the audience by lattice work, was a second and stringed orchestra. Above the alcove was a gallery, to which the characters ascended as to Heaven after having died on the stage. In front of the alcove was a small black desk at which the Chorus sat. Lying at the left side of the stage was a ladder which was used whenever a character was required to ascend to the little gallery or Heaven. Down left of the stage was the property man's box. The decorations consisted simply of long red scrolls, some Chinese landscapes hung on the yellowish walls, a large yellow lamp hung in centre, and black and gold tapestries hung over the entrance and exit. The scene was lighted in the English manner, by front battens, footlights, and side limes, the colours used being warm yellow and amber.

The Conventions

According to one of the authors, Mr Benrimo, the Chinese conventions were not rigidly adhered to. For instance, he speaks of the Chorus as an " innovation." At the Duke of York's the Chorus sat at his desk in the centre of the stage and announced each scene in turn, after each announcement resuming his seat and his cigarette till the scene ended. In the true Chinese manner the change of scene would be indicated in such notices as " This is a Forest," or " This is a Sea-shore." But at the Duke of York's the Chorus announced the scene, such as " A Courtyard in the House of Wu Sin Yin," or " A Room in the House," or " A Road leading to the Palace " ; and the only difference in the scene was a change of furniture, stools, etc., which were carried on and off by assistant property men.   But if the Chorus was " invented," the Property Man was the real thing. He externalised, indeed, the great principle applied by the Chinese to their plays, that of the Invisible expressed by the Visible.   He sat at the left side of the stage ready to hand out the primitive props as they were required.   When the dead wished to ascend to Heaven the Property Man placed the ladder for him.   When the hero needed a snow-storm, the Property Man provided one.   No matter what was required,—a mountain, a cataract, a cushion representing a severed head, " a flower-boat floating down the river of love " (symbolised by a seat, a carpet, and some bamboo sticks), swords, willow-trees, even a cup of coffee,—there was the Property Man to supply it in his quaint, scornful, and imperturbable fashion.

Its Contribution to Current Reform

In spite of its obvious fakes, *The Yellow Jacket* makes a distinct contribution to the movement in the theatre.   It comes as a strong challenge to a public accustomed to the fallacies of a movement aiming to express the materialistic realities of life. It comes at a moment when the drama is busy turning towards a new Reality—the Reality of the Imagination, and away from the old Reality of the Intellect.   And the mind of the spectator who witnesses it cannot fail to be awakened to the immense possibilities of its spirit of simplicity and child-like make-believe, in adding a much-needed impulse to creative authorship and creative acting ; as well as in stirring the public to a consciousness of the seeming reality and apparent genuineness of the gigantic shams which pass in our midst for the drama and dramatic representation. It emphasises the truth that the drama is concerned with the Invisible expressed by the Visible, and not with the Visible expressed by the Visible, as in contemporary realistic plays.

" HAMLET "

Hamlet has been produced three times in Germany by Max Reinhardt, the first occasion being at the Munich Theatre in June 1909. The productions were notable for the performances in the leading part, of Bassermann, Kainz, and Moissi. They were also distinguished by technical progress, each production being an advance on its predecessor. The third one was given at the Deutsches Theater, Berlin, in November 1910. In the attempt to make it surpass his two previous efforts Reinhardt spared neither time nor money. He endeavoured to grasp the fullest possibilities of the new freedom offered by the open stage with a curtained background that came first from England *via* Munich, followed Sir Herbert Tree's example, and experimented in a revival on Elizabethan lines. It is not clear how much Max Reinhardt derived from Sir Herbert Tree's *Hamlet* production ; but there is no doubt that he was influenced by it to some extent. It will be recollected that when Sir Herbert went to Berlin some years ago he took *Hamlet* with him, and departing from his usual custom of presenting Shakespeare in the splendid manner, did *Hamlet* in simple hangings. And he did so, not because he had changed his theory that Shakespeare should be sumptuously dressed, but because he was of the opinion that *Hamlet* lends itself to a treatment different from that of the other Shakespearean plays. Hence after playing *Hamlet* in Berlin in simple hangings, he did not hesitate when he revived the play in London, four or five years ago, to do it in tapestries. Thus the Court scenes were played in plainly painted tapestries of a conventional mediæval kind, such as might be hung in a castle, the outdoor scenes being played in tapestries on which were painted tall pine trees stretching right up into the proscenium. Reinhardt also derived from Sir Herbert Tree's production of *A Midsummer Night's Dream*, doubtless in the way that all talented men derive from each other. But if he employed principles applied by Sir Herbert Tree in *Hamlet*, he also went beyond him at least by carrying his stage into the auditorium. He built in the orchestra and removed three rows of stalls for the purpose. By this means he got a much enlarged stage and was able to work the three divisions into which he divided it with greater freedom, either for interiors or exteriors, for scenes containing one or two characters, or crowds, as the case might be. The formation of the stage, in details of build and fitment, resembled that of the stage used by Mr

Granville Barker for his production of *A Winter's Tale*, as described in the Appendix on " Recent Developments in England." Thus the stage was worked on equally rapid lines answering to the action-structure. The violet curtain before which Laertes takes leave of Polonius was raised and the scene became the " Throne Room," which, by the dropping of a dark green curtain changed to a scene in which the King appears, and which in turn was transformed, by the raising of the dark green curtain, into a room hung with a red curtain, representing the chamber of Hamlet's mother. By changes of light, scenes were also changed. So throughout the play the scenes changed and moved swiftly by an ingenious interchange of curtains and lighting.

HIS CONTRIBUTION TO THE CONTEMPORARY STAGE AND HIS INFLUENCE

HAVING examined the immense activities of Max Reinhardt, it becomes of importance to inquire, What contribution is Max Reinhardt making to the contemporary artistic movement in the theatre, and what is his influence upon England ? The answer to the first question is that he is demonstrating that a theatre may be run successfully on a commercial and artistic basis. In doing so he is really opening the door upon the purely art theatre. To-day there are three classes of theatre with which the minds of reformers are occupied. They are :

1. The commercial theatre, run by the actor-manager, a syndicate, or a successful financier who owns and controls innumerable theatres. For example, the Charles Frohman and the Schubert Trusts, who between them control nearly the whole of the theatres in the United States.

2. The commercial-artistic theatre, managed by an intelligent director working in harmony with a number of co-operators, who, though recognising the impossibility, under our present social conditions, of running a theatre on purely artistic lines, yet is able

to lift the theatre out of the rut of purely commercial enterprise.

3. The art theatre, which has yet to be born. Its aim will be Creative-Illusion, not Realism or Actuality.

The artistic reformer would destroy the first, but would support the second till the third arrives. The second is an intermediary which does cater for a critical (though not hypercritical) minority among playgoers, players, and decorators. Perhaps the author may complain that it does not cater for him. Still, it certainly indulges the artistic taste and satisfies the mind that seeks for style in cohesion and uniformity. This, then, is the value of the Theatre of Max Reinhardt. It offers us something infinitely better than the theatrical establishment run by the financier out for shekels, by the actor-manager in search of gold and silver and vanity, by the literary and moral person and the social reformer out for words and discussion. In short, it is a solution to the artistic problem of the theatre, which we ought to accept till we are offered a higher one. If we do accept it, it will lead the school-teacher mind to abandon the hope of making the theatre an "improving" academy, while inducing the artistic mind to endeavour to make it a temple of illumination.

The answer to the second question is that signs are not wanting that the influence of Reinhardt is beginning to be strongly felt in this country. Alert minds are conscious that the German producer is offering us a more potential theatre than our own sadly and rightly neglected dialectical one.

Thus Mr Granville Barker is beginning to work towards a more artistic playhouse, and the Liverpool and Birmingham Repertory Theatres are pulling in the direction of the Deutsches Theater, with the avowed object of surpassing that energetic institution if possible. Mr Barker first definitely extended his welcome to Reinhardt's ideas in a production of Professor Gilbert Murray's translation of *Iphigenia in Tauris* by Euripides. It was a Greek production entirely on Reinhardtian lines, bearing, in fact, the closest resemblance to the Covent Garden Theatre production of *Oedipus Rex*. The search for intimacy was carried on in the same manner. There was a stage that had passed out of the picture-frame and invaded the audience. There was the scene composed of a temple front leading to an inner shrine, the platform built out over the first three or four rows of stalls, and the altar placed centre. There was the emotional and moody colour, the same attempt at lighting and colour effects, the same movements of the chorus, the same mingling of the players with the audience. And there was the principal part played by the same actress, Miss Lillah M'Carthy. In fact, it seemed as though Mr Barker had come to the conclusion that Max Reinhardt's method of producing Greek plays is the right one, and there is an immense gain in reality by taking away the proscenium and allowing the players to step out of the frame and become part of the audience.

The production of *Iphigenia* was only one instance out of several of the influence of Reinhardt on the English stage. Others are given in my volume on *The New Spirit in Drama and Art*.

In short, the ideas of Max Reinhardt have had a marked influence upon the methods of play representation and interpretation in this country ; and this influence would have been far greater if only the work of the German producer had been seen at its best. That is to say, if instead of consenting to try and fit to one sort of environment the London theatres, productions which have grown naturally out of another, the Deutsches Theater (a proceeding which necessitated and ensured the complete failure of more than one of these productions), he had demanded a suitable environment for them, he would not have offered such a broad front to adverse criticism. But he seems entirely to have neglected the fact that not only were the physical conditions of the London theatres unadaptable to the fullest requirements of four of his plays at least, but that these limitations were bound to be reinforced by the censorship of English taste, by the stupid economies practised in the English commercial theatre, and by the prevalent inartistic slovenliness of English methods of representation. Acting thus, it is needless to say that he took risks, and he did himself a great injustice. He invited criticism, and certain critics are not wholly to blame if, when faced with indifferent spectacle, they charged Reinhardt with an alleged and harmful indifference to the drama. That he has not been indifferent to the drama the *Table of Productions* will show. All he has been guilty of is demonstrating what this book sets out to prove, namely, that the real Max Reinhardt is to be seen at Berlin.

SUPPLEMENTARY CHAPTER

THIS supplementary chapter contains certain matter bearing on the subject of this book, which has come to hand since the book was written.

SHAKESPEARE AND SIMPLIFIED STAGING

The present-day controversy on the manner of staging Shakespeare, to which a new impulse has been added by Max Reinhardt's visit to this country, has called forth two books of equal merit from the producer's point of view. In the first, *Thoughts and Afterthoughts*, Sir Herbert Tree says much " in extenuation of those methods which have been assailed with almost equal brilliancy and vehemence." The author examines The Splendid *v.* The Adequate, or The Fat *v.* The Thin method of production, and argues in favour of the former. Thus he meets the argument of the Adequates that the splendid manner of producing Shakespeare tends to banish him altogether from the stage, seeing that the huge cost of production forbids frequent productions, with the argument that one production in the splendid manner is worth a dozen in the adequate manner. He argues, moreover, that Shakespeare wrote for the public ; that the public demands the splendid manner, as the box-office receipts can show ; and therefore the public demands what Shakespeare would give it if he were alive to-day. And he examines the conditions of his Shakespearean plays, which have governed his choice of interpretation.

In the second book, *Shakespeare in the Theatre*, Mr William Poel defends the non-scenic method of producing Shakespeare, and deals with the questions which he set himself to answer thirty years ago. The questions may be stated thus :

1. What is the Shakespearean theatre really like ?

2. What are the dramatic conditions in which Shakespeare worked ?

3. What are Shakespeare's intentions in :

    (*a*) The construction of his plays ;

    (*b*) The method of their representation ;

    (*c*) The method of their interpretation ?

A conclusion to which the book leads the reader is that the current movement towards Shakespearean simplicity has sprung from Mr Poel's long and unswerving faith in his ideal of a Neo-Shakespearean stage, his attempt to give Shakespeare in the purely suggestive surroundings of curtains having begun in 1881, or eight years before the reaction against the elaboration of scenic details of the Meiningers set in at Munich.

With regard to the Munich Shakespeare Stage, the following facts sent by Director Kilian are of interest :—

1. The Munich Shakespeare Stage of Lautenschläger and Savits was the first German Stage to

play Shakespeare in the simplified manner. It did so in 1889.

2. The new Munich Shakespeare Stage of 1909 differs from the other in that the first proscenium is done away with, that proscenium scenes are not played in front of decorations, but generally in front of the curtain, and that modern scenic principles are applied to decorative scenes played at the back part of the stage, such as those of the round horizon, plastic architecture, etc.

3. The Munich Shakespeare Stage has so far found but few imitators in Germany.

Full particulars of the Munich Stage may be found in Amundsen's *The New Munich Shakespeare Stage*, published at Munich in 1911.

THE NATIONAL THEATRE MOVEMENT

This movement, which is inspired to some extent by the example of Germany, has found an opponent in Mr Henry Arthur Jones. For some years Mr Jones has been in favour of the establishment of a national theatre in this country, but after investigating the failure of the Millionaires' Theatre, New York, he has formed the opinion that the time is not ripe for an experiment on the lines proposed by the large and influential English committee. His objections form the new matter in a book of collected essays and lectures entitled *The Foundations of a National Drama*. Mr Poel also has something to say against the proposals of the National Theatre Committee in his afore-mentioned *Shakespeare in the Theatre*.

Symbolism in the Theatre

The interchange of Eastern and Western ideas of the theatre and the drama continues, and new books explaining Western methods of representation and interpretation are constantly appearing. In *Plays of Old Japan*, Miss Marie C. Stopes deals with the history, character, and staging of the " Nō " plays, and makes a further contribution to the subject of simplified staging.

The Re-interpretation of Ibsen

There are signs that a re-valuation of Ibsen is about to be attempted in this country, and one book at least has appeared to point the way. Mr Henry Rose's *Henrik Ibsen : Poet, Mystic, and Moralist*, provides a key to the symbolist in the great Norwegian dramatist.

The English Repertory Theatre

The new repertory habit to which London, after Germany, became addicted, and which for a variety of reasons London did not long retain, has shown a slight increase in the English provinces. The Birmingham Repertory Theatre was opened in February 1913, with a production of Shakespeare's *Twelfth Night* after the Reinhardt manner. The theatre was built for Mr Barry Jackson, to whose enthusiasm and munificence England owes the first theatre constructed for the new artistic repertory purposes. In this connection it carries on some of the reforms coming from abroad. For instance, its seating comes from the Bayreuth

Theatre, where the rows of seats rise gently one above the other ; and its lighting from the Deutsches Theater, Berlin.   The latter was introduced by Mr Basil Dean, who also applied Reinhardt's system of lighting to the Liverpool Repertory Theatre.   It should be mentioned that Mr Dean has recently resigned his directorship of the Liverpool Theatre.   Sheffield followed Birmingham with a repertory theatre, and other centres are to have experimental repertory seasons.   Meanwhile the repertory theatre habit which deserted London for the provinces, promises to return to London by the suburbs.   Croydon, for instance, has reached the new repertory stage under the direction of Messrs Keble Howard and Dick Adams.

Otto Brahm

Otto Brahm died in November 1912.   He was born in Hamburg in 1856, and became a pupil of Wilhelm Scherer, the philologist and historian of literature, soon after the latter's arrival at Berlin in 1877.   Later, as critic, he contributed to several journals, and in 1889 became closely associated with the Freien Bühne movement.   For the rest, he devoted himself to the psychological drama, the ensemble, and to the claims of newcomers to whom he believed the future belonged.   His death called forth an extraordinary manifestation of feeling from intellectual Germans, including an eloquent tribute from Gerhart Hauptmann.   According to the *Times* report of his speech, Herr Hauptmann said : " I do not believe that in the whole history of the German Theatre there was ever before him such a union of practical force and ideal force. He compelled the theatre to serve serious, true, and living Art. He brought it near to life, and life near to it, as had never been done before. . . . There may be people who regard a fight for the prestige of the German Theatre to be not important enough to justify belief in its seriousness. It is Brahm's service that he recognised its importance and gave himself to the work. He burdened himself for it with labours, cares, and duties of all sorts, undertook campaigns and experienced victories and defeats, successes and disappointments, unknown to the life of the peaceful citizen. The sense of responsibility of an important statesman entrusted with the fortunes of his Fatherland cannot be greater. It requires no greater sum of labour, endurance, insight, and courage. . . . How shall we do honour to this man ? By maintaining and continuing his vital work, the importance of which is ever more and more profoundly realised. In a certain field he achieved the unity of Art and People. In him the Theatre became the breathing organ of the People's life. To an art in itself apart and remote from the people's world he gave the simple force of a natural function."

The Spread of Reinhardt's Influence

Reinhardt's increasing influence may be noted in two directions. In the present revival of the religious form of drama may be traced the influence of the production of *The Miracle*. Mrs Dearmer's *The Dreamer*, and Mr Louis Parker's *Joseph and His*

Brethren are types of a " new " religious play.   The production of the first revealed an application of the Reinhardt principles of staging.   By the cinematograph adaptation of *The Miracle* and other Reinhardt productions, it is conceivable that Reinhardt's principles of ensemble acting are becoming widely known to player and public alike.

APPENDICES

I. A NOTE ON THE LIMITATION OF THE CULTURE MOVEMENT IN THE THEATRE

THERE has been and are several objections raised to the attempted representation of classics on the modern stage. One is the objection of the artist to the archæologist. As sources of archæology, Greek, Roman, Chinese, Japanese, Elizabethan, early French, German, and Italian plays have a profound interest, and as studies in literature and dramatic design they have both a literary and dramatic interest for historians and students. But for the playgoer the attempt of the modern producer to turn the stage into an up-to-date British museum is a challenge to undergo unlimited instruction or complete transformation. Though he is invited to the theatre to see a play, he is really offered an illustrated lecture on folklore, anthropology, civics, and Heaven knows what else. To take the Greek drama, for example, it is obvious that without prolonged and (perhaps expert) study, or without the possession of peculiar mental characteristics, no modern mind can be expected to realise the mystic whim which governed ancient Greece. It would be the same with plays based upon primitive African or Australian customs. The whole thing would be foreign to us. Even if we remove the mystic element from the Greek drama, the objection remains. There is the essential difference of the conception of life, of character, and especially of the purpose of the drama—

a purpose not capricious, but emerging from the spirit of the time—to be fully understood. It must not be overlooked that the great tragic dramas sprang from the need of the moment. The *Œdipus* had its origin in one set of circumstances. *King Lear* had another origin. Each had its own dramatic basis. The structure, emotion, representation, and interpretation of these dramas vary according to race, temperament and epoch. If, then, the Greek drama was produced by a peculiar set of circumstances, it follows that it cannot stir anyone who is not intimate with these circumstances, that is, produced by the same set of circumstances, or who possesses the same spirit that produced it. If it is true that the drama which came from ancient Greece, or China, or Shakespeare's England can be made to draw large audiences to-day, it is because producers like Max Reinhardt succeed in putting more of the human power of to-day into it, and leaving out the peculiar human power of the age to which it belongs. Each drama is, in fact, an up-to-date, not an original product ; an impurity, not a purity.

An excuse has been put forward for these representations, in the excuse that the dramas were written in great language and in an incomparable style. But so too were the great Indian epics. These, however, have not been represented on our modern stage. No intelligent person desires that they may be. And as for the language of Greek tragedies, of which but fragments remain, we have only translations to listen to.

Possibly the greatest advantage may be derived from the Greek dramas, not by seeing them acted, but by studying their form and content. This is an occupation for a certain class of modern authors and critics, but not for the general public, to whom technique should ever be a mystery. In their construction, the Greek dramas are exceptional examples of the co-ordinating power of the Greek dramatists. They have an extraordinary unity, every detail being subordinated to a single end. They were designed, and successfully, to leave a single effect on the mind of the Greek spectator, in whose ears one moral was left ringing. Like La Fontaine's fables, they were directed to point and to drive home a single idea. It might be the idea of sacrifice, or of patriotism, or of revenge, or of justice, or of peace ; but in any case it was a simple and a single idea.

The modern uncreative dramatist may then turn profitably to the Greek construction in its broadly simple and rhythmic side. But the creative author will leave Greece and its drama severely alone. He will shun the tyranny of the Greek influence as he would a plague, remembering that the advanced men of to-day do not build Greek temples, but temples of their own, having a form springing from the inner necessity of creation, not from the outer necessity of imitation. The creative dramatist has no need to revive Greek ideas, but he has every need to work his present material in a new and inspiring way. What the Greeks did and how they did it is no longer the business of such an author. And this is a fact for producers to understand. Classics are not the stuff upon which to breed vital authors. On the contrary, they are the food for re-incarnated souls. Strictly speaking, only re-incarnated souls should produce, interpret, and witness them. Managers ought accordingly to provide themselves with Shelleys for Greek plays, and Landors for Roman plays, while for German ones Carlyles would be needed, but not Carlyles with livers.

It should be mentioned that the movement in the theatre to-day is more Greek than Renaissance, owing to its feeling for unity. But the unity sought is not the same. For whereas the Greeks sought unity of unity and obtained it, the moderns are seeking unity of variety. For one thing, they are trying to get a unity of settings, every setting being subordinated to a dominant mood. All the settings are brought and bound together by mechanical processes, such as lighting, which were unknown both to the Greeks and Shakespeare and the Renaissants.

Possibly the search for unity is the great thing in the theatre just now. In any case, the present conceptions of unity and methods of attaining it are many and varied. The following table will show the variety of unity sought after :—

CONCEPTIONS OF UNITY.

Max Reinhardt	Emotional.
William Poel	Archæological.
Gordon Craig	Æsthetic.
Raymond Duncan	Greek beauty.
Granville Barker	Intellectual.
Russian Ballet	Physical.
Moscow Art Theatre	Cultural-æsthetic.
Munich Art Theatre	,,

METHODS OF ATTAINING IT.

Reinhardt	Big spaces. Elemental passions.
Poel	Scholastic-actuality.
Craig	Atmosphere.
Duncan	Movement.
Barker	Æsthetic-actuality.
Russian Ballet . . .	Colour (music, dance, decoration).
Moscow	Stylisation.
Munich	,,

The present failure to attain unity is due to the attempt to force it on plays that were not prepared for it.

II. RECENT DEVELOPMENTS IN ENGLAND

THERE are two recent events in London which deserve to be mentioned as having a direct bearing on the matter of this book. One is Mr Granville Barker's production of *A Winter's Tale* at the Savoy Theatre ; the other the exhibition at the Leicester Galleries of Mr Gordon Craig's "screen." The interest of Mr Barker's presentation of Shakespeare's play lies in the fact that it brings the modern stage a step nearer to the actual structure of the Elizabethan theatre than either Jocza Savits of Munich

or William Poel has done, and thus introduces the latest
tendencies of simplified staging in London and carries on
the tradition that Max Reinhardt has set up in Berlin.
This means that Mr Barker has at last come definitely into
line with those who are opposed to the showman-shop-
keeper representation of Shakespeare, and who, while re-
fusing to support the non-scenic extreme seen in the plain
curtain background of Mr Poel and Herr Savits, vigorously
attack the extravagances and excesses of modern scenery and
stage decoration. His view, as gathered from his production, appears to be that Shakespeare must come first, and
whatever scenery or " decoration," as he terms it, is essential to the right understanding of Shakespeare must come
after. This is reversing the conventional view that scenery
must come first. In a letter on his intentions to the
Daily Mail, Mr Barker told us he was led to detestation
of excessive scenery largely by the influence of Mr Craig.
The latter's " production twelve years ago of Mr Laurence
Housman's *Bethlehem* destroyed for him once and for all
any illusions he may have had as to the necessity of surrounding every performance of a play with the stuffy,
fussy, thick-bedaubed canvas which we are accustomed to
call stage scenery, while he opened my eyes to the possibilities of real beauty and dignity in stage decoration."
Further, he informed us that his path to the possibilities
of Elizabethan blank verse was pioneered by "Mr William
Poel—that other destructive idealist—who taught me how
swift and passionate a thing, how beautiful in its variety,
Elizabethan blank verse might be when tongues were
trained to speak and ears acute to hear it." Acting
under these influences, Mr Barker hastened to give
us a Shakespeare without cuts, without localities, and
without act-divisions, without scenery, except in the
nature of " decoration," played swiftly and spoken with
the skill of modern players accustomed to modern
dialogue, and lacking the essential sense of rhythm
which Shakespeare's lyricism demands.

In preparing his version of *A Winter's Tale* for the

stage, Mr Barker quite overlooked the lyrical element, of which it is full, and which alone gives the play coherence and uniformity. Apart from its lyricism, for which it was seemingly written, *A Winter's Tale* has but little to recommend it. Though "it belongs to the final period of Shakespeare's work," it is nevertheless one of Shakespeare's poorest plays. The plot is a mixed affair, being composed of several odd stories bearing little or no relation to each other. Apparently the plot was too short, seeing that Shakespeare has had to resort to padding. The padding is, however, the best part of the play. For in the Shepherd's affairs, the dances, the giving of flowers and favours, and the amusing doings of that Commedia dell' Arte figure, Autolycus, Shakespeare demonstrates how he could turn himself loose as lyrically and rhythmically as he pleased. At the time he wrote this play he was well under Marlowe's influence. He had learnt the latter's tricks of rhythmic prose, and knew how to avoid the "tinkling end rhyme" which Marlowe scorned. Besides being short of plots, Shakespeare was also short of characters, for those in *A Winter's Tale* are characters from other plays retouched up for the purpose. They are stock figures, shadows of their former selves. Even Perdita compares unfavourably with other types. To produce *A Winter's Tale* as a plot drama would therefore be disastrous, as former experiments in this direction have proved. Only the representation and interpretation of its lyricism could ensure success, since it is this " musical element " that makes a universal appeal.

Mr Barker goes for dramatic contrast. He reads *A Winter's Tale* as "a tragi-comedy," and treats it accordingly as a two-mood play. He places tragedy in Sicily and comedy in Bohemia, with Time between; founds the first part on jealousy, and gives it the atmosphere of an *Othello* tragedy; the second part on rusticity, and colours it with rural life.

Having made this contribution to the controversy of the structure of the play-action, he next proceeds to make

a contribution to the formation of the stage for the purpose of continuous performance. He takes the present
obsolete picture stage and divides it into three—a front,
middle, and back stage. The front or platform stage is
formed by covering in the orchestra with an apron stage ;
the middle stage is got by dividing off the front of the
main stage by means of two gold proscenium frames having
the appearance of one box fitting within another. Behind
the second frame is the back or main stage. These alternate stages preserve the structure of the action of the
play, just as they did in the Elizabethan playhouse. The
entrance to the apron stage is made through the stage
boxes. The entrance to the middle stage is made sometimes through the stage boxes and sometimes through
the prompt and opposite prompt openings ; while the
approach to the main stage is made from all entrances.
When this stage is being used Mr Barker allows his players
to walk through the frames into the picture, thus moving
them away from the audience instead of towards it. Mr
Craig expresses a similar idea of approaching the scene
from the audience in some of his sketches for the theatre
of the future, where he represents the player passing into
a scene apparently isolated from the audience. May be
it is a new way of solving the problem of intimacy, and
one peculiarly adapted to the illusion stage. If so, it is
of no use to the realistic stage, where the proper method
of solving the intimacy problem is either by the use of
the " flower path " through the auditorium or by extending the apron or platform stage into the auditorium as far
as it will go, thus allowing the players to mingle with the
audience. From the formation of the stage at the Savoy
Theatre it would appear as though Mr Barker is seeking
intimacy, and perhaps unity, but from the use of it his
chief aim would seem to be a variety of pictorial effects.

His aim concerning the function of the background
is clearer, although not altogether correct. He is rightly
convinced that the background or environment ought not
to out-act the actors, but he has not yet discovered that

the environment should not be merely decoration, something pretty added to the play and designed to conceal
the naked walls of the stage. It should be a vital
necessity to the play, essential to its inner life, and
moving and acting with it so as to give it the widest
expression. In Mr Barker's hands the background becomes the merest suggestion of the locality of the action
of the play.

Or I may put it another way. Mr Barker, aiming at
an original treatment, finds himself in a dilemma. He is
between the empty stage and the conventional scenery.
Now he does not want the empty stage, and he does not
want the conventional scenery. Finding himself in this
position, he effects a compromise. He does not set to
work and evolve an environment that springs naturally
from the fundamental note of the play—that is, the lyrical
note—but he adopts Mr Craig's method of putting a
screen round the stage. He does so with this difference,
that whereas Mr Craig frankly calls his screen a screen,
and sees to it that it screens off everything, walls, lighting apparatus, and so forth, Mr Barker calls his screen a
decoration, and makes it a part of the three bare walls.
He devises, in fact, a *décolleté* stage. In the first place,
he clears the stage and whitewashes the walls. In the
second, he calls in the aid of Mr Norman Wilkinson, who
proceeds to fill in the space thus obtained with a three-
sided frame of white classical columns shaped like
Cleopatra needles, and held together at the top by a
thin round rod. The rod is hung in the spaces between
the columns, with green-gold curtains which add a warmth
and a sumptuousness to the white walls and columns, and
form a pleasant background for the colours to move
against. In the centre of the stage he places a square of
gold settees. Almost all the scenes in Sicily are played
in this environment, which represents the Palace of
Leontes. For the Bohemian half of the play Mr
Wilkinson constructs a scene by removing the columns
and substituting a low thatched cottage or shepherd's hut,

having two chimneys and being surrounded by a wicker-
work fence. The cottage reaches right across the stage.
It is drab, with a green door centre. By means of this
cottage the decorator gets a local effect. But unfortunately the structure has no relation to the figures.
The two never come together. In fact, the characters
exist solely to advertise the cottage. Then the principle
of the newer unity in variety of stage-setting is not successfully applied. Indeed it is noticeable that there is
very little attempt to differentiate the colour of this scene
from that of the first scene. The drab of the cottage is
merely a variation of the white, and does not mark off the
joyous seductiveness of Bohemia from the fierce jealousy
of Sicily.

Nor do the colour and line of Mr Albert Rothenstein
—whom Mr Barker next calls in to design the costumes—
help materially to maintain the contrast which the producer has in mind. Throughout the colours are worked
on an arbitrary system of complementaries. They have
almost a black and white value. For instance, you find a
canary yellow having a relation to white, not to light or
real colour. The colours are, in fact, simply thrown on
in spots. They are very charming spots, ultra-refined,
purely æsthetic, and far removed from the very barbarous,
vital colours of the Russian Ballets. The fault of Mr
Rothenstein's colours is there is no vital reason for them.
Like the columns and curtains and cottage, they do not
spring from a vital necessity. When savages go to war
they smear themselves with red in order to terrify their
enemies. Their colour has a vital reason. When decorators
colour a scene of jealousy they should so smear it with
the colours of jealousy as to draw the audience into it.
But Mr Rothenstein smears his characters with colour
to create a sense of prettiness. In doing so he gives
expression to the prevailing æsthetic delusion. Nor have
the designs for the costumes any distinction; they are
merely copied from the Renaissance pattern-book of
Giulio Romano.

Mr Barker gives further practical shape to the principles of Elizabethan staging by the employment of drop curtains in the second frame. These curtains are painted with flat Japanese landscapes to represent exteriors, and with designs—leaf pattern, square and round, etc.—to represent interiors.

As in the attempt to ignore tradition much depends upon the lighting of the "scene," an elaborate and complicated system of lighting is devised. Mr Barker places in the centre of the first circle two box lights, violet in colour, this being the most powerful light ; round the front of the dress circle six cylinder lights, a light in each stage box, and four white arc lamps above and running across the centre of the main stage. By this arrangement footlights are done away with, and the effects of the differentiation as well as the mixing of colour obtained. Thus the violet and the yellow rays meeting on the stage produce warm shadows, while other effects are got by mixing the violet with yellow and white rays. The whole effect of the lighting is certainly a great improvement on that obtained by conventional methods, and suggests great possibilities in the future, when lighting is intelligently applied to the stage. But it is too much to hope that artificial lighting will ever produce the same effects as natural lighting, say, of the open-air Elizabethan theatre. It is noticeable that the best appreciations of Mr Barker's production came from the German press, one Berlin critic going so far as to remark that "the passion for new forms and for perfecting the scenic form of art has undergone a mighty awakening in England in recent years." The fact does not, however, appear to have been noticed by the London critics seeing that they offered a fairly violent and characteristic opposition to Mr Barker's application of the modern principle of the simplification of the stage for the production of Shakespeare's plays.

The representation of *Twelfth Night* followed closely on the lines of that of *A Winter's Tale*. The piece was done in curtains and a built scene (Olivia's Garden).

The stage was unaltered. The first two sections were narrower than the third. The first section or platform was formed by taking in the orchestral well and covering it with an apron stage. It had entrances or openings in the stage boxes. The second, or middle stage, was got by dividing off the main stage by two gold proscenium frames having the appearance of one box fitting in another. This stage had openings at the side. The third section was the large back or rear portion of the main stage. The back stage had entrances up right and left. The walls of the back stage were whitewashed as in *A Winter's Tale* to form a background for simple touches of colour, such as the golden throne and its pink canopy and columns, golden seats, and dark green yew trees. Messrs Shakespeare and Granville Barker were joint producers, and accordingly the play was acted without any cuts or waits whatever. Perhaps the most disconcerting thing about the production was that the characters and details of costume were reproduced with an unnecessary fidelity to the actualities. This was doubtless Mr Barker's fault, for although there is evidence that Shakespeare, in the old days, occasionally sought realisms, it is probably true that he depended largely on the imagination of the spectator. Shakespeare also demanded variety, and, had he been actually present at the Savoy Theatre, would have approved the variety got by Mr Barker by means of decorated curtains. At the same time, he would have demanded the new unity in variety, if, as some producers maintain, he had a forward-looking mind. Living to-day, he would be conscious that the movement in the theatre is more Greek than Renaissance because of its feeling for unity. Wherever there is this feeling, there may be traced a Greek influence. Take Shakespeare's plays, for instance, and we shall find that the plays which are most Greek are most unified, while those which are mere Renaissance lack unity and predominate in variety. *A Winter's Tale* may be quoted as an unsuccessful attempt to get unity. Now there is a tendency among some neo-Shakespearean reformers to add Greek unity to the Renaissance variety of setting, by taking a lot of scenes, such as a Shakespearean play contains, and binding them together with curtains. Such curtains are designed to express and sustain the predominant motive of the play. For instance, if the play is *Romeo and Juliet,* then the passionate love-motive would be seen running through all the lines and colours of the curtains, in conflict with the opposition motives (whatever they may be). Just as the Russian decorators have introduced the motive into the act-drop, curtains and background of the Russian Ballets, so a Shakespearean decorator here and there is seeking to introduce it to the Shakespearean curtain and screen scenes. But Mr Barker does not go as far as this. He makes an arbitrary use of curtains. Under his direction they are designed merely to harmonise with the costumes of the players, or perhaps to express a mental movement ; they are not bound together by a leading motive, as they should be in order to avoid the distraction set up by unrelated intervals in stage settings. Thus the first curtain, with its landscape and houses painted in the flat on a yellow ground, has no relation to the second curtain, with its composition in pinks, greens, yellows, and blues. Nor has the zig-zag curtain any relation to those that preceded and followed it. What is needed is a rhythmical unity of action, speech decoration, and lighting. The dialogue of the leading character affords a key to the rhythm of the scene. If it is a zig-zag rhythm, that is, full of a combative spirit, then everything in the scene should express it ; if a flowing rhythm, that is, of a peaceful character, then the scene should have this character. The deliberate amplifications of curtain surfaces designed to indicate the passage of a great emotion or passion, throughout a play, is the principle on which the Shakespearean decorator should work.

This advance should undoubtedly be made in the treatment of Shakespeare on the English stage, and it is not unreasonable to suppose that it will be made as soon as decorators are acquainted with its importance and are encouraged to co-operate in the work of the theatre. That more than one decorator is accessible to the new ideas is incontestible. After some talks with Mr Alfred Wolmark, an English painter of great ability, I had the satisfaction of seeing him set to work to design a set of Shakespearean curtains having the requisite element of unity in variety. These curtains were sent to an exhibition of theatrical devices, held at Warsaw, where they awakened considerable interest ; they stirred up the general opinion among people who are instinctively decorators, that Mr Wolmark is a decorator with the strength and colour vision peculiarly suited to the work of the theatre. This agrees with my own view that, if he once enters the theatre, he has a big career before him.

It should be mentioned that the lighting of the *Twelfth Night* was similar to that of *A Winter's Tale*, being obtained by means of projectors, lenses, coloured lights from tinted globes, etc.

To the attempt to solve the problem of stage lighting is largely due the appearance of Mr Gordon Craig's novelty—the latest portable screen. The arrival of the screen means that Mr Craig has thrown overboard his curtained background, and will doubtless cease to lament the fact that the German theatres have been borrowing it for some considerable time past. He has now got a contrivance entirely different from any stage device that Max Reinhardt employs, and having thus, as it were, come into a scenic kingdom of his own, will no longer prefer charges against more or less harmless persons. At the exhibition at the Leicester Galleries it was seen that the new device, which Mr Craig maintains is wholly new and wholly his own, consists of a grey portable jointed screen to be used together with some cylinders, cubes, squares, rostrums, and some white and coloured limelights. Here Mr Craig demonstrated in seven little scenes how these "bricks" are put together to form backgrounds. The plain wooden screen is adaptable to any stage. It is made to reach above the proscenium, and thus not only serves to represent the scene, but to mask in anything that the audience is not required to see, such, for instance, as the lighting apparatus. Beyond this it can be folded to form interior and exterior settings, suggesting battlements, ramparts, pillars, walls, and so on, according to the need of the drama. It can also be folded so that the light may fall at the desired points between the folds, being worked from the top, side, back, front, as the case may be. As a clue to Mr Craig's intentions regarding the setting of the scenes, let me give a description or two of the arrangements at the Leicester Galleries. Supposing a " mad " scene for Ophelia is required. All that the stage-manager or carpenter has to do is to run the screen round the stage in a semicircle, place a cylindrical column in the centre of the stage with a number of square columns colonnading round it, sprinkle a yellow light on either side at the back of the centre column, and the scene with its classical architectural features is ready to receive Ophelia. Another unaccustomed setting is got by arranging the screen to form an inverted V, with two long passages running off at left angles, middle and up stage, and by placing a huge square column in the centre of the V. This scene was lighted by a violet light (representing daylight) placed off and flooding the middle passage, and by a yellow light off, and flooding the top passage. The yellow light was so arranged as to be thrown right across and reflected on the wall right, thus filling two-thirds of the upper space. Further, the yellow ray of light coming from the upper passage and received on the wall right met the violet ray coming from the middle passage, in the space in front of the centre column, thus tending to give the column height and to create a seductive effect. Mr Craig plays with his lights from these two points in the endeavour to obtain the effects he is after. If a tragic mood is sought, doubtless he would flood the scene from these points

with reds ; if a nun coming from a cloister, he would keep
the scene white. So by a change of light he secures a
change of mood or change of time—day or night, summer
or winter, as the case may be. But of course the
architectural " environment " always remains the same. It
was remarked by the *Times* critic when dealing with the
lighting of these scenes that " a change of light makes a
change of scene." How can a change of light alter a
series of sets which in build and fitment are all alike ?
Though the V-shaped scene is very ingenious, yet it is not
without serious faults, both from the point of view of
the actor and the spectator. How the actor is to make
any intelligent use of the scene with its high column
blocking up the centre of the stage is a question which
even Mr Craig might find a difficulty in answering.
Another obvious question is, How are the spectators to
view such a scene as this as a whole, rather than in
sections ? How can a person on the right-hand side of
the theatre see what is happening in the opening and
space behind the left of the column ? The spectators are
obliged to view the scene from different angles. Thus a
spectator seated right would have the upper opening left
and a part of the space up stage cut off. The spectator
seated centre would have the whole of the space up stage
cut off, while the spectator right could see neither the
lower left passage nor an angle of the space up stage. In
short, it is apparent to anyone who views this scene from
all parts of the house, right, centre, left, stalls, pit, boxes,
circles, and gallery, that the problem of sight line is
largely increased instead of being diminished, and thereby
a great deal of unnecessary friction is set up in the mind
of the audience.

Returning to the building of the scenes, another unconventional effect is obtained by stretching the screen
right across the stage near the footlights, leaving it partly
folded into copper-colour zig-zags in the centre, with
a plain part at each end in warm grey. The screen is
lighted by a single ray of light, a double effect being

obtained by throwing the light on one side of the zig-zag sections. Thus the copper on one side becomes old gold, while the copper on the other side turns to violet. In another instance the screen is utilised to form a battlement. It is drawn across the stage to represent the exterior of a castle wall. The centre opening of the wall is occupied by a tall flight of steps reaching up to a deep blue sky. At the bottom of the steps to the right is a complementary rose-colour light. In the colouring of all these scenes it is noticeable that Mr Craig works in complementaries. Another simple arrangement is made by throwing the screen right across the stage and folding it so as to suggest the unbroken exterior of a castle wall.

The value of Mr Craig's device, as a contribution to the solution of the scene problem, is doubtful. It certainly does not solve the new problem of unity in variety, seeing that the screen is one thing and the figures that move against it are another. Mr Craig's dominant idea, it seems, is movement, and the screen is intended as a medium for emphasising this movement. But the " scene " obtained by its aid is not really a " scene." It is simply " an environment of light and shadow." The inference from this is that the lighting is the " scene," and the only unity attained is that of atmosphere. The screen is simply an instrument for receiving the light. It has no relation to the characters of the play and does not spring from the inward necessity of these characters. It is an annexe to a fully expressed movement and might be dispensed with altogether if the bare walls of the theatre could be prepared to receive the necessary lighting. As a device in stage mechanics it is ingenious, but considered in relation to the characters of a play it is not dramatic but æsthetic.

Moreover, it has no distinct economic value, seeing that before a touring company could travel the provinces with it, it would be necessary for every provincial theatre visited to have a special lighting plant, and an intelligent and expensive staff of limelight men and stage-hands. The most that can be said for it is that it is a break with the inventor's earlier tradition. Herein Mr Craig claims to make an advance upon himself, though the advance is not apparent. Looking at the screen settings, the designs for *Hamlet* and other scenes, and those for costumes and masks, the intelligent observer inquires, What does one get towards a theatre of the future? The answer is nothing vital. In all these things there is only a bloodless cloistered æstheticism. They reveal that Mr Craig is obsessed by the idea that the purpose of drama is the representation of the beauty of beauty, not the beauty of truth ; of ancient beauty by means of æsthetic movement, not present beauty by means of the unfolding of personality. They show that he has arrived at the surface, where he is trying to gild a classical cause. His screen and designs do not open a door upon the future, but upon the past. The whole thing is Greek to the core, and bad Greek. In fact, the smell of Greece is so strong as to obscure whatever little modern light Mr Craig has undoubtedly obtained in other directions. He has both gone beyond the Greeks and failed to realise the best that was in the Greeks. In short, Mr Craig has arrived at a point where he creates a desire in the spectator to look on, but never a desire to participate. The latter is the precious secret which vital minds alone possess.

Still, if Mr Craig's present line of research is not likely to assist the theatre in one way, it may do so in another. It seems to foreshadow the coming of the much needed art-drama critic.

III. GERMAN INFLUENCES ON ENGLISH DEVELOPMENT

As may be gathered from the chapter on the "Influences on Max Reinhardt's Development," the modern Repertory Theatre movement in England was largely initiated by

Germany. But Germany, although the pioneer of the modern movement, was not the first in the repertory field. Historically, the movement began with the Commedia dell' Arte. The name was given to a group of creative players who broke away from the dead formalism of the Italian theatre of the sixteenth century, and succeeded in giving the drama a new expression through freedom, creativeness, and spontaneity. These actors were so intelligent that, given a creative scenario, they could fill in its general design while communicating themselves individually to the spectator. They created their own form of expression instead of having it created for them, as is now the custom. Here was a group which appealed to the individual and collective intelligence, and which gave birth to the greatest repertory movement. In the course of time these vagrant revolutionists invaded all Europe, firing many a creative group as they went. They visited Elizabethan England, where English authors (Shakespeare among them) and players came under their direct influence. About the beginning of the seventeenth century many English comedians found their way to the German Royal Courts, and were retained by the German princes. Thus was founded the Endowed Repertory Theatre of Germany. In time this endowed system began to spread, and by the end of the eighteenth century it was firmly established in Germany. Thereafter it swept forward and was moulded in turn by Schiller, Goethe, the Saxe-Meiningen Court Company, the Freien Bühne, Brahm, Ibsen, Reinhardt, and the Court, State, Municipal, People's, and Private Endowed Theatre, and coloured by Wagnerian, Russian, Scandinavian and English artistic influences. So it swept on, adopting many and varied reforms—naturalistic, realistic, symbolic—of stage-crowds, of acting, of ensemble, of speech, of intimacy, and so forth. With the establishment of the Freien Bühne the movement crossed to England.

It came in response to a demand for the reform of the English Theatre. Some persons had seen it worked to advantage in Germany, while others were growing tired of the two principal abuses by which the English theatre was tyrannised. One abuse was the star-system or system of self-aggrandisement which, starting with the actor-manager, had passed through Kean, Phelps, Irving, and had reached its culmination in the group of private managers who controlled and still control their own theatres. The other abuse was the commercial system initiated by speculators, syndicates, and capitalists, American and other, headed by Charles Frohman. Springing up and running parallel with these were the beginnings of an economic and intellectual movement in the theatre, intended to act as a disinfectant to the said abuses. Such were found in the People's Stage Societies founded by Watts, Morris, and other artistic and social reformers, and in the establishment of small private societies. It was not, however, till the early 'nineties that the first definite step towards an organised movement in this country, aiming to bring cultural reform into the theatre, was taken. In 1891 Mr J. T. Grein started the Independent Theatre, and laid the foundation of the present literary and moral theatre in England. The sub-title of this theatre might appropriately have been the Entente Cordiale Theatre, seeing that it aimed not only to provide an open door for English plays of an independent character, but to bring foreign plays of the same character before the free and independent playgoer. After struggling along for six years, supported by a thin membership, never reaching two hundred, and by a slender income never exceeding £400, it finally succumbed, having contributed to the English stage the first batch of international literary authors, and very little by way of acting or scenic reform. The Independent Theatre was followed in 1897 by the Stage Society (later rechristened the Incorporated Stage Society), which was founded on similar lines to that of the Independent Theatre, namely, for the purpose of providing a theatre to which authors of any country might go when they had anything to say which they could not say in the conventional theatre. In this respect it strongly resembled the new so-called advanced journals which are springing up to-day, and which serve as a dust-hole for literary and moral outpouring—some of it very good and some of it very bad. The Stage Society dust-hole has suffered from a glut of mixed goods. The Society was, I believe, initiated by Mr Frederick Whelen, a gentleman possessing the requisite business capacity and dramatic enthusiasm for launching a scheme of the sort. Assisted by others equally enthusiastic, especially by members of the dramatic profession, he organised it into being, and it burst forth in all its youthful promise at the Royalty Theatre, opening with Mr Bernard Shaw's *You Never Can Tell*. It is not clear whether the play was chosen because its title seems to suggest the doubtful career of the Society. With the incorporation of the Society in 1904, its objects were defined as follows : " To promote and encourage dramatic art ; to serve as an experimental theatre ; to provide such an organisation as shall be capable of dealing with any opportunities that may present themselves or be created for the permanent establishment in London of a Repertory Theatre." The activities of this Stage Society have continued to the present day, but the London Repertory Theatre is as far off as ever. (It is true that all the London theatres combined served to form a Repertory Theatre, of a sort.) These activities have been mainly devoted to the exploitation of original home and foreign produce. They have not included any attempt to organise the theatre. From the beginning the Society has been homeless, and without an organised body of players. It has, in fact, given scratch performances of classical and contemporary (some of them banned) plays interpreted by all sorts and conditions of players, having nothing in common but a desire to make the most of their separate parts. In short, its main characteristic has been variety without unity.

For the first attempt to organise the theatre on a

clearly defined ground we must turn to the Court Theatre while under the joint management of Messrs Vedrenne and Barker from 1904 to 1907. In the activities of this theatre we see the first attempt in London to establish a repertory theatre on a combined intellectual and commercial basis, just as the Deutsches Theater is a successful attempt to run a theatre on commercial and artistic lines. Beyond the attempt to demonstrate the practicability of breaking away from the artistically disastrous long-run system and substituting a short-run system designed to please playgoer, players, and box-office alike, there was the attempt to establish an experimental theatre wherein experiments could be made in reforms that had long been making their way to this country from Germany and elsewhere. Among the reforms were those of staging plays, acting and speech. In this way the new ideas of simplified environment, crowd effects, ensemble, and uniformity of diction were introduced to London and began to make themselves felt. The result of the three years' work was, from the point of view of the promoters, highly satisfactory. Apparently it stimulated imitation in all directions. For a time London was threatened with an epidemic of repertory theatres run on the Court lines, as the movement spread from West-end theatre to theatre, from the Adelphi under Mr Otho Stuart's management, to the Criterion under Mr Grant Allen's management, to His Majesty's Theatre, where it contrived to follow Mr Whelen. This tendency to spread was further promoted by Messrs Vedrenne and Barker themselves, who, at the height of their Court Theatre management, moved to the Savoy Theatre. The change of house, however, proved a failure. Unable to meet the increased expense, the partnership came to an end in 1907. Thereafter the repertory "theatre" began to accompany Mr Barker from place to place, appearing in turn at the Queen's, Duke of York's, Little, and Kingsway Theatres. At the Duke of York's Theatre another determined attempt was made to establish the London movement on a lasting basis. Mr Barker, no doubt aided by Sir J. M. Barrie, obtained the assistance of Mr Charles Frohman. A powerful body of authors and a strong stock company were formed. Mr Frohman lent his theatre, Sir J. M. Barrie guaranteed the funds, and with the press beating the big drum, the first season was inaugurated. The season lasted for seventeen weeks, during which time one hundred and seventeen performances of ten plays were given. At the end of the first season the experiment collapsed. Mr Frohman retired, and the patience and capital of other enthusiasts being exhausted, the Duke of York's Repertory Theatre came to an end. The London movement has never recovered from this set-back.

If one feels assured that the aforementioned Repertory Theatre movement in London is made of German shreds and leavings of the past, one also feels that without these ready-made traditions it might be worse off than it is, with an impulse or two less than it possesses. The introduction of these traditions, partly by the Stage Society and more fully by the Court Theatre management, does enable us to experience to-day a sensation of animation running through the country, through cob-webby theatres, stimulated directors, authors, players, and public. Everywhere in the provinces, as well as in the Colonies, repertory theatres are springing up, bringing forth every possible form of local, intellectual, and moral gospel. The first local movement in the English provinces—a movement sworn to carry on the London tradition — was initiated by Miss A. E. F. Horniman, who made a start at Manchester in 1908. Long previous to this, however, Miss Horniman helped to pioneer the movement first in London and thereafter in Dublin. Her first enterprise was the discovery and exploitation of Mr Bernard Shaw, and the financial support of a season at the Avenue Theatre, London. Thereafter, ten years later, she came to the

rescue of Ireland, assisted the Irish Literary movement, took the Abbey Theatre, Dublin, subsidised that
national speciality, the Irish Theatre Society, and,
generally speaking, set the Repertory Theatre movement
on its legs. Three years later she purchased the Gaiety
Theatre, Manchester, which, under her direction, became
an understudy of the Vedrenne-Barker enterprise in
London. The task she had outlined was not difficult of
fulfilment. During the last twenty years there has been
a steady growth and increase of private dramatic societies
—debating, propaganda, and other—not only in London,
but in all the provincial cities. Local groups of enthusiastic playgoers—play, rehearsal clubs, societies, etc.—
were thus formed who eagerly awaited the establishment
of a central institution that should give widest expression
to their burning ideals. In Manchester these ideals had
been fed by local enterprises, such as those of Charles
Calvert, Michael Flanagan, and Robert Courtneidge.
Consequently when Miss Horniman set out to provide
Manchester with an organised theatre, there was the fairly
" advanced " playgoer waiting to receive her and fully
prepared to co-operate in promoting the objects of her
undertakings. These objects were :

To provide Manchester with (1) a Repertory Theatre,
with a regular change of programme, not wedded to any
one school of dramatists, but thoroughly catholic, em-
bracing the finest writings of the best authors of all ages,
and with an especially wide-open door to present-day
British writers, who will not now need to sigh in vain
for a hearing, provided only that they have something to
say worth listening to and say it in an interesting and
original manner. (2) A permanent Manchester Stock
Company of picked front-rank actors. (3) Efficient production. (4) Popular prices.

The life of the theatre is still assured. Its repertory
has been a long and varied one, including classical and
modern plays. It has paid special attention to ensemble
acting, and unearthed some native talent by way of

authors. Miss Horniman has apparently conquered Manchester in a literary and moral way, and now it is pleasant to see her contemplating a descent upon London.

Not much need be said concerning the spread of the Repertory Theatre movement in other directions. As I have stated, Dublin took the infection before Manchester, and the Irish National Theatre was the result, but not before the usual small beginnings had been made. These beginnings at an intellectual theatre were initiated by W. B. Yeats and others in a small hall in Dublin in 1899. Thence emerged the " school " of Irish authors, which was afterwards to be so closely associated with the Abbey Theatre when it entered upon its intellectual career in 1904. A further step in this national movement was taken when Mr W. G. Fay organised a company of exclusively Irish players in 1902. In this way the Irish National Theatre was founded and an impetus given in Ireland to the " new " Repertory Theatre traditions. The sight of Dublin organising its literary theatre and putting it in working order for the use of its own playwrights stirred up other centres, and led more than one—Ulster among them—to follow the fashion in literary theatres and groups of local writers and authors.

Following Manchester came Glasgow with its Citizen's Theatre in 1909. In the Citizen's Theatre we have a break from the privately endowed to the publicly owned theatre —such as Germany possesses in abundance. In the case of the Glasgow Theatre, the concern was floated as a company with a nominal capital of £3000, of which 2000 shares of £1 each were offered for sale. The objects of the company were stated as follows :

" 1. To establish in Glasgow a Repertory Theatre which will afford playgoers and those interested in the drama an opportunity of witnessing such plays as are rarely presented under the present touring company system ;

" 2. To organise a Stock Company of first-class actors

and actresses for the adequate representation of such plays ;

" 3. To conduct the business of theatrical managers and play producers in Glasgow and other places so as to stimulate a popular interest in the more cultured, important, and permanent forms of dramatic art ; and

" 4. To encourage the initiation and development of a purely Scottish drama by providing a stage and an acting company which will be peculiarly adapted for the production of plays national in character, written by Scottish men and women of letters."

These objects disclose that the Glasgow Repertory Theatre is designed to be a literary and moral theatre, aiming to express Glasgow through its own authors and to foster the latest principles of interpretation, naturalistic and realistic.

With the foundation of the Liverpool Repertory Theatre in 1911 we reach a new departure and a more hopeful stage of the Repertory Theatre movement. Hitherto the provincial branch of the repertory movement had occupied itself almost solely with the new problems of interpretation, such as ensemble and psychological acting, but with the coming of the Liverpool Theatre a period of experiment with the problems of representation is inaugurated, and, as I have mentioned in another chapter, Mr Basil Dean begins to inquire into reforms in staging, lighting, and decoration with which Max Reinhardt is actively engaged at Berlin. To these reforms he proposes to add some of his own, and to-day being invited to co-operate in the foundation of Birmingham's Repertory Theatre, he commences to set that city expanding along desirable artistic lines.

It is not too much to hope that Mr Dean's initiative may lead to the spread of the artistic-commercial Repertory Theatre in the English provinces, and that Sheffield, Leeds, and Bristol may organise their new theatres on really advanced lines. London tried its hand at something of the kind, but as usual could make nothing

lasting of an advanced movement. The attempt of the
Haymarket and Little Theatres to organise themselves
artistically into being has been a failure, as yet. Appended
is a chronological table of the intellectual movement in the
German Theatre and the modern corresponding one in
the English Theatre.

17th English comedians reach German Courts and Endowed Theatre, and
cent.   repertory system established.

19th State and Subsidised Theatre   Reform of theatre architecture.
cent.   Movement

20th The Progressive Municipal   Reform acting = ensemble.
cent.   Theatre (Düsseldorf)   „   drama = { literary.
                                                      { symbolic.
18th–19th Schiller   „   { drama = { cultural.
cent.   Goethe   „   { theatre = intimate. { naturalistic.

19th Saxe-Meiningen Co.   „   { acting { ensemble.
cent.   {   { crowds.
                                          { speech = natural.
                                          { scenery = historical accu-
                                                      racy.

19th Wagner   { staging = highly realistic.
cent.   { production = syntho-æsthetic.

19th Savits)
cent. |— Munich   staging = simplified (New Shakespearean).
20th Kilian)
cent.

19th Freien Bühne   Reform { acting = natural.
cent.   { drama = literary.

19th Otto Brahm = Psychologi- Reinhardt
cent.   cal acting. " Brille " { Naturalism.
                   Ensemble.   { Intimacy.
                   Repertory.
                                " Schall und Rauch " Realism.
20th Reinhardt.   Kleines Theater   Symbolism.
cent.   { Syntho-
                                Neues Theater   {   æstheticism.

                                                     (Ensemble.
                                                     | Repertory.
                                                     | Theatre
                                Deutsches Theater   {   Organisation.
                                Kammerspielhaus | The Spectacle
                                                     (Play.

1891. Independent Theatre . . . (J. T. Grein).
1894. Avenue Theatre . . . . (Miss Horniman).
1899. Stage Society . . . . . (Frederick Whelen).
1904. Court Theatre . . . . (Vedrenne and Barker).

Criterion Theatre . . . . (Grant Allen).
Adelphi Theatre . . . . (Otho Stuart)
Kingsway Theatre . . . . (Lena Ashwell).
Savoy Theatre . . . . . (Vedrenne and Barker).
Queen's Theatre . . . . (Vedrenne and Barker).
His Majesty's Theatre (Afternoon) . (Whelen and Dana).
Royalty Theatre . . . . (Vedrenne and Edie).
1884. Growth of private debating societies, ⎫ Playgoers' Club, O.P. Club,
to   play-producing, rehearsal clubs, etc. ⎬ Dramatic Debaters,
1910.   ⎭ Gallery First Nighters, etc.

Provincial Repertory Theatres, focussing activities of private societies :—

1899. Irish Literary Movement . . . (Yeats).
1904. Irish National Theatre . . . (Yeats and Miss Horniman).
1907. Manchester Literary Theatre . . (Miss Horniman).
1909. Glasgow Literary Theatre . . (Alfred Waring).
1911. Liverpool Repertory Theatre . . (Basil Dean).

Colonial Repertory Theatres :—

Adelaide Literary Theatre . . (Bryceson Treharne).
Sydney Stage Society.
Melbourne Repertory Theatre . . (Gregan M'Mahon).

Attempt to found an artistic Repertory Theatre in London :—

Haymarket Theatre . . . . (Herbert Trench).
Little Theatre . . . . (Gertrude Kingston).

Growth of propagandist play societies :—

1907. The Play Actors.
1911. The New Players, etc.
1911. Foundation of the Cabaret Theatre, "The Golden Calf."

Other movements contributing to the dramatic movement. Foreign enterprises of comparative and educational value :—

German Theatre in London.
French Theatre in London.
Japanese Players.
Sicilian Players.

English enterprises :—

Shakespeare Festival . . . (Tree, Benson).
Folk Song and Dance Revival . . (Cecil Sharp, Mary Neal).
Morality Play Revival . . . (Poel).
Pageant Plays . . . . (Louis Parker).
Village Drama Movement . . (M'Evoy, The Devonshire Players).
Music Hall Enterprise . . . (Coliseum, Palace Theatre).

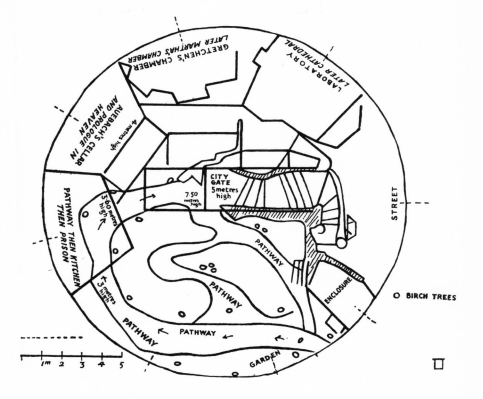

LATER MARTHA'S CHAMBER
GRETCHEN'S CHAMBER
LABORATORY
LATER CATHEDRAL

AUERBACH'S CELLAR
AND PROLOGUE IN
HEAVEN

4 metres high

PATHWAY THEN KITCHEN
THEN PRISON

3.50 metres
high

3 metres
high

CITY
GATE
5 metres
high

7.50
metres
high

PATHWAY

STREET

ENCLOSURE

PATHWAY

PATHWAY

PATHWAY

PATHWAY

GARDEN

O BIRCH TREES

1m 2 3 4 5

Ground-plan of the "Faust I" Setting on
the Revolving Stage at the Deutches Theatre

[*Sketch by Machinery Inspector, R. Dworsky*

IV. EXPLANATION OF THE REVOLVING STAGE SET FOR A REPRESENTATION OF THE FIRST PART OF *FAUST*

IN order to judge the advantages and disadvantages which the revolving stage offers to the producer of drama with a great variety of scenes, it is necessary to consider it in relation to various productions worked out according to a number of plans. The plan reproduced in this book gives, nevertheless, a sufficiently definite idea of the complication of the mechanism and different resources of the system.

In the installation of the first part of *Faust* at the Deutsches Theater, Berlin, the revolving stage is utilised both in its upper and lower part. Thus the Prologue commences in Heaven, in a scene built on the arch of the Cave of Auerbach, twelve feet above the stage. For the second scene the revolving stage is turned one quarter of its circuit and the Laboratory of Dr Faustus appears. Another quarter of turn and the Promenade faces the footlights. The part of the Promenade situated before the City gate represents an undulating ground rising gradually fifteen feet till it reaches the gate. Behind this gate, hidden from the eyes of the spectators, is a construction in iron, twenty feet high, which can contain sixty men. This cage is just the height of the mountain upon which the Walpurgis Night scene will take place. The structure, moreover, contains, at a height of ten feet, several spaces designed to represent the Sorcerer's Kitchen, later the Prison and the Cave of Auerbach. A roadway passes to the left of the scene leading to stone steps by which access is gained to the top of the iron structure.

The play commences with the following sets :—The Prologue in Heaven ; the Laboratory ; the Promenade ; Marguerite's Chamber ; the Enclosure.

After the first interval, the Garden takes the place of the Promenade, the Prison replaces the Kitchen, the

Laboratory is replaced by the Church, and Marguerite's Chamber by that of Martha. The scene of the second act is prepared by removing the accessories of the Roadway, the Chamber of Marguerite, the Church, the Enclosure, and completing with rocks and trees the ground prepared for the Walpurgis Night.

V. TABLE OF PRODUCTIONS

Taken from *Das Deutsche Theater*, *Berlin*, and supplemented by a list supplied by Mr Siegfried Jacobsohn.

KLEINES THEATER   NEUES THEATER

1902

Aug. 19. Opening performance. Three one-act plays by Fel. Schneider, Gustav Wied, Max Dreyer, already played 1901–2 in "Schall und Rauch."

Sept. 25. *Serenissimus*, by Leo Feld.

Oct. 13. *Rausch* (*Intoxication*), by Strindberg.

Oct. 29. *Ackermann*, by Felix Holländer and Lothar Schmidt.

Nov. 15. *Salome*, by Oscar Wilde.

The Importance of Being Earnest, by Oscar Wilde.

Both plays in the afternoon before an invited audience.

Dec. 17. *Erdgeist*, by Frank Wedekind.

1903

Jan. 16. *Erdgeist*, 25th performance.

Jan. 23. *The Lower Depths*, by Maxim Gorki.

KLEINES THEATER

1903

Feb. 22. (Matinee, private performance for the Lessing Society) *Salome*, by Oscar Wilde.

April 12. Afternoon, *Serenissimus-Zwischenspiele* (aus "Schall und Rauch"), 300th performance.

June 23. *The Lower Depths*, 150th performance.
July 15. End of season.
Aug. 1. Beginning of new season.

Oct. 14. *The Lower Depths*, 250th performance.

NEUES THEATER

1903

Feb. 25. *Die Lokalbahn*, by Ludwig Thoma.
Mar. 19. *Die Kreuzelschreiber*, by Ludwig Anzengruber.
April 3. *Pelleas und Melisande*, by Maurice Maeterlinck.

May 1. *Pelleas und Melisande*, 25th performance.
May 15, till the end of the month. Han Nieses' Company from the Josefstadt Theatre, Vienna.

Aug. 16. Beginning of new season : *Pelleas und Melisande*.
Aug. 25. *Doppelselbstmord*, by Ludwig Anzengruber.
Sept. 4. *A Woman of No Importance*, by Oscar Wilde.
Sept. 18. *Pelleas und Melisande*, 50th performance.
Sept. 29. *Salome*, by Oscar Wilde.
Sept. 30. *Der Kammersänger*, by Frank Wedekind.

KLEINES THEATER

1903

Oct. 16. *The Raven*, by Henri Becque.
Oct. 30. *Elektra*, by Hugo von Hofmannsthal.

Dec. 31. *Untersich*, by Hermann Bahr.

1904

Jan. 13. *The Lower Depths*, 300th performance.

Jan. 16. *Die Doppelgänger-Komödie*, by Adolf Paul.
Feb. 9. *Elektra*, 50th performance.

Feb. 27. *Mutter Landstrasse*, by Wilhelm Schmidtbonn.

NEUES THEATER

1903

Nov. 24. *Logik des Herzens*, by Robert de Flers and G. de Caillavet.
Nov. 27. *So ist das Leben*, by Frank Wedekind.
Dec. 9. *Fruits of Enlightenment*, by Leo Tolstoi.
Dec. 19. *Der Strom*, by Max Halbe.

1904

Jan. 5. *Salome*, 75th performance.

Jan. 14. *Minna von Barnhelm*, by G. E. Lessing.

Feb. 10. *Sister Beatrice*, by Maurice Maeterlinck.
    The Man of Destiny, by Bernard Shaw.
Feb. 19. *Medea*, by Euripides.

Mar. 3. *Candida*, by Bernard Shaw.

KLEINES THEATER

1904

Mar. 12. *Des Pastors Rieke,* by Erich Schlaikjer.

April 6. *Märtyrer,* by Georg Reicke.

May 10. *Miss Julia,* by August Strindberg.

July 15. End of season.
Aug. 1. Beginning of season.
Aug. 14. *The Lower Depths,* 400th performance.

Nov. 9. *Elektra,* 75th performance.

Nov. 22. *Der grüne Kakadu,* by Arthur Schnitzler.
  Der tapfere Cassian, by Arthur Schnitzler.
Dec. 8. *Die stillen Stuben,* by Sven Lange.

NEUES THEATER

1904

Mar. 19. *Königsrecht,* by W. A. Paap.

April 12. *Koketterie,* by Raoul Auernheimer.
April 22. *Kabale und Liebe,* by F. Schiller.

May 18. *Einen Jux will er sich machen,* by Nestroy.
July 15. End of season.
Aug. 1. Beginning of season.

Sept. 14. *Salome,* 100th performance.
Sept. 23. *Erdgeist* (reproduction). Prologue by Frank Wedekind.
Oct. 7. *The Pretenders,* by Henrik Ibsen.
Oct. 21. *The Merry Wives of Windsor,* by Shakespeare.

Nov. 15. *Die Morgenröte,* by Josef Ruederer.

Dec. 23. *Der Graf von Charolais,* by Richard Beer-Hofmann.

KLEINES THEATER

1904

Dec. 30. *Die Neuvermählten*, by Björnstjerne Björnson.
Dec. 31. *Abschiedssouper*, by Arthur Schnitzler.

1905

Feb. 4. *Angele*, by Otto Erich Hartleben.
  Abschied vom Regiment, by Otto Erich Hartleben.
Feb. 12. *The Bear*, by Anton Tschechow.
Mar. 10. *Sanna*, by Hermann Bahr.

April. 28. *Rosmersholm*, by Henrik Ibsen.

May 5. *The Lower Depths*, 500th performance.

July 7. *Vater Riekmann*, by Karl Strecker.
July 15. End of season.
Aug. 1. Beginning of season.

Aug. 31. Last performance under Reinhardt's management at the Kleines Theater.

NEUES THEATER

1905

Jan. 31. *A Midsummer Night's Dream*, by Shakespeare.
Feb. 1. *Graf von Charolais*, 25th performance.

Mar. 31. *Meta Konegen*, by Hermann Stehr.

April 30. *A Midsummer Night's Dream*, 75th performance.

May 11. End of season.

Aug. 16. Beginning of season.

Oct. 12. *A Midsummer Night's Dream*, 150th performance.

DEUTSCHES THEATER	NEUES THEATER
1905	**1905**

Oct. 19. Opening performance. *Käthchen v. Heilbronn*, by Heinrich von Kleist.

Nov. 9. *The Merchant of Venice*, by Shakespeare.

Nov. 25. *A Midsummer Night's Dream*, 150th performance.

Dec. 30. *Liebesleute*, by Maurice Donnay.

1906	**1906**

Jan. 3. *The Merchant of Venice*, 50th performance.

Jan. 12. *A Florentine Tragedy*, by Oscar Wilde.

　The Well of the Saints, by J. M. Synge.

　Der Herr Kommissär, by Georges Courteline.

Feb. 2. *Œdipus und die Sphinx*, by Hugo von Hofmannsthal.

Mar. 16. *Boubouroche*, by Georges Courteline.

　(Originally produced, 5th April 1902, by " Schall und Rauch.")

Mar. 28. *The Merchant of Venice*, 100th performance.

Mar. 31. *Cæsar and Cleopatra*, by Bernard Shaw.

April 12. *Œdipus*, 25th performance.

April 25. *Die Mitschuldigen*, by Goethe.

　Tartufe, by Molière.

May 11. *Orpheus in the Underground*, by Cremieux-Pserhofer. Music by Offenbach.

DEUTSCHES THEATER

1906

June 30. End of season.

Aug. 23. Beginning of season.
Sept. 15. *A Winter's Tale*, by Shakespeare.
Oct. 17. *Der Liebeskönig*, by Leo Greiner.

Nov. 30. *A Winter's Tale*, 50th performance.

Dec. 20. *Ringelspiel*, by Hermann Bahr.

1907

Jan. 4. *Die Geschwister*, by Goethe.

Jan. 29. *Romeo and Juliet*, by Shakespeare.

Mar. 8. *The Inspector General*, by Nicolaus Gogol.

NEUES THEATER

1906

June 30. Last performance under Reinhardt's management at the Neues Theater.

KAMMERSPIELE

1906

Nov. 8. Opening performance. *Ghosts*, by Henrik Ibsen.
Nov. 20. *Frühlings Erwachen (Spring's Awakening)*, by Frank Wedekind.

Dec. 6. *Man and Superman*, by Bernard Shaw.

1907

Jan. 7. *Das Friedensfest*, by Gerhart Hauptmann.

Feb. 7. *Frühlings Erwachen (Spring's Awakening)*, 50th performance.

Mar. 11. *Hedda Gabler*, by Henrik Ibsen.

DEUTSCHES THEATER

1907

Mar. 19. *Der Gott der Rache*, by Schalom Asch.

Apr. 25. *Robert und Bertram*, by Gustav Raeder.

June 7. End of season.
Aug. 8. Beginning of season.

Sept. 14. *Prinz Friedrich von Homburg*, by Heinrich von Kleist.

Oct. 17. *Twelfth Night*, by Shakespeare.

Dec. 20. *Der Arzt seiner Ehre* (*The Doctor on his Honour*), by Calderon de la Barca (Presber).

1908

Jan. 10. *Die Räuber* (*The Robbers*), by Friedr. Schiller.

KAMMERSPIELE

1907

Mar. 25. *Love's Comedy*, by Henrik Ibsen.
April 15. *Aglavaine und Selysette*, by Maur. Maeterlinck.

May 2. *Gyges und sein Ring*, by Friedrich Hebbel.
June 7. End of season.
Aug. 8. Beginning of season.
Aug. 29. *Fräulein Julie* (*Miss Julia*), by Aug. Strindberg (reproduction).

Sept. 19. *Liebelei* (*Light o' Love*), by Arthur Schnitzler.

Oct. 26. *Esther*, by Franz Grillparzer.
The Servant of two Masters, by Carlo Goldoni.
Nov. 9. *Der Marquis von Keith*, by Frank Wedekind.
Dec. 9. *Catharina, Gräfin von Armagnac*, by Vollmöller.

DEUTSCHES THEATER

1908

KAMMERSPIELE

1908

Jan. 23. *Hochzeit*, by Emil Strauss.

Feb. 9. *Frühlings Erwachen* (*Spring's Awakening*), 200th performance.

Feb. 27. *Lysistrata*, by L. Greiner (Aristophanes).

Mar. 7. *Der Kompagnon*, by Adolph l'Arronge (celebration of l'Arronge's 70th birthday).

Mar. 30. *Der Tor und der Tod*, by H. v. Hofmannsthal.
Nju, by Ossip Dymow.

April 11. *Twelfth Night*, 100th performance.

April 22. *Die Räuber* (*The Robbers*), 50th performance.

May 16. *Ulrich Fürst v. Waldeck*, by Herbert Eulenberg.

May 24. *Lysistrata*, 50th performance.

June 7. End of season.

June 7. End of season.

Aug. 8. Beginning of season.
Des Meeres und der Liebe Wellen, by Franz Grillparzer.

Aug. 8. Beginning of season.

Aug. 25. *Medea*, by Franz Grillparzer.

Sept. 4. *Sozialaristokraten*, by Arno Holz.

Sept. 9. *Kettenglieder* (*Links*), by Hermann Heijermans.

Sept. 14. *Terakoya* (*Die Dorfschule*). *Nach Takeda Izumo*, by Wolfgang v. Gersdorff.
Kimiko, by Wolfgang v. Gersdorff.

Sept. 16. *King Lear*, by Shakespeare.

DEUTSCHES THEATER

1908

Sept. 29. The 25th anniversary of the Deutschen Theaters. *Kabale und Liebe.*

Oct. 21. *Die Verschwörung des Fiesco zu Genua,* by Schiller.

Nov. 5. *King Lear,* 25th performance.
Nov. 14. *Revolution in Krähwinkel,* by Joh. Nestroy.

KAMMERSPIELE

1908

Oct. 16. *Clavigo,* by Goethe.

Oct. 30. *Eine Heiratsgeschichte,* by Nicolei Gogol.

Nov. 21. *The Doctor's Dilemma,* by G. B. Shaw.
Dec. 5. *Niemand weiss es,* by Theodor Wolff.
Dec. 22. *Der Graf von Gleichen,* by Wilh. Schmidtbonn.

1909

Jan. 29. *Die Lehrerin,* by Alexander Brody.
Feb. 26. *Revolution in Krähwinkel,* 100th performance.

Mar. 11. *Medea,* 25th performance.
Mar. 25. *Faust.*

April 27. *Faust,* 25th performance.

1909

Mar. 6. *The Doctor's Dilemma,* 50th performance.

April 25. *Wolkenkuckucksheim,* by Josef Ruederer.
April 26. *Der Graf von Gleichen,* 50th performance.

May 4. *Der unverstandene Mann,* by Ernst v. Wolzogen.

DEUTSCHES THEATER	KAMMERSPIELE
1909	1909

May 31. End of season.

DEUTSCHES THEATER:
Hamlet, by Shakespeare.
Don Carlos, by Schiller.
The Taming of the Shrew, by Shakespeare.

May 31. End of season.

KAMMERSPIELE:
Major Barbara, by Bernard Shaw.
Das Heim, by Octave Mirbeau and Thadé Natanson.

1910

DEUTSCHES THEATER:
Der gute König Dagobert, by Andre Rivoire and Felix Galton.
Christinas Heimreise, by Hugo von Hofmannsthal.
Judith, by Hebbel.
Die Braut von Messina, by Schiller.

1910

KAMMERSPIELE:
Der Naturliche Vater, by Herbert Eulenberg.
Hilfe! Ein Kind is vom Himmel gefallen, by Wilhelm Schmidtbonn.
Gawân, by Eduard Stucken.
Sumurûn, by F. Freksa.

ALPHABETICAL LIST OF AUTHORS[1]

Anzengruber, *Die Kreuzelschreiber*.
— *Doppelselbstmord*.
Aristophanes, *s. Greiner*.
Asch, *Der Gott der Rache*.
Auernheimer, *Koketterie*.

Bahr, *Ringelspiel*.
— *Sanna*.
— *Untersich*.
Becque, *Die Raben (The Raven)*.
Beer-Hofmann, *Graf von Charolais*.
Björnson, *Die Neuvermählten*.
Brody, *Die Lehrerin*.

Calderon, *Der Arzt seiner Ehre*.
Courteline, *Boubouroche*.
— *Der Herr Kommissär*.

Donnay, *Liebesleute*.
Dymow, *Nju*.

Eulenberg, *Ulrich Fürst v. Waldeck*.
Euripides, *Medea* (übers. v. Wilamowitz-Möllendorf).

Feld, *Serenissimus*.
Flers, de (u. G. de Caillavet), *Logik des Herzens*.

[1] It has not been possible to carry this list beyond May 1909, up to which date it is complete.

Gersdorff, v., *Kimiko.*
Goethe, *Clavigo.*
— *Faust.*
— *Die Geschwister.*
— *Die Mitschuldigen.*
Gogol, *Eine Heiratsgeschichte.*
— *Der Revisor (The Inspector General).*
Goldoni, *Der Diener zweier Herren.*
Gorki, *Nachtasyl (The Lower Depths).*
Greiner, *Der Liebeskönig.*
— *Lysistrata* (Aristophanes).
Grillparzer, *Esther.*
— *Medea.*
— *Des Meeres u. der Liebe Wellen.*

Halbe, *Der Strom.*
Hartleben, *Abschied vom Regiment.*
— *Angele.*
Hauptmann, *Das Friedensfest.*
Hebbel, *Gyges und sein Ring.*
Heijermanns, *Kettenglieder.*
Hofmannsthal, v., *Elektra.*
— *Œdipus und die Sphinx.*
— *Der Tor und der Tod.*
Holländer, *Ackermann.*
Holz, *Sozialaristokraten.*

Ibsen, *Die Gespenster (Ghosts).*
— *Hedda Gabler.*
— *Kronprätendenten (The Pretenders).*
— *Komödie der Liebe (Love's Comedy).*
— *Rosmersholm.*

Kleist, H. v., *Käthchen v. Heilbronn.*
— *Prinz Friedrich von Homburg.*

L'Arronge, A., *Der Kompagnon.*
Lange, Sven, *Die stillen Stuben.*
Lessing, *Minna von Barnhelm.*

Maeterlinck, *Schwester Beatrix (Sister Beatrice).*
— *Pelleas und Melisande.*
— *Aglavaine und Selysette.*
Molière, *Der Tartüff (Tartufe).*

Nestroy, *Einen Jux will er sich machen.*
— *Revolution in Krähwinkel.*

Offenbach, *Orpheus in der Unterwelt (Orpheus in the Underground).*

Paap, *Königsrecht.*
Paul, *Die Doppelgänger-Komödie.*

Raeder, *Robert und Bertram.*
Reicke, *Märtyrer.*
Ruederer, *Die Morgenröte.*
— *Wolkenkuckucksheim.*

Schiller, *Kabale und Liebe.*
— *Fiesco.*
— *Die Räuber.*
Schlaikjer, *Des Pastors Rieke.*
Schmidt, Lothar, *Ackermann.*
Schmidtbonn, *Mutter Landstrasse.*
— *Graf von Gleichen.*
Schnitzler, *Abschiedssouper.*
— *Der grüne Kakadu.*
— *Der tapfere Cassian.*
— *Liebelei.*
Shakespeare, *König Lear (King Lear).*
— *Die lustigen Weiber v. Windsor (The Merry Wives of Windsor).*

Shakespeare, *Romeo und Julia* (*Romeo und Juliet*).
— *Kaufmann v. Venedig* (*Merchant of Venice*).
— *Sommernachtstraum* (*Midsummer Night's Dream*).
— *Das Wintermärchen* (*Winter's Tale*).
— *Was ihr wollt* (*Twelfth Night*).
Shaw, *Arzt am Scheidewege* (*Doctor's Dilemma*).
— *Candida*.
— *Cäsar und Cleopatra* (*Cæsar and Cleopatra*).
— *Mensch und Übermensch* (*Man and Superman*).
— *Der Schlachtenlenker* (*The Man of Destiny*).
Stehr, *Meta Konegen*.
Strauss, *Hochzeit*.
Strecker, *Vater Riekmann*.
Strindberg, *Fräulein Julie* (*Miss Julia*).
— *Rausch*.
Synge, *Der heilige Brunnen* (*The Well of the Saints*).

Takeda Izumo, *Terakoya*.
Thoma, *Die Lokalbahn*.
Tolstoi, *Früchte der Bildung* (*Fruits of Enlightenment*).
Tschechow, *Der Bär* (*The Bear*).

Vollmöller, *Graf von Charolais*.
— *Katharina von Armagnac*.

Wedekind, *Erdgeist*.
— *Frühlings Erwachen* (*Spring's Awakening*).
— *Der Kammersänger*.
— *Der Marquis von Keith*.
— *So ist das Leben*.
Wilde, *Bunbury* (*Importance of being Earnest*).
— *Eine florentinische Tragödie* (*A Florentine Tragedy*).
— *Eine Frau ohne Bedeutung* (*Woman of No Importance*).
— *Salome*.
Wolff, Th., *Niemand weiss es*.
Wolzogen, *Der unverstandene Mann*.

INDEX

329